THE IDOLS ON THE HILLS

Rae,
I hope you will be
blessed by this book.

Burt Barnes
10/7/2018

THE IDOLS ON THE HILLS

Values, Choices,
and the Battle
for the Hearts of Mankind

Phillip C. Brainerd

Xulon Press

Xulon Press
2301 Lucien Way #415
Maitland, FL 32751
407.339.4217
www.xulonpress.com

Printed in the United States of America.

Edited by Xulon Press

ISBN-13: 9781545625712

Table of Contents

Introduction

A Personal Story

One of my favorite writers, J. I. Packer, wrote a book which influenced me mightily. In his introduction to the book *Knowing God*, he wrote these words:

> As a clown yearns to play Hamlet, so I have wanted to write a treatise on God. This book, however, is not it. Its length might suggest that it is trying to be, but anyone who takes it that way will be disappointed. (Packer 2010, preface).

That such a thoughtful, intelligent, and well-read man should be humbled by what he was about to do should add extra consideration to someone such as me. The book you're about to read is potentially life-changing; to explain why I'm writing it, let me share some experiences.

As a child, I once received an unusual gift: a King James Bible with my name on it. Now, Bibles with names on them aren't unusual. What made this one unique was its age—it was older than me. The name was embossed on the cover long before I was born. As it turns out, it once belonged to an uncle who died young, passing away before he could marry and have children; I was named after him in his honor. Someone discovered this Bible in an attic and thought *Certainly little Phillip would like to have his uncle's Bible*. For many, the story would stop there. Many Bibles are placed in prominent locations on bookshelves and never read, acting as a sort of ennobling decoration for a room. For me, the story got longer when I later learned my uncle owned several Bibles; those who stumbled upon them also sent them to my door. By late elementary school, I owned a stack of Bibles about a foot high. Perhaps I was an odd child (some would say certainly so), but it occurred to me that God might be trying to say something.

When I was young, my family attended church, but that stopped before I entered elementary school. Having no church service to attend, I started going down to our basement on Sunday mornings to read my Bibles. Not having any idea what else to do, I opened one of them, a King James Bible, and started reading at the beginning. Now the King James Bible was written in the 1500s and reflects the speech of that time. As such, I saw words like "begat" and "smote" and "Thee" and "Thou", and others that make reading clumsy. Owing to this difficulty, the "Church of little Phillip" ended.

As I grew older, I started having experiences with religion. I had a number of Jewish friends, and I was invited on several occasions to attend their Bar Mitzvahs. I always enjoyed seeing the pride in parents' faces as they watched their sons take on the mantle of their religion. In my family, my sister started attending a Methodist church, so I went along for the ride. A few years later, I showed some vocal talent, so I took a job singing tenor in an Episcopal church choir.

Having grown up in the 1960s, and now coming of age in the 1970s, I was exposed to the explosion of religions and philosophies that swept America. I remember taking money given to me as a high school graduation gift and visiting the local center for transcendental meditation. There, I paid to learn this practice; I was taught to meditate twice a day and did so faithfully for three years. Furthermore, I eventually become a vegetarian and came to believe I could meditate myself to higher plains of existence.

I went away to college, and grew long hair and a beard (older readers may recall a day when good kids didn't do this). As a double major in voice and theater, I sought opportunities to sing and act, so I auditioned for a local production of the musical *Jesus Christ, Superstar*. Why? Since I had long hair and a beard, I looked like Jesus, and I could sing. There you go.

This was meant to build my performance resume, but I wound up with a profound religious experience. In my drama classes, I learned every good actor researches his/her characters, so I researched Jesus. This involved reading the Bible. Whereas my childhood experience ended far short of the entire text, this time I read the whole thing.

As I read, I found myself in a dilemma. I was raised in the modern age and had been taught the Bible is one of many books you can read if you want to be religious. By this time, I had been exposed to multiple religions and philosophies. The Bible should have been one of many books on my spiritual pilgrimage; however, it became more—much more. As I read, I found things written in its pages that were just *right:* they made sense. Certainly some sections were harder to understand than others, but overall, I was very impacted by what I read.

Something else occurred to me as I read these ancient texts. I found *much of what I had heard about the Bible was different than what I read*. Most of the things I heard people say about the Bible were spoken by individuals who could not possibly have read it themselves.

A year later, I had what Christians call a "born-again" experience, accepting Jesus Christ as my Lord and Savior. From there, I finished college and felt a call to the ministry, attending seminary and holding various positions in Christian organizations. Sometimes my work looked traditional, serving on the staffs of evangelical churches: at other points, I participated in activities ranging from social work with the mentally handicapped to playing keyboard in a Christian rock band.

But enough about me; suffice it to say I found the writings of the Bible to be profoundly important in my life. From here, I need to share two more experiences.

Connections

The first is the result of reading authors who noticed a sad trend among people of faith. Many have what I call a "compartmentalized" life. They attend worship services and experience religious feelings. After this experience, they leave; upon doing so, a sort of curtain falls behind them. Life on the street and life in the house of worship become two different things.

For some, this is unintentional. This group of people doesn't realize they do it and would be saddened if they realized what was happening. For others, it's a deliberate, important part of their philosophical approach to life. What makes this compartmentalization possible? As I observed the lives of people at different points along their spiritual journeys, I began to see a need for *connections;* many need to see how their faith connects to modern life. Every generation has issues that call for points of connection between spiritual life and daily life. Every generation has personalities who try to demonstrate those points. That's part of the reason for this book: to point out today's connections.

Values and Choices

To make these connections, people need to see the "why" behind the connections. I learned this in the next experience involving a message given by a man named Joshua many centuries ago:

> Joshua said to all the people, "This is what the LORD, the
> God of Israel, says: 'Long ago your forefathers, including
> Terah the father of Abraham and Nahor, lived beyond the

River and worshiped other gods. But I took your father Abraham from the land beyond the River and led him throughout Canaan and gave him many descendants. I gave him Isaac, and to Isaac I gave Jacob and Esau. I assigned the hill country of Seir to Esau, but Jacob and his sons went down to Egypt.

Then I sent Moses and Aaron, and I afflicted the Egyptians by what I did there, and I brought you out. When I brought your fathers out of Egypt, you came to the sea, and the Egyptians pursued them with chariots and horsemen as far as the Red Sea. But they cried to the LORD for help, and he put darkness between you and the Egyptians; he brought the sea over them and covered them. You saw with your own eyes what I did to the Egyptians. Then you lived in the desert for a long time.

I brought you to the land of the Amorites who lived east of the Jordan. They fought against you, but I gave them into your hands. I destroyed them from before you, and you took possession of their land. When Balak son of Zippor, the king of Moab, prepared to fight against Israel, he sent for Balaam son of Beor to put a curse on you. But I would not listen to Balaam, so he blessed you again and again, and I delivered you out of his hand.

Then you crossed the Jordan and came to Jericho. The citizens of Jericho fought against you, as did also the Amorites, Perizzites, Canaanites, Hittites, Girgashites, Hivites and Jebusites, but I gave them into your hands. I sent the hornet ahead of you, which drove them out before you—also the two Amorite kings. You did not do it with your own sword and bow. So I gave you a land on which you did not toil and cities you did not build; and you live in them and eat from vineyards and olive groves that you did not plant.

Now fear the LORD and serve him with all faithfulness. Throw away the gods your forefathers worshiped beyond the River and in Egypt, and serve the LORD. But if serving the LORD seems undesirable to you, then choose for yourselves this day whom you will serve, whether the gods your forefathers served beyond the River, or the gods of the Amorites, in whose land you are living. But as for me and my household, we will serve the LORD. (Joshua 24:2-15)

The phrase, "as for me and my household, we will serve the Lord" is one of the best-known phrases in the Bible. It can be found on plaques hanging proudly in the homes of religious people, but what is its meaning? Do the owners of those plaques really understand its significance? Just prior to these words, Joshua encouraged the people of Israel to do something very important. He wanted them to *choose* something; this choice was to play a key role in their faith. Joshua warned the Israelites to flee the worship of other gods. He encouraged them to choose instead to worship the God that he, his mentor Moses, and all the faithful of Israel considered the one true God. He gave several reasons for his belief; let's look at two of them.

First, it was the reason for Israel's existence. In the time of Abraham's youth and before, the ancestors of Israel worshipped the deities Joshua called "other gods". Abraham was brought out of that land so he could learn to worship the true God instead. *Second, God had shown himself to be far more powerful than the gods in the surrounding countries.* He showed this by bringing Moses and the Israelites out of Egypt. The mightiest of Egyptian deities failed to prevent the people of Israel from leaving. Even the highest rulers of the land suffered tragic loss when they resisted Israel's God; this was repeated every time nations opposed the Israelites and their God.

To Joshua, this was an easy choice: "As for me and my house, we will serve the Lord" (Joshua 24:15).

What did the choice involve? According to Joshua, it involved *serving* someone. Serving God means seeking to do things that are pleasing to Him. To please God, you must learn His laws and His values, and dedicate yourself to live in conformity with those things. It also involves enjoying the blessings God chooses to give His followers. Ironically, serving the other gods involves something similar; in some ways, the only difference is the target of service. The other gods also have laws, which followers must learn and obey. They also have values, which must be understood and honored. Followers of the other gods seek to receive rewards offered by those gods.

We'll talk about the other gods later. For now, we must understand one important thing: in Joshua's mind, there was a major difference between serving God and serving the other gods. One was the *right* thing to do; the other was the *wrong* thing to do. People needed to make a decision. They needed to *choose*.

The Battle

For the people of Joshua's generation, it seemed right to follow his advice. Sadly, after a short time, these noble words lost their meaning. The Scriptures state that later generations fell into worship of the other gods on numerous occasions; this created a series of cycles. One generation was faithful to God; the next was disobedient. Disobedience made the Israelites vulnerable to attack and subjugation from their neighbors. After a period during which God allowed them to experience the results of their faithlessness, God would raise up someone to lead the people away from their oppressors. A time of spiritual renewal followed. Sadly, the cycle would start again only a few years later.

This cycle repeated over and over again. Spiritual renewal and zeal for God were followed by deterioration into disobedience. At some points, there was faith and triumph; at other points, rebellion and failure.

During the high points of this cycle, the home of worship was the temple of Jerusalem. The builder of the first great temple, Solomon, understood God didn't actually live there: "But will God really dwell on earth? The heavens, even the highest heaven, cannot contain you. How much less this temple I have built!" (I Kings 7:27)

Still, there was symbolic value in a place for centralized worship; this value was quickly demonstrated during the low points of the cycle. The other gods made no claim to infinite qualities like omnipresence; in fact, they were considered local and territorial. As such, their shrines proliferated all over the landscape. At the points of greatest deterioration, shrines were found "on every high hill and under every spreading tree" (I Kings 14:23).

The periods of disobedience often ended with bad leadership being replaced by good. Under the leadership of the good kings, the other gods were shown the exit. As you read these histories though, there is one group of gods that usually survived these times—a very curious group. These were *the idols in the high places.*

Something was difficult about the high places, which allowed them to become entrenched. Perhaps it was their number? In the worst of times, they were on "every high hill". Perhaps it was the geographical advantage hilltops and mountainous terrains gave to devotees who, in many cases, would choose to fight for their deities. To this day, such terrains make the most confident warriors sober and the most advanced armies careful. Taking out all the high places by force could be a costly and potentially risky venture.

Whatever the reason, spiritual revivals often stopped at the edges of cities. The reader is left asking, repeatedly, "Will there be a time when someone is courageous enough to remove the high places? When will someone throw down *the idols on the hills?*"

To most, idolatry conjures up images of statues—some small and some large. Some are simple and appear to be carved from common materials with the simplest tools. Some are beautifully crafted by artists who could compete with the best talents of the modern age.

Some of those statues can be seen in textbooks or quiet museums. Their antiquity makes them worthy of study, but their age makes us overlook something. We miss the fact that they represented something important to their original owners. We forget these images were created to represent something of another world—symbols of great meaning to their creators. Because we forget this, we sometimes make simple replicas and place them in our homes, restaurants, and places of business. We think they're only interesting conversation pieces. The originals may have sat on the windowsills of small huts, or they may have stood in the centers of grand temples, erected by the greatest builders of the ancient world. However, they always represented something important; something to be given intense devotion; something thought to be *alive*.

Some of these statues stood at the heart of civilizations. Sometimes their worshippers carried them into monumental battles. Sometimes they received sacrifices of the most precious things available in their day, *including human lives.*

Far more fantastic, and perhaps more incomprehensible to the modern mind, is the idea these idols were involved in a battle fought on planes higher than our earthly habitat. These statues represented the other gods mentioned in the records we now call the Bible. They competed with the one true God and called for allegiance in a cosmic conflict that has vied for the hearts of mankind from our earliest days.

The heart of that conflict, the temptations and challenges people faced long ago, still exists today. Although the forms of the images have changed, much of what energized the hands of idol makers centuries ago still energizes people today; and God, the one true God who watched the conflict over the centuries, still lives.

One way of describing human history is to look at it as a competition spanning millennia. The one true God, the God who created humans, reaches out to them, though they run from Him in every direction. He competes with the idols to which the humans run. Sometimes the competition is quiet; sometimes it's explosive. I hope we can learn more about Him by studying His actions in the ancient competition: *the battle for the hearts of mankind.* In addition, we can learn some things about ourselves.

With these things in mind, let's enter the battlefield.

7

Chapter 1

In the Beginning—Who Is God; Who Are Human Beings?

The State of Our Modern Culture

A friend of mine runs something called a backyard Bible club. School children in the United States take much of the summer off from their studies and often have abundant free time. Harried parents are often glad for an activity that keeps the kids out of trouble; my friend provides such an activity in her home. Children visit and are given opportunities to play games, sing songs, and learn things from the Bible. One morning, one of the participants brought a friend. After the games and songs came the learning time. Not having been exposed to any of the material, the friend sat quietly and politely through the session. At one point, the child began to look perplexed. After a time, she raised her hand. Always happy to answer questions, my friend called on this child and asked what she wanted to know. Here is the question the child had patiently held back for most of the morning:

"Who is this 'God' guy you're all talking about?"

For those born in the Western world, any time in the mid-twentieth century or earlier, this is a stunning question. For most, the presence of God is a common assumption. There are many, of course, who challenge this; and the challenge is nothing new. Either way, the beliefs of parents are usually passed along to children. If parents have some belief in God, their children have visited a place of worship at one time or another. If parents don't believe in God, they warn their children about their "superstitious" neighbors. Either way, children are at least aware of the notion of God, but here was a new development: a child who grew up in a home where God was not even mentioned. God was neither a basic assumption nor a concept to be avoided. There was simply no mention of such a being: no friend, no relative, no teacher, or anyone else brought up the idea of God in the presence of this child.

For those who consider the concept of God as outmoded thinking, this moment should bring excitement; it's the result of years of hard work by atheists. To those who believe in God, this is a sad moment. It's not a hopeless moment, mind you. Remember, this occurred in the context of a backyard Bible club. The child heard all about God from that moment on. Sorry, atheists.

The reason for this being a sad moment for believers is that much of Western civilization held strongly to belief in a one true God for centuries. Certainly, there was disagreement about what He was like and who should be considered as His authoritative representatives; but how did we get to the point where there are growing numbers of people who have never set foot in a place of worship, and who are not inclined to even mention God to their children? The answer is one of the topics of this book. To discover that answer, we must visit the question of who God is, who we are, and what both of us desire. To do that, we need to do nothing harder than open the book of Genesis at the beginning of the Bible. This book is believed by three of the largest religions in the world (Judaism, Christianity, and Islam) to be inspired by God. As such, it is honored on some level by billions of people.

What We Read "In the Beginning"

There are two fundamental teachings given to us in the early chapters of Genesis. These truths govern everything else taught in the Scriptures. They are found in the following two statements: "In the beginning God created the heavens and the earth. . . . Then God said, "Let us make man in our image, in our likeness" (Gen. 1:1, 26).

The first truth is God is our creator. Second, He created humans in His image. The first truth would be an amazing thing in itself and worthy of our attention; the second, though, is even more awe-inspiring. There is something about God that He wants to demonstrate in human beings. This is not said of any other created thing; this means human beings are *special*. We are not just one more item in a long list of accomplishments credited to the creator God. Later in history, Jesus Christ would make the following statement: "Look at the birds of the air; they do not sow or reap or store away in barns, and yet your heavenly Father feeds them. Are you not much more valuable than they?" (Matt. 6:26). Birds are part of the created order, so they have value, but humans are worth much more.

In its very first set of statements, the Bible sets itself apart from any other religious system.

If you're starting from a perfectly clean slate, there are few possibilities when attempting to study the source of the universe. One way of looking at the universe is to say it has no origin; it has always existed in one form or another. Those who hold this belief would say everything in the universe is a random happening. The forces and laws of the universe are ruled by nothing; everything is the product of chance. On the extreme opposite of philosophies is pantheism; (everything is God – Matthews 2013, 3). God is everywhere, and everything is part of God.

As different as these viewpoints would seem, they share a striking similarity: there is no one thing more important than anything else. To the atheist, a bird is just as important as a human; they're both worth nothing. To the pantheist, the bird and the human have equal value; they're both worth everything, because each is a part of God. To the pantheist, humans shouldn't consume a bird because the bird has just as much worth as the human. In fact, the essence of the bird may someday reside in the body of a human. To kill a bird is as much an act of murder as the destruction of a human. To the atheist, the bird only has value as it has value to humans. Does it make us feel good when we look at it? Does it taste good and does it provide nutrition, should one choose to consume it? Does it play a part in balancing the environment of the planet that allows us all to live?

Against these two philosophical viewpoints, the biblical view of a Creator stands in stark contrast. Humans and birds have value, *but humans have much more*. Humans have this great value because God assigned it to them when they were created.

Values

In our current culture, we become nervous when discussions turn toward *values*. We don't like to hear that one person thinks his values are better than another's. However, values are an important part of God's creative act; in fact, *the creation expresses God's values*. Every act during the creative process reveals a set of priorities. Consider the second day of creation:

> Now the earth was formless and empty, darkness was over the surface of the deep, and the Spirit of God was hovering over the waters. And God said, "Let there be light," and there was light. God saw that the light was good, and he separated the light from the darkness. (Genesis 1:2–4)

It is said God created *ex nihilo* ("out of nothing"). As far as we can tell, the stuff of the universe that God created "in the beginning" didn't have any shape. We don't know exactly what it was like, but we're told it was "formless". In other words, God starts with something, which is the equivalent of a lump of clay. God's next step is to *improve* it; to do so, He created light.

Today, we know light and dark are not separate entities per se. When you say you have light, you're saying the stuff that makes light has been gathered into one place. In another place, there is less of that stuff, or none of it. (Note: The word *stuff* isn't terribly sophisticated, but the word *matter* doesn't precisely describe everything in the universe, especially when you talk about light. The word *stuff* is more fun, so I'll ask the kind indulgence of more scientifically oriented readers.) We call the area where there is no stuff that makes light "darkness". So, when God made light, God did so by moving things around. When He did this, He made a decision involving His values. Moving things in the universe from one place to another made the universe *better*. The separated stuff that comprised what was now light and darkness God called "good". If you're not agreeing with the idea of values to this point, you have to grab on here. To call something "good" is to assign a value. The universe was now better than it previously was in God's way of thinking.

Often, we understand God's values. We see the improvement God made to the universe, and it makes sense to us. In its most fundamental form, light allows us to see the creation. God could have seen it very well without light, but we need light to experience the creation. So we like light; it makes sense to us.

Also, in this first action, God created the beginning of something fundamental to the life of the universe. He created *energy*. Energy is one of those words we take for granted. We hear it often, but if you were to ask what energy is, few could explain it. Here is a definition that would be used by a physicist: energy involves the potential to do work. It appears in the universe when one area of space contains more stuff (there's that word again) than another. For some reason, the universe doesn't "like" to have more in one place than another, so the stuff tends to move around in such a way that it can equalize. When it moves from one place to another, the flow represents potential. To the sailor, this quality of physics is enjoyed when winds strikes his sails. The meteorologist would say there is an area of high air pressure in one place and an area of low air pressure in another. When the air attempts to equalize, moving from the high-pressure area to the low, the manifestation is called wind. It can be experienced as a simple pleasure on a summer day, or it can be put to work. The sailor hoists his sails to catch the wind and propel his ship forward.

Other kinds of stuff occur in disproportionate ways in the universe, creating amazing potentials. When electrons are gathered in one place, such as the end of a battery, they tend to want to equalize, moving from one pole to the other; we call this manifestation *electricity*. When a light bulb is placed in this flow, we get light. When circuits are placed in this flow, we can get all manners of electronic activity, from radios to computers. We have discovered a multitude of energy sources in the universe, and we'll certainly discover more.

When God moved the stuff of light from one place, the formless place, to central locations, He was in essence charging the batteries of the universe. It was as though He was pulling a pendulum of unimaginable size to its highest position, and releasing it, so all the gears of the universe would be powered.

When He gave power to the forces of the universe, He revealed another important aspect of his being: He is "power-full". He is so powerful, He can take nothing and create everything we know of in the universe (and more, which we haven't discovered yet). He has the power to take all the pendulums of the universe and pull them to the highest they can go, and then give them a push. As such, He is (at least) more powerful than the sum total of all the power in the universe He created. Today, with the help of telescopes, we can peer into distant corners of our galaxy. The images that come back are striking and fantastic. There are celestial bodies, which pump out more raw power in a second than the human race has consumed in all of its existence. Our telescopes view images of stars whose mass far exceeds our own sun, which is somewhat small in comparison to the great powerhouses of our galaxy; yet, our sun is so powerful we dare not draw much closer to it than our own planet. Interplanetary probes have shown us that the surfaces of the inner planets are hot enough to melt metals like lead; yet, our star is only one of billions that exist in our galaxy alone. Our galaxy is one of billions in the universe. Our minds can only begin to grasp this much power; yet, God is more powerful than all of these things combined.

There's more. If God's purpose was to create some sort of cosmic light show, He could have stopped there. He didn't stop, though, because He wasn't done yet.

This introduces the next thing we learn about God: He creates with a *purpose*. Each of the early steps of creation leads to something higher, better, and even more valuable than the steps that precede it. Size and power don't fulfill God. He turns next to the earth where He creates oceans of water. He causes the gases and clouds of the early atmosphere to become clear, so an earthly observer can view the stars. Evaporation returns some of the water to the skies, so it can be sent back to the earth as rain. The rain waters parched ground, and eventually forms rivers and lakes. All of this is powered by the newly activated sun, which pours radiant energy onto the earth. God causes plants to appear on the planet, living off the waters and gases of the atmosphere. He then follows with animals, which live off the plants. With each step, God looks at what He has created and pronounces it "good". His creation is getting better and better with each step; it's becoming more and more valuable. In particular, it's becoming more and more valuable to the Being who is in the process of creating it.

With values and purpose comes another of the characteristics of God, revealed through his creation; we call this characteristic *God's sovereign will*. When God chose to create a universe, and to put certain things into it, He made decisions. He made these decisions in accordance with his values. Certain things would exist; they would exist in certain places. Other things would never exist. There were numerous things God might have created, which He chose to skip because they didn't represent the highest expression of his values. In addition, we have no record of him asking anyone for help or directions. Everything that happened was the result of his will. Nothing would ever happen which is outside of his will and his plan.

Finally, God created what, for the time being, would be the final step. He created the first human beings. When He did so, He made some amazing statements: "Then God said, "Let us make man in our image, in our likeness" (Gen. 1:26).

Let me repeat: God made a statement about human beings not made of any other thing in the created order. Human beings are made *in his image*. Once again, God communicates his values. The human creature is different from any other. Some components that God used in humans are similar to other creatures, such as blood and flesh and bones. Nevertheless, the sum total of what these parts become, when assembled, is far superior to the other creatures. Man is special — very special.

So, what does it mean to be made in the image of God? We may never fully realize what this quality entails, but God shows us much in these first few chapters of Genesis. He states some plainly; He implies others.

Making Things

Humans love to make things. Although we can't create *ex nihilo*, we share God's desire to improve upon what lies around us: we move things, shape things, and assemble things. In New York City, not far from my home, examples abound. You need only stroll down any Manhattan street to see thousands of structures: some are massive; others are smaller, but they express the plans of master architects and are built by hundreds of craftsmen. Almost every building is within walking distance of landscaped parks dotted with statues. Walk a little further, and you'll see massive museums filled with the artwork of centuries. When people aren't building, molding, or painting, they're singing, acting, or dancing.

This is one area where the religious get lazy. Once I shared this point with a group of young adults. Their eyes rolled as if to say, "Yes, we know God made everything. OK, we like to make things. Please move on to something more sophisticated." Sadly, some have realized the value of this idea after believers have passed by. Karl Marx, the originator of communism, conceived a principle he called "alienation". In this theory, humans start out unified, with their labor expressing their being. "Our products would be so many mirrors in which we saw reflected our essential nature" (Karl Marx 1988, 34). Unfortunately, according to the theory, humans are separated from their essential natures by corrupt social and economic systems. In the best world, every person would make things. They would make things because they could enjoy what they made and share freely with others. This innocence is corrupted when people make things in order to purchase the creations and possessions of others (a.k.a. bartering). Further alienation occurs when people's creations are replaced with abstractions, like currency. At worst, people become pieces of machines in factories, never seeing, much less owning, the fruits of their labor. I don't mention this to suggest I agree with Marx's conclusions. I mention it because one of the dominant philosophies of the modern world is strongly influenced by the recognition of our desire to create, and by the acknowledgment that this desire lies close to the core of our being. We are taught this important truth in the first chapter of the Bible; we marginalize it at great risk. Others have been quick to pick up treasures the "religious" carelessly leave behind in their quests for sophistication.

Choices

Inherent in the love of creating things is the ability to make *varied choices*. I chose that phrase carefully, and I'll explain why soon. For now, consider what happens when we create. We'll use a sculptor working with clay as an example. The sculptor takes a formless lump of clay and begins by manipulating it, moving some of it around. In some cases, he adds a little clay; in other cases, he removes a little. Each motion represents a decision based on values. In the artist's eye, each relocated piece of clay is an improvement. That describes us as humans; we improve things. We move things around and rearrange them according to our values. We make choices based on what we believe will be better after we complete our actions. With each motion, we express ourselves. Our creative motions become a language of sorts.

It's the same with God. The psalmist writes:

> The heavens declare the glory of God;
> the skies proclaim the work of his hands.
> Day after day they pour forth speech;
> night after night they display knowledge.
> There is no speech or language
> where their voice is not heard.
> Their voice goes out into all the earth,
> their words to the ends of the world. (Psalm 19:1–4)

When God chose to rearrange the material of the universe, He was expressing himself in a way that, to him, was as sure as language. We, too, express ourselves in a way, which to us is as sure as language. The only problem is humans don't fully understand the creative language of God. Still, God has shared with humans the ability to express themselves through creating things.

As I said, I use the phrase *varied choices* in association with this creative process. Some would note that many creatures move things around and build things. The birds build nests; the bees build hives. Some of these structures are complex, like a beaver's dam. However, there are limits to the variation of structures created by any one species of animal. If you observe the nests of birds, most look much the same. There is some variety between subspecies, but the structures built by birds of the same type are rather uniform, depending on the sources of building materials nearby. The "creations" of birds appear to be functions of genetics. The birds don't teach their young how to build; they just start to build when they're ready. The fundamental design is hard-wired into the bird. As such, birds don't really have a choice; they follow mechanistic instincts.

However, humans are different. We choose on a much wider spectrum than even the most intelligent animals. We resemble God in this sense more than we resemble the lower created things.

Rest

Let's consider this thing called choice: the ability to have values and to express them in our actions. All of us assume it, fight for it, and cling to it. The ability to choose stands at the core of modern governmental systems.

However, we haven't begun to comprehend its value. That value is expressed in the next Scripture passage:

> Thus the heavens and the earth were completed in all their vast array. By the seventh day God had finished the work he had been doing; so on the seventh day he rested from all his work. And God blessed the seventh day and made it holy, because on it he rested from all the work of creating that he had done. (Gen. 2:1–3)

To readers born into Western culture, the idea above seems to be another commonplace subject. God worked and then stopped for a while—a whole day. Because we are made in God's image, we are told to do likewise. "What's unusual about this?" asks the modern reader. "Doesn't everyone take time off? Hasn't this always been?" The answer to these questions is no. If you move the walk we mentioned earlier from the city to the forest, one thing becomes apparent: there are no "days off" in nature. There is the cycle of day and night; action followed by sleep to gain energy once again for action. The cycle of live/work and sleep/recharge grinds on every day. Each day, the animals awaken, leave their shelters to hunt for food, and return. This pattern doesn't break unless broken by circumstances, like a change of season or cataclysmic events.

Why is this? Because animals don't appreciate their work as we do. Their work gains for them enough sustenance for the moment. In some cases, God has given animals instincts to gather extra for seasonal change. However, animals don't value their work and their creations as humans do. God created and then stopped to enjoy it; He did so because He chose to dedicate time to enjoyment. He watched the sun rise and stood back, as it awakened the spectrum of colors that bathed the surface of the earth. He gazed on the faces of the flowers and the frolic of young animals leaping in the fields. As an all-present Being, He could feel the power of the forces bound by gravity at the core of the earth, where molten magma stirs in mesmerizing patterns. He could stretch his hand to the sun and run his fingers through the flaming plasma on its surface, as easily as we run our fingers through the water of a mountain stream, shimmering as it reflects the light from the sun millions of miles away.

God has the ability to enjoy beauty. No animal has this. No animal has ever stared at the sunset from the time the sun sits just above the horizon to the time its final ribbons of light disappear, but God shared this ability with us. He didn't create the universe for himself to enjoy alone. With us, his special creation, He shared this monumental gift.

Rulers

More than this, humans would rule:

> Then God said, "Let us make mankind in our image, in our likeness, so that they may rule over the fish in the sea and the birds in the sky, over the livestock and all the wild animals, and over all the creatures that move along the ground." (Gen. 1:26)

If any doubt remains concerning mankind's privileged status, it's dispelled here. The earth was created to be ruled by humans. Humans were created to hold a higher position than any of the earth's other inhabitants. Humans were not only to make decisions for themselves; they would make decisions involving everything on the earth.

Yet More Gifts

The gifts that God gave to mankind were amazing. Could He give anything more? The answer is yes, and we'll talk about that in the next chapter.

Chapter 2

God's Most Important Gifts

Up to this point, God gave the newly created humans incredible gifts, but He wasn't done. There were yet more gifts to be bestowed on mankind, but what could be greater than a planet? What privilege is greater than dominion over this immense creation? Considering the actions of humans throughout history, you'd think there was nothing greater than riches and real estate. Terrible wars have been fought over the right to rule the parcels of ground that cover this planet. Treasures have been depleted and blood spilled to fight over what God gave to humans for free; but yes, there are things greater—things that, to this day, many can't comprehend.

The unveiling of this new group of gifts can be found in a plant, which has confounded people from the time of its appearance.

> Now the LORD God had planted a garden in the east, in Eden; and there he put the man he had formed. And the LORD God made all kinds of trees grow out of the ground—trees that were pleasing to the eye and good for food. In the middle of the garden were the tree of life and the *tree of the knowledge of good and evil*. (Genesis 2:8–9; emphasis mine)

Adam and Eve had all kinds of wonderful fruit to eat. They could sit under an orange tree, enjoying bite after bite of the same thing, or gather an armful of varied flavors from different trees for a gorgeous fruit salad. Some effort would be involved. "The LORD God took the man and put him in the Garden of Eden to work it and take care of it" (2:15). This, too, is understandable if you've ever worked with plants. Gardening can be very fulfilling. To top this, there were no weeds. There was only meaningful effort, resulting in growth and multiplication of beautiful plants.

Two trees were mysterious, though. The Tree of Life is merely mentioned. At this point in the story, we know nothing about it.

With the Tree of the Knowledge of Good and Evil, we know a little more. We only know one thing associated with it—a prohibition:

> And the LORD God commanded the man, "You are free to eat from any tree in the garden; but you must not eat from the tree of the knowledge of good and evil, for when you eat of it you will surely die. (Gen. 2:16–17)

Here was something new. Up to this point, God commanded Adam to do things that all resulted in pleasurable experiences: eat delicious fruit, give names to the animals, and rule. Implied were a host of enjoyable activities— explore, enjoy, learn, and play. Swim with the dolphins. Run with the gazelle. Laugh with the monkeys. Lay in the sun with the lizards. Climb with the squirrels and wrestle with the lion cubs. Adam and Eve's whole experience was a long list of *do's*. Here was something different: *don't*. Along with this strange new thing was a stranger concept; doing the *don't* would result in something called *death*.

Death? What was that, anyway? All other experiences in the Garden were beautiful or fun or tasty, or in some way positive. This was dark and foreboding.

Now, why would God do this? From our perspective, this raises lots of questions. Why would He take this beautiful, sunny paradise and darken it with such a prohibition? Why did there have to be such a tree as the one named Knowledge of Good and Evil? If it must exist, why put it in the Garden? If it really had to be in the Garden, why not build a fence around it, so the new human creatures would be kept away? God has fallen under considerable criticism for this strange and, I dare say, inconvenient choice of landscaping.

As we said, there was yet more God wanted to share with humans. Something more valuable than the sum total of everything a planet had to offer; something more valuable than a universe filled with pleasurable experiences. It was something not shared with any other member of the creation.

Above everything else God gave was the most special gift of all. When God gave humans the ability to experience beauty and joy, He wasn't just sharing the things He created; He was sharing *Himself*. When you look at what God created, you learn things about God. At night, you can gaze into the expanse of the heavens and sense God's size. He is far greater than the distance to the farthest star. You can look at the forces of nature and get a sense of His power. Locally, He controls volcanoes and ocean waves. Further into the heavens, He controls the immense furnaces we call stars, which generate the energy needed to power solar systems.

God's creation is awesome in its size, but also in its intricacy. The same God who created stars created the smallest of living things. The complex mechanisms of a single cell put the finest watch to shame, but all these pieces are incomplete in themselves. Together, the creation points us to the Being who made it. God offered to mankind not only the things He made— He offered Himself. Even more than this, He offered *His heart*. Humanity's purpose wasn't just to wander through the world, learning things about God. Humans weren't just going to have a series of experiences by themselves. They were going to walk through the earth *with* God. Humans would enjoy all the experiences God had for them, with God Himself sharing in their joy.

We could stop here and be content to fall on our knees in worship, as we consider this incomprehensible gift; but if we jump forward thousands of years to our time, we realize somehow this isn't the way our modern world works. Why not? Because even with this, the gifts of God weren't yet complete. There was more of Himself He wanted to share with His special creation—mankind.

This is what He wanted to share: *the ability to make choices based on godly virtues*. These virtues include (at least) humility, wisdom, faith, and love. These virtues exist in the person of God, and He wanted to share them with His special creation, humans. In doing this, God was offering to mankind a magnificent gift; a gift of generosity larger than the universe. *God was offering mankind the ability to participate in his own divine nature.*

To understand this, we'll look at the parts of the prohibition God gave.

Humility

"You must not eat." Responding correctly to this, or any prohibition, requires the first godly virtue: humility. Humility involves two things: first is an accurate understanding of who we are. We'll expand on this later, but for now, this means understanding that we're the created ones, not the Creator. The person who has humility treats their Creator with deep respect. God is God. When He says something, it's right. He's the highest authority in the universe. Some time ago, I saw a bumper sticker that read "Because I'm the mommy, that's why." In our society, we understand the concept of authority. Children should respect parents and elders. They should show this respect first and foremost, because it's right. How much more should we respect our Creator when He says something?

I mentioned earlier God was sharing Himself with us; this leads to the question, "Is God humble?" If we define humility, at least partially, as having an accurate understanding of who we are, God certainly does that. He's the Creator of the universe and is worthy of being its ultimate ruler. There's nothing arrogant about this; He deserves to be the rule-maker. It's right for any created thing to follow the rules God makes.

As I said, there's a second aspect of humility; this is the *ability and the desire to attribute value to others*. In fact, the humble person attributes more value to others than to themselves. The apostle Paul stated, "Do nothing out of selfish ambition or vain conceit, but in humility consider others better than yourselves" (Phil. 2:3). God definitely displays this quality. He displays it to His entire creation on different levels. When He created His universe, and placed living things in it, He obligated Himself to its maintenance. He chose to spend the rest of eternity providing for what He created. The sun would be made to rise each morning and set each night whether there was something more interesting to do or not. The plants would have to grow and provide food, whether it was fun or not. In providing for His creation, God chose something remarkable: *He chose to be a servant to what He created*. Without His constant attention, nothing in the creation could continue to exist.

This represents a turning point in the experience of Adam and Eve. Previously, they could be wholly selfish. They could make each decision in terms of what was best for them. What action would bring the most pleasure? The most fun? The best flavor? The most exhilaration? If they continued this way, they would think, "*We* are the most important beings in the universe. We can act as we please whenever we wish. We have no limits. We don't need to value anything above how it can serve us." Now, they were instructed to make decisions based on God's values. Would they choose to demonstrate humility and learn to make decisions based on something other than their own interests? If they responded to the prohibition in a positive way, they could receive God's offer of this wonderful attribute.

We should note this first of the godly virtues offers an important delineation between mankind and the rest of creation. Consider the animals. As we noted before, animals exist with far fewer choices than humans. However, within their limited abilities, they, too, can make choices of sorts. If you put a piece of fish and a piece of chicken in front of a cat, the cat will choose whatever it likes best at the moment; but whatever choice it makes, it will make the choice based on itself and its impulses. If God were to allow humans to continue in a state where they made all choices based on themselves and the impulse of the moment, humans would be no different than animals, except in complexity. Making choices based on external standards given by God is one of the qualities making humans different than the animals—and not just different; God offers humans the opportunity to be higher than the rest of creation.

What would Adam and Eve choose? Would they choose to respond in a way that differentiated them from the lower life forms of earth, or would they choose to be the same?

Wisdom

Wisdom is the second godly virtue. Consider the next phrase: "...for when you eat of it, you will surely die." (Gen. 2:17) This wasn't merely a prohibition. It wasn't, "Don't do this because I say so." It was "Don't do it because you'll get hurt." More than a prohibition, it was a *warning*.

J.I. Packer suggests the following definition of wisdom: "Wisdom is the power to see, and the inclination to choose, the best and highest goal, together with the surest means of attaining it." (Packer 2010, 90) There are two ways to learn wisdom; one is to experience things firsthand. When a small child enters a kitchen and sees fire on the stove, the fascination may cause him/her to reach out and touch the glow under the pots. A watchful parent sends a stern warning: "Don't do that, or you'll be burned." At this point, the child can respond in two ways. They can disregard the warning and reach into the fire. In this case, they'll experience firsthand the consequences of the warning and experience pain—a lot of pain. Hopefully, this experience would be sufficient to cause the child to act more wisely in the future. On the other hand, there is another way to learn about fire. This involves *the ability to accept instruction and warning from others*. (Proverbs 1) The child who listens to the warning of parents can avoid excruciating pain and possibly disabling injury (Proverbs 1:8-9). The wise child listens and receives instruction; the foolish child insists on learning for him/herself.

In this "Introduction to Wisdom", God offers this type of instruction to Adam and Eve. If they choose the path of wisdom, they can avoid something called "death". They don't know what this is any more than a small child knows what it's like to be burned. They only know God has warned them. Because God is the Creator who knows how everything in the universe works, He always knows the best way to accomplish things. He offers to share this knowledge with humanity; it's always wise to respond to God's offer.

This is another opportunity for humans to act differently than animals. Animals know to avoid things that hurt them. Unfortunately, they often need to experience those painful experiences at least once. Sometimes, pets respond to stern warnings from owners: but this happens only after spending significant time with people, and after multiple attempts to associate stern warnings with something unpleasant like a loud clap. This is simple behavioral conditioning. Often, the learned behaviors deteriorate quickly after the owner walks away. I once owned a cat who fully understood it wasn't to jump onto the kitchen table. If I was in the room, a stern warning would keep the cat on the floor. It wasn't unusual to find the cat on the table if I stepped out and returned minutes later.

Another note: God didn't state that Adam and Eve would never eat from this tree. He only said they should avoid it for the time being. I sometimes compare the tree to the streets and roads that pass through our neighborhoods and in front of our homes. We teach small children to stay out of the streets. Someday, they'll be old enough to learn to cross the street. Later, they'll learn to drive automobiles or ride buses on the streets. Their lives will be greatly enhanced by these wonderful things, but only when they're ready. Prior to that time, streets can be very dangerous places for little children. It was the same with the Tree of the Knowledge of Good and Evil. What choice would Adam and Eve make? Would they choose wisdom, or would they choose to experience something painful by disobedience?

Faith

The third godly virtue is faith. If you ask a hundred people to define faith, you'll likely get a hundred different definitions. To many, faith is a warm emotion. If someone mentions God and others in the room have warm feelings, this is thought to be faith. The faith God was seeking to impart to humans through the prohibition involves the idea of *dependability*. The other day, I needed something high on a shelf. I couldn't reach it, so I got a ladder. I believed the ladder would hold my weight, so I was able to climb and obtain the object I wanted. You could say I had faith in the ability of the ladder to hold me. My faith was demonstrated in the fact that I climbed the ladder. Imagine, on the other hand, if I had looked at the ladder and said, "I have faith. I'm experiencing warm feelings. I certainly like the idea of a ladder. However, I don't think I can depend on the ladder to hold me, so I'll look for another way to reach that shelf." That would be an odd mismatch of feelings and reality; it certainly wouldn't be faith.

In other words, *faith involves an object*. In the case of the prohibition, faith would mean believing that when God says something is going to happen, it will. Faith would be demonstrated in obedience to the prohibition.

Love

Love is the final godly virtue. As with faith, to many people, love is another warm emotion. We think of others, and we feel something good. Love certainly involves that sometimes, but love is something much more. When you truly love someone, you value them. You value them so highly, you willingly give up things you consider valuable for their benefit. The greater the love, the more willing you are to give up things. This kind of love is *sacrificial* love. When you love someone and you're aware something pleases him/her, you make it happen. The young man who loves a young woman sends flowers, knowing the gift will make her happy. On the flip side (and, sadly, a bit rarer in young romance), if the lover knows certain things are unpleasant for the beloved, those things are avoided. A good way for Adam and Eve to show love for God would be to say something like, "I don't know why it would displease God if we ate the fruit from that tree, but if it makes Him unhappy, that's good enough for us."

Once more, this would involve an even further turn for Adam and Eve outward from themselves. To eat from the tree would mean ignoring God's feelings; it would make Him unhappy (to say the least).

More on the Virtues

The four godly virtues offered to humans through the Garden prohibition are wonderful things in themselves. We could build a book around them alone. For now, there are just a few more things.

First, let me restate some things: (1) the virtues are gifts that can, when grasped, differentiate mankind from the other members of creation. With them, humans can be something much higher than the animals; and (2) they're possessed and expressed by God Himself.

Next, there are two more important points about the virtues. First, they're important attributes of rulers. Humans were created to rule earth, and God intended them to be the best kind of rulers. A humble king seeks to serve his subjects, not oppress them. He values them, even over himself. A wise king seeks to learn how to serve his people. Wisdom also tells the king he's insufficient by himself to rule; he needs God's help. Thus, he needs faith. A king who does all this would be a great gift to any nation, but if he does these things because he genuinely loves his people, it's truly wonderful.

The second point is something very important for humanity to realize. *Without these godly qualities, humans would be destroyed by their limitations.* Let me explain. As we watched the unfolding story of God's creation, we learned that this creation involved the expression of His values. Things are different from one another. Placing one thing in one location and another someplace else was better than the other way around, at least at the time they were created.

An important expression of God's values involved *limits*. The ocean stops at a certain point, and the dry land appears: water has limits. Higher up is a point where the atmosphere thins and empty space begins: air has limits. There are reasons for these limitations in the mind of God. When God created humans, He shared something of Himself with His special creation, but there is one thing He cannot share: his size. God is infinite. Humans are limited.

We don't currently know the exact limits of human beings. Every time the Olympics take place, someone breaks a record—they run faster or jump higher than those before them. The limits of a human are hard to nail down, but one limitation was made clear by the prohibition: *a limit on our ability to perceive and to judge ultimate reality*. When God told Adam and Eve about their roles in the Garden; the wonderful privileges they had, the responsibilities they would undertake, and the one prohibition they should observe; *God did it with spoken words*.

When God intended for humans to learn about the forbidden tree, He didn't sit Adam down in the Garden and say, "Well now, Adam, look around. Does anything stand out to you? Say, do you notice that one tree over there? Does it *look* a little unusual? Does it *feel* different to you? What emotions are you experiencing when you look in that general direction?" No, God didn't do that. He spoke, and He spoke plainly. God's words were sufficient to instruct Adam about what he should and shouldn't do. This isn't to say humans are incapable of learning by observation, or that their feelings are unimportant. Minds and emotions are powerful things; it's just that humans are limited. The gap between this limitation and ultimate reality must be bridged by something theologians call "special revelation". God speaks. Humans listen.

If Adam and Eve had chosen to exercise the four godly virtues God sought for them to experience through the prohibition, they would have said something like, "Well, God, I can see You don't want me to eat any fruit from that tree. It doesn't look or feel bad, but because You are God and I am the created one, I respect You, and I'll do what You say. I'd surely prefer to listen to You than to find out on my own what this scary thing You call 'death' involves. I have confidence it's going to happen because You said so. Because I love You, I want to make You happy."

Perhaps these affirming statements would even be followed by a question: "Come to think of it, are there any *other* restrictions You want us to know about?"

With this final question, the prohibition could have introduced mankind to wonders we may never fully understand in our journeys through this life. There were many more things humans would need to avoid. If they climbed to a high place and saw before them a steep precipice, they couldn't simply step out and fly as the birds did. They would experience severe pain if they did. At the edges of volcanoes is something called lava, a substance so hot, humans dare not jump in and swim like they might at the local lagoon. Even on this wonderful gift of a planet, there would be many potentially painful experiences. They could all be avoided if Adam and Eve would have learned to listen to their Creator.

So, the prohibition concerning the Tree of the Knowledge of Good and Evil wasn't a random occurrence or the product of incomplete planning. It was an incredible gift intended to elevate humans to heights they could never attain without this first stage of learning. The human ability to make choices based on godly virtues would differentiate them from the other creatures they were created to rule. This ability would keep them safe, while they journeyed through the seemingly endless wonders of God's creation.

Once again, if we jump forward to the modern day, the world we live in looks much rougher than the perfect garden offered to Adam and Eve. What went wrong? We'll learn this in the next chapter.

Chapter 3

What Went Wrong?

So, we have two perfect people placed in a perfect garden on a perfect planet in a perfect universe. However, we don't see much perfection today. War, poverty, hurricanes, and earthquakes are only the start of horrible things pervading the human experience. If I didn't include a disaster affecting everyone, I can summarize by simply saying that sooner or later, we all experience pain. Granted, we still see beauty and goodness: sunshine, flowers, calm majestic forests, and a mother tenderly caressing a newborn child. Somehow though, the bad, the ugly, the dirty, and the dangerous have a way of creeping in and ruining the good, the beautiful, the pure, and the safe.

What went wrong?

Those who follow the story of Scripture trace the imperfection of our day back to a tragic event in the early world. Previously, we learned about the prohibition given by God that Adam and Eve should avoid a certain tree. We continue in Genesis chapter 3:

> Now the serpent was more crafty than any of the wild animals the LORD God had made. He said to the woman, "Did God really say, 'You must not eat from any tree in the garden'?" The woman said to the serpent, "We may eat fruit from the trees in the garden, but God did say, 'You must not eat fruit from the tree that is in the middle of the garden, and you must not touch it, or you will die.' "You will not surely die," the serpent said to the woman. "For God knows that when you eat of it your eyes will be opened, and you will be like God, knowing good and evil." (Genesis 3:1–5)

They say, when talking about a book, you should never reveal the ending or big plot twists, unless all your listeners have read it. Doing so spoils the story. I'm going to work on the assumption that many people already know about the next development. If you don't, please forgive me for revealing a major turning point:

> When the woman saw that the fruit of the tree was good for food and pleasing to the eye, and also desirable for gaining wisdom, she took some and ate it. She also gave some to her husband, who was with her, and he ate it. (Gen. 3:6)

Tragically, Adam and Eve disobeyed. Here is a vital fact that everyone must understand: *this failure has resulted in everything wrong or evil in the world.*

For the resident of the modern age who reads this, the questions are strikingly simple. How did this happen, and how did the result of this one act influence the entire modern world?

Let's examine what happened. First, we see a new actor identified as the serpent. Before we get too deeply into this topic, we should mention that this is where things get hard, if they haven't already. The serpent represents an individual known as Lucifer, the Devil, or Satan. At this point, some would say, "Surely you're not going to talk about the Devil as though modern, scientific-minded people should take him seriously."

Well, yes, we are.

It seems there is more to our reality than we can see. Along with humans, we are told in the Scriptures that God created a race of beings called angels. They are spirit beings with intelligence and power, but not with the same kind of corporeal bodies humans possess. The greatest of the angels was known among other names as Lucifer. At some point, he rebelled against God and took with him a large number of his kind, who are now generally known as "fallen angels" or "demons". They are responsible for much pain in our world. The angels who did not fall remain to this day as faithful servants of God.

It's a funny thing—if you were to ask the average, scientifically minded person whether life can exist in outer space, most would reply "probably" or even "yes". If you were to ask whether such life might be more intelligent than us, again you would get positive responses. Affirmations continue if you ask whether such beings would look very different from us and even if they could have visited us by now. So, let's say someone makes the following statement: "There are beings who are very different than we who have vast amounts of power and intelligence. They were created by God alongside of us and have existed on our planet for thousands of years. They're known as angels and demons." For some reason, the immediate response of the

29

scientific mind is, "That's impossible!" If they come from outer space, beings with angel-like features are fine. If they appear in the Bible, they're nonsense.

Unfortunately, there isn't time to explain the existence of angels or the philosophic reasons making their existence entirely reasonable. We will make some comments along the way, but for now we have to assume their existence and state that the worst of them appeared in the Garden to cause trouble. The only further point of note with Satan is *he has a deep hatred for God and anything God considers valuable*. This made the newly created creatures called humans prime targets. The forces of creation who rebelled against God were about to declare war. The hearts of the first two people on earth were to be the first battleground.

Imagine the scene: Lucifer appears in the Garden, wanting to sabotage paradise. He doesn't have much time. He has one shot, and it must be effective. Note: I suggest he uses tools that match his nature, and which he still uses to this day in his dealings with humans. Among those tools are what I call "The Three Doubts".

The First of the Three Doubts: Doubt God's Word

The serpent starts with the following question: "Did God really say, 'You must not eat from any tree in the garden'?" (Gen. 3:1) The Creator desired to give humans a stepping stone to the four godly virtues, one being faith. The serpent's first attack attempted to undermine this virtue with its polar opposite: doubt. Consider that phrase, "Did God *really* say . . . ?" Why would he start with that question? Answer: This question is intended to cause Adam and Eve to *doubt the ability and willingness of God to communicate in meaningful ways to humans*. At first, it seems to question whether we can dependably receive any communication from God at all. In other words, the serpent might be saying, "I know that the big guy said something to you, but are you sure you heard it correctly? Maybe when you were swimming with the dolphins, you got some water in your ears."

Believers have presumed for centuries that God communicated to people in accurate and dependable ways. As I stated earlier, this communication is essential because humans don't have the ability to fully and accurately sense reality on their own. Believers have historically felt the writings found in the book known as the Bible comprise the main recordings of people who received special communication from God. When those writings were originally recorded, they were infallible. There may be debate about the ability of any individual human to understand and interpret these writings perfectly. However, there is common agreement among those who hold a conservative form of faith that the writings themselves represent God's will for us. If there are any disagreements about what to do with the writings, those who form the community of faith stress it's our fallibility that leads to those disagreements, as opposed to any problem with the writings themselves. It's the task of believers to thoughtfully and diligently seek the meaning of the writings with God's help.

As a last note on this topic, I will build the foundation of this book on writings that are agreed upon by members of the Jewish and Christian faiths — the writings of Moses and the following histories of the Hebrew people (the Tanakh to the Jews and the "Old Testament" to Christians). As a member of the Christian faith, I will also include the writings of the followers of Christ (the New Testament), which in many cases expand the earlier teachings.

Having said this, the first statement of the serpent implies we need not even bother starting on this quest. It's impossible to hear anything from God correctly, according to the serpent; and many in the modern world heed this advice. I've had numerous conversations with friends in which a suggestion that they consider the Bible is met with a response something to the order of "Why bother? No one can figure out what God wants!"

This assumption misses some important points regarding God's abilities. If God created the heavens and the earth, isn't it reasonable to assume He can accurately share a few of His thoughts when He wants to? When you stop to think about it, it's silly to assume otherwise. It may have been the serpent's hope that he could stop there. This ploy certainly works well in the modern world. However, there was more potent poison to be fed to the newly created human couple.

Notice that the first question raised by the serpent was a terrible exaggeration of what God said in the prohibition. "Did God really say, 'You must not eat from *any* tree in the garden'?" That's not what God said; He said there was only one tree to avoid. The rest of the Garden was a sea of wonderful things to eat, all perfectly allowable. Here's the point; if God had created a wonderful paradise, and then told Adam and Eve they weren't allowed to enjoy *any* of it, that would be *silly*. Eve calls him on it, at first. She answers, "We may eat fruit from the trees in the garden, but God did say, 'You must not eat fruit from the tree that is in the middle of the garden, and you must not touch it, or you will die.'" The serpent skillfully leaves the statement hanging. There is no "Oh, you're right — I'm sorry." There is only the dangling suggestion that when God speaks, He may be sharing things that aren't worthy of serious consideration.

We said another of the godly virtues is *wisdom*. The wise person hears wisdom and responds appropriately, but how do the wise respond when they hear foolishness? They ignore it; and this was the sharp end of a wedge that the serpent was attempting to drive between humans and God. The serpent introduced doubt that God is able to share things with humans; and if He does share things, Adam and Eve should doubt that He has anything worthwhile to say.

Although the answer given by Eve would appear at first to be sufficient rebuttal to the serpent, it indicates she may have had some doubts about this odd rule. She not only states God told her and her husband to avoid eating the fruit, she adds they must not *touch it*. God didn't say anything about touching in the prohibition; only eating was forbidden. For some reason, Eve decided to add something to the clear revelation of God. We are not told why, but with some reasoning I'll label as speculation, we can possibly draw nearer to the meaning. Perhaps Eve was thinking something like, "I wouldn't say God was so silly as to tell us we can't eat anything in this garden, but it does seem odd He would leave something said to be dangerous hanging within easy reach. It's clearly insufficient to merely avoid putting it in our mouths. It seems reasonable to keep some distance." In other words, Eve viewed the prohibition not as completely absurd, only slightly questionable. God was somehow coming up short in His provision here. If Eve got too close, she felt that fruit could jump right into her mouth. There was something somehow *unfair* in all of this. How could God make such a rule and then give so little help in obeying it?

Let me repeat—some of the above is speculation. It's clear, though, that Eve thought it a good idea to bolster obedience with some extra rules; it's also clear this didn't help anything. Adding additional rules to God's clear instruction is called *legalism*. We'll talk about it later in the book. At any rate, with the wedge now firmly inserted, the serpent is ready to drive in more damaging attacks.

The Second of the Three Doubts: Doubt God's Power

"You will not surely die," said the serpent, "for God knows that when you eat of it, your eyes will be opened, and you will be like God, knowing good and evil." (Gen. 3:4-5)

The next virtue to be defiled was *humility*. As we stated, when the Creator of the heavens and the earth speaks to the created ones, it's right to listen; but the serpent has successfully suggested that sometimes God says things that aren't very wise. Is it right to listen to someone who says foolish things? Maybe in the overall scheme of the new universe, God isn't as lofty as He supposes. Maybe *He* needs a little humility, in terms of accurately understanding

His status? As troubling a thought as this might be, there's more. In this case, God says (or so it is charged) that something is going to happen that absolutely won't occur. "Die?" blasts the serpent. "That's never going to happen. It's totally false."

Let's think about this. What kind of person says things that aren't true? What kind of person would predict something that can never happen?

Erroneous predictions are the product of people who don't have the ability to accomplish what they say they'll do. Here the serpent extends doubt to the area of God's *power*. The serpent, who previously questioned God's ability to communicate in accurate ways, now, tacitly, admits God is in fact fully capable of sharing His thoughts. He's just not capable of following through on what He says.

I once had a friend who suffered from a debilitating illness. In the latter years of his life, he was limited to a wheelchair and lacked the strength to lift more than a small spoon to his mouth. He could feed himself when food was placed in front of him but could do little else. During one visit to his home, I overheard an argument he was having with a man who rented a room from him. As part of the rental agreement, the tenant agreed to help around the house but wasn't fulfilling his responsibilities. The argument got very loud, and eventually the tenant walked away. In a tragic burst of anger, my friend yelled out, "You come back here! I'm going to kick you across the room!" He actually used more colorful language, but we'll keep the censored version for now. One observer in the room, normally a very kind person, found himself doing something unthinkable—he had to suppress a laugh. No, he shouldn't have laughed, and later felt bad for doing so; but there was something so outlandish in this scene, he couldn't help himself. With some fear of sounding mean, a man confined to a wheelchair who threatens extreme bodily harm to another is *pathetic*. Most sad was the reaction of the intended victim; he let out a derisive laugh (which, unlike my kinder friend, he made no attempt to suppress) and arrogantly sauntered away.

The Third of the Three Doubts: Doubt God's Character

"You know," said the serpent, "this fellow who's been barking out commands is pathetic. He says things he can't possibly make happen." Could there be a more demeaning charge? Maybe not, but there are even more serious charges you can make, and one of them came next. You can charge someone with being *dishonest*. Behind the implied series of charges submitted before these two unsuspecting courtroom jurors lay the intimation that

God is a willful liar. "He knows what He's saying won't happen," charges the serpent.

"But why?" someone could ask. "Why would God make up such a thing?" The serpent's answer: *because He's hiding something.* With this charge, the serpent leaps forward and plunges his dagger of doubt into the heart of Adam and Eve's faith. He wanted them to doubt God's *character.* If the young couple in the Garden were to take from the tree and eat, they could be *like God.* "Forget all of this humility nonsense!" proclaims the serpent. "Forget about this business of accurately judging your place in the universe and respecting those higher in the chain-of-command. You can make a bold leap right up to the top." The serpent goes on, "And why wouldn't you? This pathetic being who calls himself 'God' can't (or won't) communicate meaningful things to you in meaningful ways. He says things that can't possibly happen because He doesn't have the power to make them happen. And worst of all, He's doing all of this because He's holding back on you. There are wonderful, incredible things you could have that He hides behind nothing more than a bald-faced lie! He is something far less than benevolent, something far less than loving, and something far less than good. Why would you trust *Him*?"

The Mechanism of the Fall

We were told the serpent was the "most crafty" of the creatures in the Garden, and now we see why. In just a few sentences, he's undermined any reason to reach for the four virtues. Why be humble when you can be like God? How is it wise to listen to someone who says foolish things? What was there to have faith in? How can you trust a pathetic, selfish being when he clearly has something other than your best interests in mind? Finally, how can you love someone as obviously unlovable as this?

With all objections to the prohibition nullified, Adam and Eve looked to the tree they were warned to avoid. They had no idea what "Knowledge of Good and Evil" was, but it sounded important. The thing called "death" couldn't happen, so indulgence had to be safe. Why not try it?

A note: I'm not an expert in the ancient Hebrew language of the original Genesis manuscripts, but I'm told a good translation of this passage is Adam was right there with Eve (Crabb 1995, 11). Many have placed entire blame for this action on Eve. Eve is certainly culpable for her part. However, although Eve reached out first, Adam could have stopped her if he were not as taken as she was. According to the text, he was right there quietly listening while he let his partner do the talking. This turns out to be a team effort.

In looking to the tree, Eve no longer had the revealed words of God; those words which alone enabled an adequate grasp of reality. Instead, she relied on her senses:

> When the woman saw that the fruit of the tree was good for food and pleasing to the eye, and also desirable for gaining wisdom, she took some and ate it. She also gave some to her husband, who was with her, and he ate it. (Gen. 3:6)

Adam and Eve thought the fruit was "good for food". How could they know this before they tried any? They could only use their senses and feelings. Objective scientific observation is usually thought to have been invented in the modern age, but it may have been invented by the two highly intelligent (though morally questionable) people in the Garden. When held up next to other foods, it appeared to be, well, a fruit. It had similar weight, similar color, similar feel, and similar smell to other fruits. If you walk into a produce store, there's a distinct smell; a steakhouse has another. You can tell them apart. The fruit of the forbidden tree seemed a fine fit for the supermarket produce aisle. In a more revealing amplification of what happened, we're told in the same sentence the fruit was "pleasing to the eye". When Adam and Eve looked at the fruit, they had a positive feeling. It looked appealing, if not pretty. If it makes you feel good, it must be good, right? Do we really need objective observation when we feel good? Many would say "no" to this day.

Finally, the fruit was judged to be "desirable for gaining wisdom". Again, how could this be determined before it was ingested? Again, the answer is plain: Adam and Eve based this assumption on their emotions. They were feeling very sophisticated at this point. They had come to believe that only a few short minutes ago, they were lowly lapdogs of a mean-spirited being. They were unimportant zookeepers whose job was to spend eternity cleaning up after a bothersome menagerie of countless animals one minute, while tending someone else's garden the next. All this while being conned into believing that the foolish chasing of virtue would somehow ennoble them, when in fact they were being cheated out of jewels that dangled before them within easy reach. They were about to be "like God" (whatever that meant). They certainly felt like they could be no wiser. Maybe they didn't even need to eat the fruit. They may have felt they already surpassed God just thinking about the possibilities!

But eat they did; and within only a few seconds, they discovered they had "bitten off more than they could chew". They were only moments from the beginning of a painful journey starting at the exit door of the Garden. This journey would take not just them, but their children and their children's children for millennia over dark and frightening paths.

The Plan Goes Bad

What was the sign that something went wrong?

"Then the eyes of both of them were opened, and they realized they were naked; so they sewed fig leaves together and made coverings for themselves" (Gen. 2:7). Adam and Eve thought their senses, working in conjunction with their emotions, were channels to higher realities and powers. In an instant, those channels turned into chains. These two, previously enraptured with themselves and their potential, now received a truer picture of what they were. They were naked.

Oddly, they weren't more naked than a few moments before. With clothing, you can't go further than nothing. So, what was the problem? To find the answer, we must ask, "What is now different?" It wasn't clothing. Before, Adam and Eve were "naked and felt no shame". Now, shame had awakened.

Let me offer this definition of shame: It's what you feel when you're given reason to consider yourself less important or significant than you think you should be. In particular, it's when you're made to feel there's something *wrong* with you.

Sometimes definitions don't come close to fully describing our human feelings. My definition admittedly falls short of human experience in this case. Shame hurts. In its degrees, it can range from a quick sting to something that festers painfully in the pits of our souls. We don't know how deeply Adam and Eve felt it. It could be they were feeling an emotion so new, it was closer to the sting; or it could have been much worse. Whatever they felt, they hadn't yet come to the fullest realization of this emotion. Why? Because they weren't yet debilitated. Shame does this at its worst. In their minds, there was corrective action to be taken, and they jumped right to it. They quickly tore some leaves off a nearby fig tree and fashioned a new invention called *clothing*.

Artists have portrayed this scene over the centuries. In most renderings, Adam and Eve are pictured with a single leaf covering their genitals. This is a tragically misleading picture, made sadder by the number of times it's been repeated. The text of the story says Adam and Eve took leaves, plural. You could say that picturing them each with one leaf adds up to two, so this could be technically correct. However, the technicality evaporates when we're told the couple in the Garden *sewed* the leaves together into a garment. This implies there were more than two leaves involved. I'm suggesting

Adam and Eve made something looking more like a trench coat than minimalist swimwear.

Why do I suggest this? Because we're told the creation of Adam and Eve marked the pinnacle of God's creation. When God added Adam and Eve to the universe, He was done. He had previously looked at His works and pronounced, "good." After the first couple appeared, He then pronounced, "very good." There was nothing about Adam and Eve displeasing to God. Everything about them was perfect. Why? Because *He* thought so. That point of reference was discarded by Adam and Eve. When they did this, they learned the first of many harsh realities: *It is God who assigns value in this universe, and it's only His estimation that matters.* From the first day of creation, pieces of the universe were moved from place to place because doing so reflected God's values. If He chose to move matter, floating aimlessly around the cosmos into celestial bodies, such as suns and planets, it was because it seemed good to Him. In fact, it was perfect. When He created Adam and Eve, He created them as perfect beings fitting perfectly into His perfect universe. They had value for one reason and one reason alone: God assigned it to them.

This is what changed. With God, everything about Adam and Eve was valuable. Without Him, nothing could be declared with confidence to have worth. Adam and Eve felt it right away. It wasn't just their genitalia that became questionable—it was every inch of their bodies. More than this, it wasn't simply a question of their persons lacking value. Something was *wrong*. Adam and Eve understood for the first time, at least partially, the meaning of good and evil. There was now something about them that fell under the evil part.

Their theft of the forbidden fruit was motivated by a desire for "the Knowledge of Good and Evil", and now they had it. Sadly, they discovered they had chosen to learn of evil by taking it into their very beings; they consumed it. Now, it was a permanent part of them. When they realized this, a new and complex set of feelings welled up from their hearts. They saw something displeasing about themselves. In fact, it was something repulsive; something needing to be covered up and hidden from their newly sensitized emotions.

Then, they felt something that rocked them to their cores. They felt *fear*.

> Then the man and his wife heard the sound of the LORD God as he was walking in the garden in the cool of the day, and they hid from the LORD God among the trees of the garden. (Gen. 3:8)

Prior to this, God was always a welcome guest in the residence at 1 Garden Road. We aren't told the time span between the completion of creation and the Fall. It may have been minutes; it may have been centuries. Whatever the time, God had been someone who could walk in the door without knocking. Now, His appearance down the road became reason to lock the door and hide under the bed. Adam and Eve did some creative work making garments to hide their newly discovered blemish. However, it took only a second to realize this wasn't enough. God didn't have to say or do anything. Adam and Eve realized many more leaves would be needed to hide the stains of this spill. So, they found a section of trees and cowered behind them.

I think I understand how the couple felt because of an experience I had as a child. In many ways, I was considered a well-behaved little boy. I remember listening, when warned, about the dangers of the world. One of those dangers was fire. We had a cartoon character in those days called Sparky the Fire Dog, a Dalmatian with a fireman's hat who sternly warned us: "Don't play with matches." One day, at an age when my mother felt it safe to leave me at home while she went next door for a few minutes, I discovered a book of matches. I had seen them lit from a distance, and the sparkle of the flame looked to a small mind to be a great wonder. I remembered the warnings, but I decided I was above the danger.

I remember picking up the book of matches and standing over a small trashcan in a bedroom, where I commenced lighting my first match. It sparkled and glowed with mesmerizing force. I blew it out and threw it into the trashcan. A good plan, it seemed. I felt in total control. So, I did it again. Nothing bad happened. This was fun—*really* fun. Obviously, that Sparky character had no idea what he was talking about. So, I repeated the process a number of times.

Then something went very wrong. One of the matches I threw into the trashcan wasn't completely out after I blew on it. Because I had neglected to empty the trashcan before starting, there were some pieces of paper inside of it awaiting that diabolical little match. In only a second, I saw a small flame being hatched beneath me. I tried blowing on it, to no avail. Unknown to children is the fact that the amount of blowing needed to extinguish a match is exactly the right amount to fan a newly started fire; but wait! There was hope. I ran as fast as I could to the bathroom and grabbed a small paper cup next to the sink. After filling it with water, I ran as fast as I could back to the flame. It was now bigger, but surely my little fire company had arrived in time. I threw the contents of the cup into the can and stopped to catch my breath. In a second, though, I experienced for the first time in my life a feeling of absolute horror when I saw that I had not even slowed down the flames.

Another round trip to the bathroom brought me to a fire that was climbing higher than the top of the can.

Eventually, I put out the fire. I don't remember exactly how many trips it took, but one thing I remember—it seemed an eternity. Finally, though, the fire was vanquished. I won!

Now there was a problem. The can was filled with charred pieces of paper. Certainly, they would be found. What to do? Why, hide the evidence, of course. I carefully removed each piece of half-burned paper from the can and began to hide them. There were quite a few, and it took a number of creative attempts to make them all disappear. One went behind the headboard in the master bedroom. Another went under the rug; yet another found its final resting place behind the dresser, and a few more went into banishment in the closet. What a clever boy I was! The matches had gotten out of hand, but I successfully performed a cover-up worthy of any in history.

My victory was short-lived, however. Once my mother returned home, I stood quietly, waiting to see what would happen. It was then I discovered something: God has given mothers a special tool to aid them in times of childhood misbehavior like these—something called a "nose". Within seconds, my mother knew something was wrong. She smelled smoke. She was led in a totally mysterious way (or at least it seemed to me) directly to the altar of burnt offering. She may have thought the house was still on fire. To her relief, this wasn't the case; but the relief was short-lived. She was met with the complex emotion that results when fear is relieved and replaced with anger. No, the house wasn't burning down, but it certainly might have been. There could be only one culprit: the little boy my mother thought she could trust.

I thought my poker face was sufficient to this task, but there must have been fear in my little eyes betraying my guilt. I still remember her voice as she asked, "What is *this*?" while pointing into the can that still contained ash-laden water—another small oversight in my plan. She smelled around some more and immediately found the piece of burned paper that was (or so I had thought) completely hidden under the carpet. One by one, other pieces of evidence quickly came out of hiding, as if an unseen hand was leading my mother from hiding place to hiding place.

I still remember the worst part. My mother, who had trusted me, looked me in the eye, while holding one of the charred paper remnants. She asked, "Did *you* do this?" What does any self-respecting child do at a time like this? Why, lie of course. "Noooooo," I immediately answered. Somehow, when you're a child, you think that stretching the "O" of "no" for a long time improves your chances of being believed. This "no" rang out with my very best effort and echoed throughout the room, but it wasn't enough. The evidence was too great, and my fearful countenance revealed the guilty party to any discerning eye.

If a human mother could smell the remains of failed match play, and quickly single out the culprit, how much more could the all-knowing God become immediately aware of what had just happened in the Garden? He knew exactly what had happened, and He knew exactly where Adam and Eve were.

How did He respond?

Chapter 4

God's Response to the Fall

The Surprising Episode That Followed

What should God have done at this time? He created a world. He created Adam and Eve to live in it and enjoy the awesome benefits of ruling with Him. He showered them with unimaginable gifts; yet, they rebelled against Him. They showed total disregard for His generosity and love, while showing absolute disdain for His authority.

Once I saw an enactment of this story where an angel makes the following suggestion to God: "Why not doom 'em all and start again with some other kind of critter?" Indeed, why not? Why should God have to be bothered with such nonsense? He could wipe out these annoying human beings and create something else—something more *compliant*.

He didn't do that because the existence of compliant beings wasn't His goal. Rocks are compliant. God tells them to sit somewhere, and they stay until something moves them. God's goal was embodied in the two beings He already created. As we said before, His goal was (at least) beings possessing the divine ability to make choices, and to make those choices based on godly virtues. He displayed these virtues Himself up to this point, and He was going to continue displaying them because they're part of His character. God had humbled Himself and made Himself the servant of His creation. As such, He wanted to heal, not destroy. As a God of wisdom, He knew the gift of choice meant allowing for bad choices as well as good. You see, *if bad choices are impossible, there is no real choice at all*.

Finally, God showed His love. God's love isn't shown only to those who return it after it's given. When God loves someone, He showers the benefits of love on him/her, expecting nothing in return. That's Him; that's how He is. The apostle John would later write, "God is love" (I John 4:8). Love may be the quality God desires to show to His human creation above all others. When we as humans feel powerful, we like to show it—maybe too much. If we think we know something, we like to let others know how smart we think we are; but God likes to be known best for His love.

God desired people who knew how to make decisions correctly. If they chose correctly, God could shower them with His love. Since they chose incorrectly, God would show His love *even more* by showing it to beings who didn't deserve it. Infinite power and infinite wisdom and all the other infinite qualities of God are surpassed only by His infinite love.

He showed it here. Adam and Eve deserved nothing at this point. They deserved only judgment followed by destruction. They didn't deserve a word of explanation; they didn't deserve a waiting period. They deserved only retribution, swift and sure. They deserved to be destroyed "before they knew what hit them"; but God didn't give Adam and Eve what they deserved. He gave them what they were to receive as people whom He loved. They received an amazing gift of God: *mercy*. Instead of destroying the couple, God reached out to them.

God Showed Mercy

"But the LORD God called to the man, 'Where are you?'" (Gen. 3:9) God could have reached into the midst of the trees and pulled out Adam and Eve by the scruffs of their necks, kicking and screaming. Instead, He gave the couple a chance to accept responsibility. Adam spoke up when called: "He answered, 'I heard you in the garden, and I was afraid because I was naked; so I hid'" (vs. 10).

Notice three things here: First, God had not yet asked, "Did you do something wrong?" Adam may have perceived an opportunity to escape without being caught, so he moved to the obvious. "Well, I was just looking around and happened to notice I'm not wearing anything. Then I heard You coming and assumed something bad was about to happen. Can You blame me for hiding?" There is a hint here of Adam's inner train of thought. Nakedness equals something God won't like. God hadn't provided any clothes. Therefore, *God had fallen short*. This was the beginning of an accusation. God failed to provide something in Adam's mind. The word *provision* will become very important in the future.

The second thing was the thought that all Adam had to do was hide. The aforementioned limitation of people to truly judge reality on their own became apparent here. Adam totally missed the ability of God to be everywhere and to know everything. Even more, Adam totally underestimated the size of the problem he created. Maybe it would quickly go away. Although he knew something was wrong, Adam didn't, in any way, sense the depth of what happened. Perhaps it bothered him that God barged in at such an inconvenient time. In a few minutes, the spill might painlessly evaporate.

The third thing to note: there is no "we" here, only "I". Eve was out of the picture from Adam's perspective. Adam became completely absorbed in himself. He wasn't only experiencing alienation from God; his self-centeredness had already grown to the point where he was alienated from the only other human on earth.

God refused to allow Adam to cloud the issue. He pressed on: "Who told you that you were naked? Have you eaten from the tree that I commanded you not to eat from?" (Gen. 3:11)

Here it is: "Did *you* do this?" The question is raised along with evidence of wrongdoing, much like my mother holding up the charred remnants of paper after my ill-fated match play. If Adam hadn't eaten from the tree, he wouldn't have been aware of his nakedness, much less troubled by it.

The explanation made perfect sense to Adam. There was no point in hiding the truth any longer. The man said, "The woman you put here with me—she gave me some fruit from the tree, and I ate it." (Gen. 3:12)

Adam had problems here, but stupidity wasn't one. He knew he was caught, so lying was pointless. Adam chose a more appropriate path for someone just beginning to experience the evil side of "good and evil". He chose blame-shifting; "not guilty" is usually the first defense when the unrepentant are accused. When denial doesn't work, the next argument in line is often "It's not my fault." Adam pled it right away. The woman had committed the crime and then put the fruit into Adam's hand. What could he do? Maybe Adam agreed with the "Don't even touch it" technique for avoiding bad behavior. When the fruit was on the tree, everything was fine; but when the fruit was placed in his hand, and "everyone else was doing it" (another plea thought to be helpful at times like this), how could anyone be expected to act otherwise? These were overwhelming forces. A few moments ago, Adam had completely forgotten his mate. Now, she became an important, if not indispensable, figure: a scapegoat.

There is yet another facet to Adam's argument; one largely missed by readers over the centuries (taken from *Silence of Adam*). Note Adam's first words: "The woman, who *you* put here with me . . ." (Gen. 3:12, emphasis mine). Adam wasn't just blaming Eve; he was blaming God. The finger that pointed first to the next person in line is now pointed upward to her Creator. "Well," Adam hinted, "aren't You the funny one? That was an impressive practical joke. You had me thinking this Eve gal was the best thing in the world. It turns out she's the worst thing that ever happened to me, and I have no one to thank but you! How could you have played such a dirty trick?" In Adam's mind, this was all the fault of others. Eve pulled him down, or so he thought; and who provided Eve? Why, God did. That makes this whole thing God's fault. Adam wasn't culpable in his own thinking.

The next argument following "It's not my fault" is often, "This isn't fair." Such is Adam's attitude. He wasn't an actor in this tragedy; he was a *victim*. Sadly, this has been a time-worn defense for many whenever it comes to taking personal responsibility for failures.

When people think this way, reasoning with them is usually unrewarding. God moves on to the next in line.

"Then the LORD God said to the woman, 'What is this you have done?' The woman said, 'The serpent deceived me, and I ate'" (Gen. 3:13). The spotlight now hits Eve. She's asked a simple question. Will Eve do better than her husband and accept responsibility? Not on your life. Eve decides to jump in line with the pointed fingers and moves on to the serpent. "Oh yes, I did it," Eve says, "but there is a perfectly reasonable explanation. It's all *his* fault! He misled me and made me do it." Behind the "perfectly reasonable explanation" lays a mindset not much different than Adam's. "*Someone* let that thing in here. Doesn't this place have any kind of security? Maybe a better-designed garden would have a fence. Isn't it enough that You leave that awful fruit dangling in front of our eyes, without allowing in slippery snakes to cloud our minds? I had everything under control with my 'extra measures' until that serpent came along." In Eve's mind, God failed to protect her. That word, *protect*, is another that will become important in the future.

The amplified dialogues above are speculation. What I'm trying to do through them is illustrate a point: Adam clearly didn't think the situation was his fault. Eve clearly didn't think the situation was her fault. If the fault wasn't Adam's and it wasn't Eve's, then whose fault was it? I have run into many people who are familiar with this story, and many of them have suspicions about the answer, I think. Few of them will admit it.

To many, this is God's fault. He could have stopped the serpent. He could have hung the fruit higher; or, he could have left it out of the Garden all together. He left Adam and Eve with insufficient resources to battle the serpent when their eternal safety was endangered. God failed to provide for Adam and Eve, and He failed to protect them, or so many would charge if they were honest with themselves.

When people allow this line of reasoning into their minds, they show how much we are all like the couple in the Garden; I include myself in the "we". None of us are better than Adam and Eve. I believe any of us would have done likewise were we in their situation. Sadly, to this day we continue to be quick to entertain statements that paint God as the bad guy, while excusing our own responsibilities.

There was a simple solution to this problem. At any point during the temptation, Adam and Eve could have said, "Hey, wait a minute. Let's think about this." They could have remembered all the wonderful things God had done. Best of all, they could have called to God and asked for His help. He would have gladly come. Neither of them had to face the serpent alone.

Instead, they forgot what God had done for them. They invited a lie to fill the void left when they pushed those memories out of their heads. Choosing to act on those lies, they took raw evil into their hearts. So now, they stand before God defiled. They're angry, they're fearful, and they're shifting blame: and the one they're ultimately shifting blame to is standing right before them.

If God didn't have reason enough to send them both into oblivion before this, now He has far more. Fortunately for Adam and Eve, much less the multitudes of humans that were to follow, that's not what God chose to do. That's not who He is. That wasn't His plan. He was going to show mercy to the human race that would be repeated countless times in the millennia to follow.

Immediate and Future Mercy for Adam, Eve, and Humanity

Mercy has at least one part: the painful retribution that someone deserves isn't shown him/her. At its best, mercy has two parts. Not only is retribution removed, but generosity appears in its place. God first displays His mercy when pronouncing judgment on the one individual who clearly had a part to play in this act, the serpent.

> So the LORD God said to the serpent, "Because you have done this,
> "Cursed are you above all the livestock
> and all the wild animals!
> You will crawl on your belly
> and you will eat dust
> all the days of your life.
>
> And I will put enmity
> between you and the woman,
> and between your offspring and hers;
> he will crush your head,
> and you will strike his heel. (Gen. 3:14–15)

The judgment on the serpent has two parts: one symbolic and one prophetic. It's generally believed that behind the physical animal of the Garden was the fallen angel, Satan. The animal through which he appeared became a symbol. Though they may hold some fascination to those who keep them in cages, most people don't like snakes. Some are poisonous. Even the nonpoisonous varieties cause many to shudder. It seems to be an ingrained reaction. It follows snakes will lie in hidden places, snapping at the heels of all the children of women. Gardeners and farmers of all stripes will grab a shovel and crush the heads of those biological landmines.

Behind the symbol is the question of Satan's eventual fate. We're told God would put "enmity" between the woman's offspring and Satan. In particular, we're told the offspring "will crush your head" while the serpent would "strike his heel". To have a heel bitten is painful and injurious; to have your head crushed is fatal. This statement is the first mention of ultimate justice. Someday, a human child will be born who will destroy Satan. In this, God has shown His first act of mercy to the human race. Evil entered the world with the help of Satan. Someday, Satan and all evil will be judged and destroyed.

The Hard Side of Mercy

Here we expand our understanding of mercy. Though it often results in far less pain than deserved, *mercy doesn't always mean a complete escape from the consequences of evil or unwise actions*.

In this case, God gave Adam and Eve a choice—a true choice. Being entrusted with this choice was necessary for them to grow into something higher. God still intended for them to grow, but now it would be painful. This was their choice. God would make them, and all their descendants, follow through on the decision. They chose evil, and now it was going to come.

There are many fine commentaries on the next few verses, so I'll let those who wish to dig deeper search them out. To summarize:

1. The harmony and love of human relationships would be stressed and often broken. Men and women were meant to meet, fall in love, marry, and produce families, with children in homes ruled by love. Often, familial relationships are filled with happy times, but now a new element was introduced. Marriage would include painful battlegrounds where two people would often manipulate and oppress each other rather than love and serve. The raising of children would start with a seemingly unbearable experience for the woman. The experience of raising offspring would be further tainted by children who would present various levels of rebellion sooner or later. The pure joy of new life and families would be marred forever, sometimes to excruciating levels.

2. Humans were created to grow, learn, and build up the world in ways that would be self-fulfilling and enjoyable with each new moment. Although some joy could still be achieved in this process, most would experience something that we now call *work*. For most, this is not the preferred way to experience life; to others, it's absolute torture. Previously, reasonable and meaningful effort produced abundance. Now, weeds and thorns would compete for food, causing the basic act of gathering sustenance to be a painful chore.

3. All people would eventually face a day when their physical bodies ceased to function. As God had warned, the energy of youth would be replaced with the slowdowns of aging and eventually with the complete breakdown of death. The complex and wondrous arrangement of atoms and molecules God assembled from the basic elements of the earth would cease to hold together. Human bodies would return to the materials from which they were made: "dust you are and to dust you will return" (Gen. 3:19 b).

Sadly, these three things are familiar and undeniable to anyone who looks honestly at human experience.

God's Final Acts of Mercy in the Garden

There were two more things needed before the scene could be complete. Both were immense acts of mercy on God's part. First: "The LORD God made garments of skin for Adam and his wife and clothed them" (Gen. 3:21).

Why did God do this? Didn't the couple make clothes already? Apparently, these garments were insufficient. They represented the notion that whatever was wrong with Adam and Eve, it could be hidden in some relatively simple way; but something was created in the rebellion of the Garden. It is summed up in the word *sin*. Sin is very, very serious. Adam and Eve had no idea how serious it was. Just grab a handful of leaves from a tree, do a little sewing, and *voila*, instant disappearing act for the stain of sin; but God knew Adam and Eve needed to see how serious the stains were. In order to get the skin from an animal, it has to be killed. This was the lesson: *sin and rebellion leads to death*. No amount of human effort and no combination of readily available materials can cover the effects of sin. Even more than this, since the resources to overcome sin are not within human reach, *God must provide them*.

This was the first object lesson for the couple in dealing with their decisions and its results; but one final act of mercy was needed:

> And the LORD God said, "The man has now become like
> one of us, knowing good and evil. He must not be allowed
> to reach out his hand and take also from the tree of life and

eat, and live forever." So the LORD God banished him from the Garden of Eden to work the ground from which he had been taken. After he drove the man out, he placed on the east side of the Garden of Eden cherubim and a flaming sword flashing back and forth to guard the way to the tree of life. (Gen. 3:22–24)

There was one more tree of great power in the Garden, the Tree of Life. Ingesting its fruit would place in Adam and Eve a force that would cause them to live in their human bodies forever. Previously, there had been no prohibition against eating from this tree. If Adam and Eve lived forever in their perfect states, that would have been wonderful. Now, experiencing this tree would leave them locked in their new, degraded states for all eternity.

As I said, sin leads to death. As it turns out, that's not always the worst thing. Though death in itself is tragic, it has one remarkable value: *it is part of the process that allows humans to be separated from their sin.* Knowing this, God banished Adam and Eve from the Garden and blocked the way to the Tree of Life. Something like a Tree of Life or a Fountain of Youth is the goal of many medical researchers. This goal grows out of our limited human wisdom. In the infinite wisdom of God, the death that will eventually take all humans is part of a divine plan to express His mercy. Death is not to be rushed, mind you, but it doesn't need to be feared.

Chapter 5

How Does the Fall Affect Us Today?

Different Ways of Looking at the Universe and How They Affect Values

Remarkably, much of Western thought for the last thousand years was founded upon concepts taught in the opening pages of the Bible. Before moving on, let me restate some of those things. While restating, we'll revisit the ways these concepts interface with different areas of modern thought.

According to the biblical story, the universe was brought into existence by a Creator God.

There are three ways to see the universe. Classic students of philosophy and religion might want more categories, but three will suffice for now. Each has powerful ramifications.

- As we just stated, God made it. For now, let's call this the "Creator" view (also called theism).
- The universe doesn't have a creator. It has always existed and always will. It may change form, but it has always been (atheism—no God).
- The universe and God are one. They're the same thing (pantheism—God is everywhere and everything).

For years, people who discussed religion discussed different kinds of religions. Today, atheists have proliferated; they don't see themselves as having a religion. So, a better term for the above concepts is *worldview*. Following are some of the ways the worldviews see reality.

For those in the Creator worldview, a being who could create the universe must be incredibly intelligent and fantastically powerful. The universe expresses these qualities. People who hold this view also see the universe as a cosmic workshop where a master artist expresses his *values* through the creation. Watching the universe is an opportunity to learn something about the Creator who made it. Since the Creator is incredibly intelligent, He created according to a plan.

To the atheist, since there is no God, the universe is a gigantic series of random events. As such, no one thing is more valuable than any other. No event is more special than the next. If observing a thing or an event causes an emotional response, this is simply the next random event in a long, long string of causes and effects. One thing happens; it causes something else to happen. That "happening" causes yet another. This has been going on forever and will continue forever. The important thing to remember is this: for the atheist, there is no such thing as an eternal value because *there is no eternal being to assign value*. Everything is equally valuable because everything has no value. Some atheists would suggest it's the responsibility of each person to find his/her own value.

To the pantheist, since everything is God, everything is also an expression of that god. The difference between the pantheist view and the Creator view is this: for the pantheist, everything is an expression of God's values *at the moment*. This differs from the Creator view, and it's an important distinction.

Objects in the universe change frequently. For the pantheist, this means their god is changing. It's growing; it's learning. The universe is a gigantic attempt by this god to work out things in its mind, with every thought reflected in matter and events. On the other hand, for those who see a Creator, all of the stuff of the universe can experience change without the Creator changing, because the Creator is separate from His creation. Change is *part of the Creator's plan*. For the pantheist, change *is part of their god*. Values are assigned in a wholly different way. Whatever you see at the moment is how your god feels at the moment. Everything is equally valuable because everything is God.

For those in the Creator camp, God's plan and foreknowledge are reflected in the living things He creates. Each has a different purpose that fits into a grand scheme. Each has a different value based on the Creator's foreordained plan. Each can cause more wonder in human observers than the nonliving things because they're fantastically more complex. The complexity of each living thing causes even more wonder when you realize it's part of an ecological system—a mind-boggling clockwork of living organisms that somehow work in conjunction with each other to sustain life.

To the atheist, the animals of the earth are simply more products of random chance. They're effects of the afore-described series of causes and effects. Again, all are equally valuable because all have no value. In fact, animals are no different than waterfalls or rocks. A rock was once dust floating in space. It fell into a gravitational pool billions of years ago that became our planet. It was exposed to heat and pressure and, at some point eons later, appeared where it could be seen by humans. Other atoms floating around in space also fell to earth and were shaped by other forces into animal life. The only thing important at any given time is what's around at that time. If dust is blown through the air and covers a rock, the rock silently disappears. That's it. If one animal meets another and a fight ensues, the winner is considered the "fittest"; if the winner of the fight consumes the loser, that is "survival of the fittest". The new situation is not better or worse, only different. If a gigantic meteorite were to fall to earth and destroy all life, that would just be one more change. Nothing would be better. Nothing would be worse. Everything would just be different. Some atheists would disagree. They would suggest that certainly, some things are more valuable than others. The purists among the atheists, though, would consider this way of thinking inconsistent with the heart of atheism (and I would agree).

Once more, the pantheist assigns equal value to all life because all life is a piece of their god. Moreover, a rock has the same value because it's a piece of this god, too. The important element is merely what appears at the moment. If dust blows over the rock and hides it, then the dust becomes important because that's how their god feels at the moment. If two animals meet and fight, with the winner consuming the loser, this, too, is merely the momentary feeling of the pantheist god.

Here we see a paradox forming between the pantheist and the atheist. Both assign equal value to everything within their systems. To the atheist, nothing has value. To the pantheist, everything has value. The difference is the amount of respect the follower of a worldview has for an object or an event. The atheist values things only as far as they are useful to him. The pantheist values everything as he feels his god wants it valued at any moment. This is important because of the next thing we learn from the first few pages of the Bible:

According to the biblical story, God created humans. More than that, He created humans to be very special.

For followers of the Creator, humans aren't simply one more variety of animal. Humans were created for a divinely inspired purpose. As such, they have greater value than the animals and inanimate objects of the universe. Shakespeare's character Hamlet said it well:

> "What a piece of work is a man, how noble in reason, how infinite in faculties, in form and moving how express and admirable, in action how like an angel, in apprehension how like a god! the beauty of the world, the paragon of animals."
> (Hamlet, 2.2.303–311)

The contemplative young man struggles in his musings to understand the intent of God, who placed man so high in the created order. The psalmist David understood even better the purposes of God, when he said that looking at human complexity leads to worship: "I praise you because I am fearfully and wonderfully made" (Psalm 139:14).

As if there's not enough wonder in the human status, which Shakespeare called the "paragon of animals", here is more: The Creator God calls on mankind to rule the earth. More than that, He calls on mankind to rule *with Him*. God talks with humans and gives them the ability to understand what He says. Using spoken words, God communicates His will and His feelings to mankind.

If there weren't marked differences in worldviews to this point, here's where they fly apart. Between the three, the value of human life is profoundly different. To the atheist, humans are just another animal, which is just another kind of matter; which is just another effect from a cause. Rocks have no value, animals have no value, and humans have no value. As humans are no different than animals, their lives and activity are viewed as merely extensions of the ways animals live and behave.

To the pantheist, humans have great value, but only because everything has great value. Humans are important, but no more important than the animals with whom they share a world. Therefore, it's inappropriate to kill or eat an animal because doing so is equal to the murder of a human being. As a practical matter, since rocks, trees, and other plants don't appear to care, they can be moved, shaped, eaten, and used to build things: but all moving life is sacred to the pantheist.

So why does all this disagreement exist?

According to the biblical story, humans fell away from God.

God created humans to rule with Him and offered humans the ability to be like Him. Among the most important of the gifts God offered to humans was the ability to make decisions like He does. If humans had accepted this, they would have realized their true roles as superior beings in the universe. Unfortunately, the first inhabitants of the world chose to make decisions in a manner that made them no different than the animals. Perhaps that's one of the reasons modern people find it so hard to differentiate between themselves and their fellow earthly creatures. At any rate, the Fall introduced a number of terrible problems into the world.

Effects of the Fall

Some of the results of the Fall are mentioned plainly; some are implied or expanded upon in later sections of scripture. The most obvious is:

Death

It's said, "Love is a many-splendored thing." That's true, but death is also complex. Asking for a definition from a crowd will draw painful and frightening images of accidents, illnesses, funerals, and graveyards. To start, we must view death from another perspective.

The Start of Death Is Separation from God

Once, I spent an afternoon in an orchard, picking apples with some friends. Apples start their existence as fragrant blossoms. They move slowly through growth stages, becoming small green orbs and later, upon ripening, the fruit we all know. We were in the orchard at the end of the apple life cycle. The ones we sought were different shades of red. On the ground, though, were apples which had fallen from the trees because of a storm. The journey from green to red had been interrupted when those apples were separated from the tree, their source of nutrition. As any farmer knows, the fallen apples didn't immediately disappear. Instead, they lay on the ground slowly deteriorating and suffering the attacks of weather, insects, and bacteria. The fallen apples I saw that day were corrupted to varying degrees, but all were destined for complete destruction.

Apples aren't a complete illustration, because even the best apples will be destroyed when they're eaten by the farmer's customers, but let's not be picky; they make a good illustration of what has happened to humans. Imagine an apple could reach some ideal state of perfect maturity, and afterward could hang on the tree in that perfect state forever. That would be an illustration of what humans were meant to be.

When Adam and Eve fell, they cut off the whole human race from its tree. From that time, every human is born and grows to a certain point. We spend twenty or so years reaching the peak of our strength and vitality, only to begin an immediate downward spiral. One after another, our component parts fail. Eventually, our entire bodies come to a complete halt. The only exception to this process comes when illness or injury cuts the time even shorter.

Death is a painful subject. It seems almost comic to discuss its parts and effects in a dry, sterile manner, but I'm afraid that's what we're stuck with. The most obvious of the effects of death is what I'm going to call "lack of earthly permanence".

Lack of Earthly Permanence

Some have suggested God did a bad job describing the penalty of death when He told Adam, "On the day you eat of it (the fruit) you will surely die." (Genesis 2:17) Any reader can see the players are left standing after the Fall — in fact, long after. Didn't death occur much later?

First, the Hebrew language allows for a figure of speech that could be translated: "When you do something, you have secured the effect of your action, even if the effect occurs later." That would certainly be the case here, as complete physical death followed years later. However, many of the effects of the Fall could be felt right away.

I've said, for instance, humans share God's quality of being creators: we like to make things. Prior to the Fall, Adam and Eve could outlive anything they created. They could plant a California Redwood tree as a seedling, come back centuries later, climb over three hundred feet to the top, and watch sunsets. They could carve a stone statue and show it to friends for eons.

Now, people would have to leave their creations to others; and others may not remember or understand them. The world is full of statues that had great meaning to their sculptors, but today are curiosities. Many are very meaningful for the pigeons that roost on them, but they hold little value for the masses who wander past.

Even moments enjoying the simple things of creation have become fleeting glimpses of a world that might have been. There are things that bring joy, like sunshine on flowers in the morning. Sadly, those things bring that joy one day and then dissipate into fading memories, as our eyes grow dim with age. Further, any moment we enjoy in life can be marred by the knowledge that the moment may be our last. Every joy is eventually cut short. Every happy second in the light will eventually be replaced with darkness.

Perhaps saddest is the grief we experience when friends and loved ones pass. Hamlet, who marveled at the construction of the human form, felt despair when faced with its destruction. In one of the best-known scenes from Shakespeare, Hamlet wanders into a cemetery while some gravediggers work. They accidentally unearth the skull of a court jester named Yorick, who befriended Hamlet as a child. The sight prompts Hamlet to muse:

> Alas, poor Yorick! I knew him . . . a fellow of infinite jest, of most excellent fancy: he hath borne me on his back a thousand times; and now, how abhorred in my imagination it is! (Hamlet 5.1.169-172)

In a flash, Hamlet is bombarded by all the happy moments he spent with his talented friend, who always had time to delight a child's heart. To look at the corroded skull that was once his smiling friend broke something in the heart of the pensive prince.

Centuries earlier, the great Hebrew king Solomon began a contemplative treatise with the following:

> The words of the Teacher, son of David, king in Jerusalem:
> "Meaningless! Meaningless!"
> says the Teacher.
> "Utterly meaningless!
> Everything is meaningless."
>
> What does man gain from all his labor
> at which he toils under the sun?
>
> Generations come and generations go,
> but the earth remains forever.
>
> The sun rises and the sun sets,
> and hurries back to where it rises.
>
> The wind blows to the south
> and turns to the north;
> round and round it goes,
> ever returning on its course.
>
> All streams flow into the sea,
> yet the sea is never full.
> To the place the streams come from,
> there they return again.

All things are wearisome,
more than one can say.
The eye never has enough of seeing,
nor the ear its fill of hearing.

What has been will be again,
what has been done will be done again;
there is nothing new under the sun.

Is there anything of which one can say,
"Look! This is something new"?
It was here already, long ago;
it was here before our time.

There is no remembrance of men of old,
and even those who are yet to come
will not be remembered
by those who follow. (Ecclesiastes 1:1–11)

When people lack permanence, everything about them becomes meaningless. Writers from Solomon to Shakespeare and into the modern age have attempted to grapple with humanity's lack of permanence and its effect on life. Many who assume this task slip into despair.

One way to grapple is not to grapple at all. "Why all this 'grappling'?" happier people ask. "You've got to stop focusing on all this depressing material! You simply have to put out of your mind the negatives of life and enjoy the happy things while they last." I'm not sure I could count all the songs I've heard over the years elevating this thought to glimmering heights. I certainly don't want to say you can't "take a walk on the sunny side of the street" when you're down. I just want to suggest there's something more. We'll discuss this in a moment.

Another way to grapple is to create things that have an air of eternity about them. Tourists travel from all the world to visit the pyramids of Egypt, which have stood for millennia. The ancient kings of Egypt and their builders certainly succeeded in making something that would be around for a while; or did they? Originally, the pyramids had an outer layer of polished stone. This, no doubt, gave them a spectacular shine that could be seen for miles. However, the outer layers were stripped off and used for other purposes by later builders, leaving the once-shining pyramids with a dull, stepped posterior.

These pyramids were built by the royalty of ancient Egypt to serve as their home after death. How did the inhabitants of these massive structures fare, along with those put to rest in sister tombs dotting the Egyptian countryside? Most of the tombs were desecrated and emptied by grave robbers. Many of those left after the ghoulish thieves finished their work have been discovered by archeologists, who promptly put their contents on display in museums. The bodies of the great rulers that occupied these tombs often became destination points for tourists, curious to see the dried-up remains of ancient monarchs.

At one time, the sovereigns who occupied these tombs held the power of life and death over thousands of subjects who existed for their pleasure, or so they thought. They presumed they would enter their long sleep to be awakened only when the time came to walk in eternity with their gods. Some even thought they *were* gods and encouraged their subjects to believe such. Unfortunately, their expensive plans to create gateways into eternity became something else: tourist attractions attended by gum-chewing third-graders, who will later be forced by their teachers to write a one-page essay on what they saw during their field trip to the museum.

Others have tried to create eternal legacies by creating great works of art or by exercising great acts of compassion or by making great contributions to science. We are certainly better for their efforts. Some who do this have supposed they could somehow live on in the memories of those who observe their memorials. Others have supposed this for them.

The Impact of Eternity

All these efforts have something in common: however much we all might marvel at their creations; however much our lives may have been made better; and however much we appreciate what they did, the creators of these works are all gone. They aren't here to enjoy with the rest of us what they created.

This isn't the way things were meant to be. People weren't created to be forced to leave behind their works, their lives, and their loves. They weren't meant to exist merely as memories in the finite lifelines of those who follow them. *They were meant to live forever.* Our motivation as a race to create things that live past us exists because we know this to be true. As Solomon grappled with this, he penned these remarkable words: "He (God) has made everything beautiful in its time. He has also set eternity in the hearts of men" (Eccl. 3:11).

The Scriptures give us an amazing truth: we are driven to seek eternity *because we were created to*. We know our lack of permanence isn't the way things were meant to be.

The different worldviews we discussed look at eternity differently. To the atheist, eternity is only for *matter*, not *being*. The things making up the universe have been around forever and will continue forever. Our conscious thoughts are only a few more effects of earlier causes. When our bodies stop functioning, our minds stop existing. That's it.

In the pantheistic realm, there is disagreement on what happens to us after death. Some say we come back at a different time and try again. Likely, we will come back as something different, depending on what we did with our lives. If we were "good", we come back as something "higher". If we are "bad", we come back as something "lower". I'm placing the words good and bad in quotations because these value judgements are resisted by many teachers of eastern thought. (Rahula 1984, 41) Higher and lower, good and bad are hard to settle upon, since "good" involves making a value judgment about what is "bad", and value judgments are hard to come by with a changing god.

To those in the Creator camp, there are only two possibilities. Some acknowledge a Creator, but don't see anything after death. The more common belief involves an afterlife, where we exist in some form related to our earthly beings. There is disagreement about whether we are like ghosts who wander without bodies, or whether we automatically become something better—angels perhaps?

To the Christian, there is only one possibility: resurrection. Resurrection teaches that we were created human and will always be human. In our fallen states, our human frames perform poorly compared to the perfect state, so Christians look forward to a much better life in the resurrection. We'll discuss this in more detail later.

For now, we reiterate the question: why all the disagreement? If humans long for things eternal and dream of being eternal, why do atheists so quickly give up on eternity? The answer involves one of the most difficult concepts of biblical thought. To understand death, you must understand its cause.

Sin

Sin is understood in two ways; first, it's an action. It's the act of disobeying God's commands. Early Presbyterians penned this definition in a document known as the Shorter Catechism:

> Question 14: What is sin?
>
> Answer: Sin is any want of conformity unto, or transgression of, the law of God.

All the problems of humanity can be traced back to the first decision of Adam and Eve to disobey God's clear command.

Sin has a secondary implication. This involves the results of sin; the first of which we described as separation from God, resulting in death. More than this, we are not only separated from God, we are defiled. Sin surrounds us, permeates us, and infects us. We have taken evil into our souls, and our souls are permanently stained. We don't just sin; we *are sinful*. As if death wasn't enough, this has repercussions.

An important one involves our orientation. To be sinful means we live in a constant state where not only are we cut off from God's life force, but we are also cut off from God's *direction*. To understand this, you must understand the nature of God's laws. As I've repeatedly stated, the universe is a gigantic expression of God's values. Every piece of the original universe expressed who God is. It's the same with God's words. When God speaks, He speaks from who He is. Every word reflects His character and values. When our behavior and attitudes deviate from those words, *we deviate from Him*. Incidentally, when humans fell, the universe was adversely affected. It no longer perfectly reflects God's values.

Previously, we received our orientation and our value from our Creator. Without Him, we have neither. We have nothing we can depend upon to accurately perceive values. Before, God was the standard by which we measured everything. Now, we are *self-standardizing*.

Self-Standardizing People

When people started claiming ownership of things, they had to find a way to measure what they owned. This created the need for standard measurements, like the *cubit*. A cubit was about eighteen inches, or the average length from elbow to fingertips. You can imagine someone measuring wood; just hold up your forearm and start counting. In later years, people used other body parts like the foot. This was fine for centuries past, but differences in individual size necessitated better standards. The next step involved moving up the social ladder to the most important individual in a region: the king. King's feet were important, at least to locals of the day; unfortunately, kings come in different sizes, too.

Eventually, scientists created a universal system: the metric system, using distances calculated in relation to the size of the earth. Many now agree on this *external* standard. Keeping exact standards for this system is vitally important. Early in the development of the metric system, French scientists created a one-meter bar made of platinum-iridium, an alloy known to expand or contract minimally in varying temperatures. The bar is a master for all measuring devices. It's kept in a special vault, where temperature and atmospheric pressure are kept at precise levels. Having such a high standard makes it possible to determine with certainty the reliability of all other measuring tools.

Let's go back to the days before such sophisticated standards existed, forcing people to employ body parts. Someone who wanted to buy something from his neighbor could offer to use his foot to measure. "I'd like ten feet," he says. His neighbor points to his own foot and says, "Let's go." The first notices that the neighbor's foot is much smaller than his own, so "ten feet" is much less than he wants. You could get into a fight.

If that wasn't bad enough, imagine a world with no standards at all, not even body parts. There are only individual feelings. Consider the following scene: someone walks into a merchant's shop, and the following discussion ensues:

Customer: I need some stuff.

Merchant: How much stuff do you want?

Customer: Right now, I'm having some feelings. I feel like a certain amount would do.

Merchant: OK. I have some feelings, too. Here is the amount I feel you need.

Customer: You have it all wrong. That's not what I felt.

Merchant: That's a shame. By the way, what do you think you should pay for the stuff?

Customer: I have a feeling about that, too.

If the whole world ran this way, nothing would get done. We would still live in the Stone Age.

To be sinful means we have no more certainty about our values than the trading partners in our illustration. The only thing that can be used to judge values is one's own feelings. Hence, the world has ultimately as many value systems as it has people. With the addition of each new person, you get the introduction of a new set of values.

What's the big deal about values? Why is there a problem? Oftentimes, there's no problem at all. Let's say that some friends walk into a restaurant. One person orders a salad. One person ate earlier, so he/she orders dessert.

Another wants a fuller meal and orders an entrée. There's no problem here. Each person's feelings are fine. In recognition of this, the restaurant has a helpful tool called a menu, which allows lots of people to simultaneously indulge their varied values.

The problem occurs when values *conflict*. We see this in the next chapter where we learn about more results of the Fall.

Chapter 6

The Next Generation of Mankind

In the last chapter, we saw some powerful illustrations of values: God's values and our values. When everyone's values coincide, life is good; but what happens when they don't? We learn more about this as the story of the first humans continues:

> Adam lay with his wife Eve, and she became pregnant and gave birth to Cain. She said, "With the help of the LORD I have brought forth a man." Later she gave birth to his brother Abel.
>
> Now Abel kept flocks, and Cain worked the soil. In the course of time Cain brought some of the fruits of the soil as an offering to the LORD. But Abel brought fat portions from some of the firstborn of his flock. The LORD looked with favor on Abel and his offering, but on Cain and his offering he did not look with favor. So Cain was very angry, and his face was downcast.
>
> Then the LORD said to Cain, "Why are you angry? Why is your face downcast? If you do what is right, will you not be accepted? But if you do not do what is right, sin is crouching at your door; it desires to have you, but you must master it."
>
> Now Cain said to his brother Abel, "Let's go out to the field." And while they were in the field, Cain attacked his brother Abel and killed him. (Genesis 4:1–8)

Two Children, Two Sets of Values

The next chapter begins with hope: the birth of two children. Let's stop here. In our modern world, we hear stories of new birth so regularly we don't pay much attention. We have whole segments of our medical profession dedicated to the birth and care of children and whole industries built around products for babies. It's easy to lose the wonder of a birth. What was it like when the first child arrived on earth? Though Eve no doubt experienced the pain in childbirth she was warned about, the experience of holding a child in your arms often makes the memory of pain fade (or so I am told by many mothers). Adam and Eve are given a major glimpse of God's mercy; their transgression has not prevented new generations from arriving on earth.

Then there was a second: the first child, Cain, is followed by a brother, Abel. There are always matters of import to be addressed when you have two children, such as "Do we dress the kids the same way, like matching bookends, or will they each be unique? Do we ensure that each child will be allowed to be his/her own person?" Apparently, it didn't take very long to see the answer in this case. These two youngsters were very different. They showed different inclinations and wound up working different parts of the farm.

Cain worked the ground. Digging up dirt every day isn't an easy life; and that's assuming hoes were invented. Remember, one of the pronouncements following the curse was difficulty in working the soil. Thorns filled the ground and no doubt pricked Cain's fingers. The sun that previously shined on the peaceful Garden of Eden now baked his skin while he toiled. This career can be challenging, but at harvest time, every piece of produce is a prize. Visit the home of any gardener, and he/she'll be happy to tell you the tomatoes on the table came fresh from the backyard agrarian enterprise.

Abel, on the other hand, liked the farm animals. In particular, he spent time with the animals found in flocks, better known as sheep. Shepherding is a misunderstood job. Sometimes, there's total boredom, while you watch your animals slowly chewing the grass. Suddenly, you notice one is missing. Your job is now a frenzied search for something considered a valuable commodity in those days. One minute, monotony—the next minute, panic. One minute, you're quietly watching the flock from the shade of a tree; the next minute you're chasing a stupid lamb that's getting dangerously close to that big hole at the far end of the field.

Although the two young men had different jobs, they had some common experiences. One was worship. Sadly, an experience that should have been a joyful bonding time for the boys and their parents became a point of painful departure. The following story is what happens when humans have clashing values.

The word *worship* comes from the old English word "worth-ship". Worship is the act of assigning worth to something. When you worship something, you're saying, "You're very valuable to me." Is anything more valuable than God?

Question: What is the best way to say to someone, "You're valuable to me"? Answer: Give him/her something valuable. That's why we're introduced early in Scriptures to the concept of an offering; the act of taking something valuable and giving it to God as an act of worship.

Cain and Abel both had this opportunity. When the time came to make an offering, we're told Cain brought "some of the fruits of the soil" (Gen. 4:3). Abel brought "fat portions from some of the firstborn of his flock" (4:4). The result? We're told, "The LORD looked with favor on Abel and his offering, but on Cain and his offering he did not look with favor."

Now, what's going on here? There are (at least) three possibilities:

1. There might be a hint in the term *firstborn*. The firstborn of anything was highly regarded in ancient culture. It represented the best.

The best of produce from the soil might be harder to discern. Should it be merely the first chronologically? Not always. Most produce comes in batches. You can watch it growing, so when harvest comes, you can pick out the best. I enjoy gardening, and I'll tell you nothing compares with watching your crop grow and seeing a harvest ready to come. On the day you see it, you walk over to the best of what your plants have to offer and break it off. After admiring it for a moment, you take a bite. There's nothing better.

Now imagine you're there with me on this important day in the garden; and imagine, instead of taking a bite out of that very special item, I offer it to you. That would mean something, wouldn't it? That would mean you're valuable to me. Now, on the other hand, imagine I took that first bite and then noticed you looking on longingly. I glance around and notice something on another plant that's a little inferior-looking. I break it off, pluck off a slimy-looking insect, and offer it to you. You wouldn't be very impressed at that point, would you?

Abel offered God the first of his flock. Perhaps Cain took that bite we discussed and then offered God something less. That would be disappointing, because "the first" doesn't come around until next season. Of course, God would be unhappy.

2. The Bibles we have are quite large as they are. Not every detail of every story can be included. Adding more details would balloon Bibles to unreadable size. Because of this, some suggest Cain and Abel may have had explicit instructions on the types of offerings to bring. Cain, in this case, didn't follow the rules and should have known better. He was the first of many people who feel that the worship of God involves doing whatever you like, as opposed to asking God what He likes. Again, this displeases God.

3. The last possibility involves a statement I made earlier. When Adam and Eve sinned, they grabbed some leaves and figured it would be enough to cover their sin; but God gave them animal skins. We said that when sin occurs, two things happen: something has to die, and God has to provide a solution. Abel's offering followed this pattern. When you're a shepherd, you're aware God provides a lot of what you get in the end. Although sad, watching an animal die would be a powerful object lesson about the results of sin. Death is painful. Death is permanent. On the other hand, there's something about gardening that makes it easy to assume the product is exclusively the result of your own work. You plowed, you dug, you weeded, you watered, and you pruned. So, Cain grabbed a few items from the garden, knowing they would soon grow back, and waited for God's applause. Once more, he missed the point and got the opposite of what he expected from God.

All these scenarios are what happens when a self-standardizing being has values that clash with God's, but things get worse.

More important than Cain's mistake was his reaction to God's displeasure. Cain got angry. Sadness was understandable, but anger? Anger is often caused by the feeling that something is unfair. Apparently, Cain inherited his parents' bad attitudes. To him, this was all God's fault. Cain thought his offering was just fine, thank you. In his thinking, God didn't give him enough instructions, or God didn't make things clear enough, or God set unreasonable standards and provided insufficient help.

What touched off Cain's anger? Consider God's response to Cain's attitude: "Why are you angry? Why is your face downcast? If you do what is right, will you not be accepted? But if you do not do what is right, sin is crouching at your door; it desires to have you, but you must master it." (Gen. 4:6-7) Did God respond to Cain's failure by insulting him? Did He call Cain a moron or use demeaning language? Did God cause physical injury or pain? No, God didn't do any of that. All He said was something like, "Try to do better next time." God then warned Cain: be careful of sin's power. If Cain didn't fight it, sin would overpower him.

No, God did nothing abusive to Cain. Understanding this is important. *All it took for Cain to be angry was discovering God's displeasure with his choices.* Even more important is Cain's reasoning: *Cain assumed God must be wrong, not him.*

Violence Enters the World

So, how does Cain react to God's warning? Cain doesn't fight the sin "crouching at the door", but invites it in. Rather than focusing on his own bad attitude, he focuses his anger on an innocent person. Cain lets his eyes wander to his smiling brother who enjoys God's approval. This makes Cain burns with jealousy. He has a cauldron of anger bubbling inside of him. What to do with this anger? Cain decides to unleash it on his innocent brother. He decides to cause some *pain*. We're about to see a worst-case scenario of what happens when a self-standardizing person has values that conflict with another person who seeks God's values.

This is early in human experience. No one on earth had physically died yet. As such, we're not sure Cain foresaw the results of unleashing his anger. Perhaps he just wanted to throw a few punches? On the other hand, Cain saw animals die. Remember Abel's offering? Sheep must die to provide fat offerings. The appearance of slaughtered sheep is gruesome. It's entirely possible Cain's thinking was something more than "I just want to give that guy a good punch in the nose." Instead, the thinking may have been more like, "So, something is supposed to die because of sin, huh? Maybe it should be Mr. 'Goodie-Two-Shoes' over there!"

We're told Cain went out to a field with his brother, a place his parents couldn't see. He apparently thought it was a place God couldn't see, either. Cain may have only given his brother a few punches and watched him accidentally hit his head on a stone after falling. Or, maybe he picked up a blunt object, snuck up from behind, and pounded. Maybe he kept pounding until his brother stopped pleading, stopped crying, and finally stopped moving. Cain may have looked at what he had done in horror. Or, he might have allowed himself a quiet moment of grim satisfaction, as he watched the last drops of blood drain from an innocent, unsuspecting soul who had trusted him. Violence had been born on the earth. The war that broke out between God and the rebellious had taken its first life.

Before analyzing the conversation that followed, we need to consider some points. First, why did Cain choose his brother? Sadly, it's not uncommon for people to focus anger on someone other than the cause of his/her insult, and sometimes the next person in line can be a victim. Lots of men yell at their wives, or kick the dog, after they've been mistreated by their bosses, but there's something more here. God showed approval to Abel and disapproval to Cain. Every time Cain looked at Abel, Cain was reminded of that fact. Every time he was reminded, he felt shame. His shame could have motivated him to try harder next time, but instead he decided to nurture the sin that grew inside him. His anger was primarily at God, but that presents a problem: God is hard to hurt. Sometimes, it's easier to find someone that God cares about and hurt *them* instead.

If this sounds in any way familiar, it should. You may recall that Satan, the fallen angel, entered the Garden to hurt Adam and Eve. He didn't do it with physical attack, but with stealth and cunning. His motive was to hurt the God whom he rebelled against by hurting Adam and Eve, the most beloved of God's creation. We're starting to see the depth of sin's effects. In only one generation, Adam and Eve produced a man whose motivations were no different than the serpent who tempted them in the Garden; but whereas their sin was to take a piece of fruit, their son's sin was to take a life.

Things got worse. Cain was allowed to live after his horrible deed and went on to have his own children. In only a few generations, one of his descendants, a man named Lamech, said this: "I have killed a man for wounding me, a young man for injuring me" (Gen. 4:23). Lamech killed on multiple occasions and boasted to his family about it. His boast was something to the order of "Someone stepped on my toe, so I stepped on his head!" Violence was here to stay; and it would escalate as more self-standardizing people were added to the human population, each with their own ideas of how the world should work.

Another point involves our orientations in life. Stated in its simplest form, there are two paths you can take. You can follow God or not follow God. Following Him means seeking Him, obeying His directions, and giving Him your best. Not following means avoiding Him, disregarding His directions, and giving Him leftovers or nothing. Here is where values collide. This is not chocolate and vanilla; *this is right and wrong*. Cain started a pattern that appears in each succeeding generation. I call it the Cain Principle:

People who don't follow God dislike people who do.

Those who rebel against God are reminded of their bad decisions each time they see obedience. They feel shame, but often this emotion is repressed. Instead, their outward expressions can be anything from quiet disdain to outright rage. Depending on the generation and the place, violence may follow.

There are lots of ways to cause pain other than violence, though. You can ridicule. You can mock. You can reject. You can also slander. Slandering is saying things about another person which are untrue, or which distort truth in order to destroy the subject's reputation. Sometimes slanderers are the originators of falsehood, making things up as they see fit. Other times, the soldiers of slander wait patiently until they hear anything demeaning about their unfortunate victims. The information is then gleefully passed along to others, knowing it will hurt. The slanderer is a coward who inflicts pain on someone's heart rather than injury to the body.

As serious as these points are, the next is probably the most dangerous. As people pull further and further from God, their sense of values becomes more and more distorted. With God, man is the highest created being in the universe. Without Him, man is only one more object. When this happens, each individual person has no more worth than what other people are willing to assign them. When people assign value to each other, the value can be very subjective. In short, if you help someone achieve their goals, you're valuable; your value increases or decreases in respect to your usefulness. If you block someone's goals, at that point you have negative value. You must be coerced into line or eliminated. Without God, human value evaporates. It's replaced with the feelings of the moment.

When people pull away from God, not all go the same distance. Some are overtly evil; others become mild "stinkers". Some look downright benevolent when compared to others, but the Scriptures teach that all are stained to some degree. The apostle Paul wrote, "All have sinned and fall short of the glory of God" (Romans 3:23).

An Ongoing Pattern

In this story, God has repeated a pattern. As there were no fences in the Garden, there were no fences around Abel. God didn't put chains on the first humans to prevent them from hurting each other. God gave a responsibility to someone and allowed him to make a choice. Once again, that someone failed; and once again, God didn't destroy Cain for his sin. Instead, He sought out Cain and offers him a chance to take responsibility: "Then the LORD said to Cain, 'Where is Abel your brother?' And he said, 'I do not know. Am I my brother's keeper?'" (Gen. 4:9).

Once again, someone failed to respond to God's mercy. This passage is often misunderstood; when I first read it, my response to the "keeper" question was, "As a matter of fact, you *are* your brother's keeper!" That's not the answer God gave, and there's a reason for it. The question asked by Cain was not a sincere question. *It was meant to throw God off track*. More than that, Cain intended it to intimidate. He was essentially saying, "Where is my brother? What a stupid question!" The words coming out of Cain's mouth were, in no way, the words of someone who regretted his deed.

Cain's approach is like the serpent in the Garden. "Did God really say you can't eat from *any* of the fruits of the garden?" That question distorted God's words. Eve fell for it and tried to respond, "Well, no, God didn't say that. Let's have an intellectual discussion about what He really said." Being now sidetracked, she was easy prey for deception. Cain may have been attempting something similar here. Only unlike the serpent, who used it on a naïve, young human, Cain was trying it on God.

Imagine this scene: the Creator of the heavens and the earth is standing over a mere mortal. The mere mortal doesn't get it at all. He thinks his Creator is small and stupid. In Cain's mind, God is surely not big enough to know a murder had taken place. Cain's anger is still seething, apparently not quenched in the attack on his brother; there is more pain to be unleashed. Not only has he acted despicably, but now he thinks he can toy with God. Perhaps what Cain wanted God to answer was, "Your brother's keeper? Well, no, of course not! I never told you to be your brother's keeper. How silly of Me to think you would know anything about your brother's whereabouts. That really was a dumb question, wasn't it? Sorry!" God would then wander a little further down the path where He would find His "precious little Abel" lying in a ditch. Cain could watch from a distance and gloat, as He observed the pain God would surely feel upon the discovery. Cain's reply to God may have been the beginning of a trap meant to fulfill his unholy anger.

God didn't try to reason with this impudent, wretched man. Cain had his opportunity, and he missed it.

> The Lord said, "What have you done? Listen! Your brother's blood cries out to me from the ground. Now you are under a curse and driven from the ground, which opened its mouth to receive your brother's blood from your hand. When you work the ground, it will no longer yield its crops for you. You will be a restless wanderer on the earth." (Gen. 4:10–12)

Like his parents before him, Cain chose to learn the hard way. He learned God is the ultimate judge of evil. The judgment that God proclaimed is complex, so we won't comment on the whole thing, but one aspect demands attention. God speaks of Abel's blood "crying to me from the ground." When people sin, it's tempting to think sin is a one-time act. Sin is bad, we think, but once it's done, it's done. To this, God says, "No." Sin has lasting effects. Some are visible here on earth. The body of a victim is obvious, but there are also effects in other realms of reality. The picture of blood crying from the ground denotes a spiritual or cosmic effect of sin. Things get broken that we can never see, but God sees them. As the ultimate judge, He's responsible to act when He sees sin. The more severe the sin, the more lasting the effect, and the greater the judgment. We may never fully understand the results of our actions. Sins, whether small or great, whether few or many, have lasting impacts on our world and on us. We must be reminded that God sees it all. There is no hiding from Him—not in the trees of the forest and not in the distance of the field. He sees all.

God also shows mercy. Even in the midst of this horrific scene, God heard Cain.

> Cain said to the LORD, "My punishment is too great to bear!
> "Behold, You have driven me this day from the face of the
> ground; and from Your face I will be hidden, and I will be a
> vagrant and a wanderer on the earth, and whoever finds me
> will kill me." So the LORD said to him, "Therefore whoever
> kills Cain, vengeance will be taken on him sevenfold" And
> the LORD appointed a sign for Cain, so that no one finding
> him would slay him. (Gen 4:13–15)

Could there have been a more fitting judgment for Cain than to become the object of a manhunt? Death would come at the hands of angry avengers after a tortuous, exhausting chase. God could have left Cain to the fate Cain predicted for himself; instead, God chose to protect him. Even after all of this, God extended mercy. There is still time for Cain to choose a redemptive path. Does he do so? We don't know for sure, but we get a hint in the next verses:

> Then Cain went out from the presence of the LORD, and set-
> tled in the land of Nod, east of Eden. Cain had relations with
> his wife and she conceived, and gave birth to Enoch; and he
> built a city, and called the name of the city Enoch, after the
> name of his son. (Gen.3:16-17)

Cain "went out from the presence of the Lord"; there is no record that he ever came back. He chose a location away from his parents and away from the worship of God. God granted Cain something Cain had taken from his parents: a son. Cain decided to build a city in his son's honor. What to name it? He could have named it after his parents. He could have named it in remembrance of God's kindness and mercy—perhaps something like City of Mercy. Instead, he named it after his son. It's certainly good that he was thankful for his son, but perhaps he was too thankful. He was indulging his son. Have you ever had anything named after you? The closest I've ever seen to this personally was a woodworker who made a sign for this son's bedroom that said, "Tommy's Room". Perhaps Cain felt guilty and attempted to show his son something he never gave to his own brother. Sometimes guilty people indulge their guilt by giving lavish gifts. On the other hand, perhaps Cain was saying, "I'm alive. My brother's dead. I have a son. My 'righteous' brother never will. I just got away with murder! I won!" A stretch, perhaps; at any rate, the generations following Cain were godless, and they became increasingly evil and violent over time.

An Alternate Ending

This is getting awfully depressing. Weren't there any good people in the ancient world of Adam and Eve? As I said, all humans to come from the first couple are in some way stained with sin; but God, being a God of mercy, offered Adam and Eve hope once more.

> Adam had relations with his wife again; and she gave birth to a son, and named him Seth, for, she said, "God has appointed me another offspring in place of Abel, for Cain killed him." To Seth, to him also a son was born; and he called his name Enosh. Then men began to call upon the name of the LORD. (Gen. 4:25–26)

We aren't told everything that occurred around the time of Abel's murder. Now, Adam and Eve experienced yet another new emotion: grief. They wanted to know about good and evil, and they were willing to steal from God to obtain this forbidden knowledge. When they found the body of their son, their quest became a reality. They now knew evil because they were experiencing its ugly effects firsthand.

God could have rubbed it in. He could have called the parents over and gestured toward the body, saying, "Well, there you go. This is what you asked for, and now you've got it. Enjoy!" This broken couple lost not one, but two sons in one day. One child died in brutal fashion; the other committed the crime and ran away, never to return. Perhaps the grief was causing them to reach their limits.

God didn't rub it in. As He watched the sobs of Adam and Eve, perhaps He shed tears of His own. No, instead of exploiting the situation and permitting it to drive the bereaved couple to despair, God allowed another new emotion: consolation.

Two people trapped in the throes of heartache can hold out their arms to each other and embrace. They can wipe the tears from each other's eyes, and after a time comes healing: another gift of mercy. The two, though wounded and scarred, can draw close in many ways. In the closeness of solace, two can have a quiet passion awakened that draws them to their bed. There, Adam and Eve joined under the caring eyes of God and conceived another child. When that child was born, he was born of two hearts beginning to understand God's love and mercy. "God has appointed me another offspring in place of Abel," said Eve. (Gen 3:25) She knew the source of her consolation; and this time, the child lived long enough for Adam and Eve to see grandchildren. After this, we're told, "Men began to call upon the name of the LORD." (3:26)

Why is this important? Because it's what needs to happen when you recognize your problem with sin. Humans always needed God, but now, with sin infesting the souls of every human being, seeking God's help became paramount. Later, Moses would write: "You will find him (God) if you look for him with all your heart and with all your soul" (Deuteronomy 4:29).

God says, if you're looking for Him, you'll find Him. He'll guide you. He'll help you. He'll make provision for your sins; more about that later.

The Two Lines

A new line of people appeared, seeking God instead of running from Him. The theologians who study these passages speak of the "godly line of Seth". This line stood in direct conflict with the "ungodly line of Cain". When read from the distance of millennia, the passages describing these two lines seem vague. There are numerous accomplishments in Cain's line (Gen. 4:17–24). They all appear significant, at least as far as modern people are concerned. The children of Cain discovered music, for example. They also discovered how to work metals. Finally, they developed techniques of husbandry that must have done wonders for the livestock industry of the day. On the other hand, though, some embraced violence, and none of them embraced God. They were great students of the arts and sciences, but failed in theology. Their failures caused them to gradually descend into increasing evil.

The description of the Seth's children is downright sparse. As we read Genesis, chapter 5, we hear of one child being born to another and how long they lived. That's it. It seems the writer says something like this: Seth had a son (who also called upon the name of the Lord). That son had a son (who also called on the name of the Lord). That son had another son (who did guess what?). This is repeated numerous times until we hear an unusual reference to a man named Enoch: "Enoch walked with God; then he was no more, because God took him away" (Gen. 5:24).

Apparently, the line of Seth put a lot of emphasis on matters of the heart and soul. What mattered to them? People; people who followed God. Accomplishments were, no doubt, enjoyed while they were alive, but their legacy was measured by whether they walked with God and whether their children did, too. One of their own was a man so righteous, God simply took him to heaven one day. There is no record of his death.

The comparison of these two lines reveals a tendency that exists to this day. There are many followers of God who enjoy the arts and appreciate the sciences as much as anyone. The annals of these disciplines are filled the names of such people; but when disciplines that expand the mind and the senses are pursued without concern for the heart and the soul, they become empty, succeeding only in drawing people down dark paths.

For generations, the two lines coexisted, but one day, the results of the Fall became even more blatant. When this happened, God reacted with one of the most famous events in history.

Chapter 7

When Good Compromises with Evil

The Lines Break Down

There's an easy way to resolve value conflicts: pursue the most fun. Unfortunately, this isn't always the best path.

> When men began to increase in number on the earth and daughters were born to them, the sons of God saw that the daughters of men were beautiful, and they married any of them they chose. Then the LORD said, "My Spirit will not contend with man forever, for he is mortal; his days will be a hundred and twenty years."
>
> The Nephilim were on the earth in those days—and also afterward—when the sons of God went to the daughters of men and had children by them. They were the heroes of old, men of renown.
>
> The LORD saw how great man's wickedness on the earth had become, and that every inclination of the thoughts of his heart was only evil all the time. The LORD was grieved that he had made man on the earth, and his heart was filled with pain. (Genesis 6:1–6)

Theologians debate the meaning of this text; they disagree about the "sons of God" versus the "daughters of men". Many suggest the sons of God descended from the godly line of Seth, while the daughters of men descended from Cain. If true, the generations of people who previously called upon God were wearying of good behavior while their neighbors enjoyed constant parties. There was something about life "over there" that seemed more exciting and more colorful; and oh my, how beautiful the women looked. The daughters of Cain spent significant time on their appearance, as opposed to the daughters of Seth who concentrated on character. The allure of beauty is strong. Both beholder and owner feel its power. Men who desire it in women can go insane. Desiring beauty can lead women to spend massive amounts of time, energy, and money to attain it. For both genders, it can be an all-absorbing obsession.

So, the godly children of Seth left their pursuit of God to pursue beauty and sex. The result was children born from a fusion of both cultures: a little religiosity here, a little decadence there; a little noble-mindedness now, lots of self-indulgence later.

Among this crowd arose a mysterious group of people called the "Nephilim" or giants. Remember the tendency toward violence in those days? The Nephilim were a warrior class. Only, there was no need for war because the two lines of people were merging. What do fighters do when there are no battles to be fought? In other times, they might consider other professions, but in those days the fighters became gladiators who took on all challengers. They became "men of renown" because of their awesome battle skills.

The music played by the children of Cain got louder. Musicians played at parties that grew into drunken orgies. Advances in metallurgy produced better farming implements, but also produced better armaments. Advances in husbandry produced larger and better flocks of sheep. Could it be someone got the idea that those techniques could also be used on humans? The Nephilim are reported to be giants. It could be this was a figurative way of describing their role as celebrities, or it may have been the literal result of people attempting the first "improvements" on humans through manipulative breeding over generations.

We don't know exactly what was happening. The language is terse. One thing we know: whatever happened, it grieved God's heart. The pleasure He felt over the formerly godly line of Seth was now replaced when this noble family compromised with their evil neighbors. For mankind as a group, "every inclination of the thoughts of his heart was only evil all the time." (Gen.6:5) Sadly, humans chose en masse to learn evil by immersing themselves in it. The battle for the hearts of mankind progressed to the point where most people chose to join the rebellion. Because of this bad decision, they were going to learn something about God.

Here's what they were about to learn: God wants to show incomprehensible mercy to His creations. He's patient in ways observers find difficult to understand, but, His mercy has limits. *When those limits are reached, terrifying scenes follow.*

The Flood

> Noah was a righteous man, blameless among the people of
> his time, and he walked with God. (Gen. 6:9)

Apparently, there was one man remaining among the children of Seth
who still followed God. So, the Creator called him aside one day:

> Now the earth was corrupt in God's sight and was full of
> violence. God saw how corrupt the earth had become, for
> all the people on earth had corrupted their ways. So God
> said to Noah, "I am going to put an end to all people, for
> the earth is filled with violence because of them. I am surely
> going to destroy both them and the earth. So make yourself
> an ark of cypress wood; make rooms in it and coat it with
> pitch inside and out. This is how you are to build it: The ark
> is to be 450 feet long, 75 feet wide and 45 feet high. Make
> a roof for it and finish the ark to within 18 inches of the top.
> Put a door in the side of the ark and make lower, middle and
> upper decks. I am going to bring floodwaters on the earth
> to destroy all life under the heavens, every creature that has
> the breath of life in it. Everything on earth will perish. But I
> will establish my covenant with you, and you will enter the
> ark — you and your sons and your wife and your sons' wives
> with you. You are to bring into the ark two of all living crea-
> tures, male and female, to keep them alive with you. Two
> of every kind of bird, of every kind of animal and of every
> kind of creature that moves along the ground will come to
> you to be kept alive. You are to take every kind of food that
> is to be eaten and store it away as food for you and for them."
> (Gen. 6:11–21)

Again, we don't know what people were doing, but it was bad. We're
only given the words *violence* and *corruption*. God's response: "That's it. No
more." Modern man looks back at this and asks, "What could mankind have
been doing that was so horrible?" It's here that God reserves the right to be
God. He doesn't owe anyone explanations, much less detailed ones. He saw
something that incensed Him, and it was time for what He saw to end. He
displayed mercy for centuries up to this point. Humans used God's kindness
as an excuse to push back and buck hard against their Creator.

The method of the judgment? *Water.* Water would become the weapon in the battle between good and evil.

I was once invited to the United States Naval Academy to watch the graduation ceremony. It was early June; the humidity crept up to a level that made even the most inactive people sweat. The speaker, an admiral, began his address by talking about water. The graduates were embarking on a career where they would experience much more of this substance than average. They would float on it; it would surround them. The admiral reminded his listeners of a fact: the human body is mostly water—almost eighty percent.

The admiral proceeded to mention some paradoxes of this substance. Pure water is vital for life. We must consume large amounts to survive. Add salt, though, and it becomes unfit for human consumption. Small amounts of other chemicals can make it poisonous.

Humans can do amazing things with water. We build swimming pools that cool us on hot days. We've taken substances like steel that should sink quickly to the bottom of an ocean and fashioned it into ships that take us comfortably across the surface. If we control it, water makes life good. Then, the admiral reminded us of what happens when water gets out of control: It becomes dangerous. Floods and hurricanes devastate whole cities. Water can be a life-giver. Water can be a life-taker.

God told humanity His patience was wearing thin. "My Spirit will not contend with man forever," He warned. (Gen.6:3) You can imagine the reply of a disobedient population possessing spirits like their father Cain's: "God's upset? So what? What's He going to do about it?"

What He was going to do was change the way the forces of nature worked. For centuries, people took nature for granted. In the first days of creation, God ordained a line where the water stopped. Rivers, lakes, and oceans remained obediently behind their borders. Until now, the shepherds of Cain led their animals to the quiet water's edge to drink. Farmers relied on the irrigation channels they dug to bring life-giving moisture to their fields. People could build beautiful homes overlooking serene lakes. The inhabitants of earth could peacefully grow in corruption and violence without fear. God didn't matter; He was a patient lapdog who could be depended upon to keep the universe serving humans, while they became increasingly independent of their Creator.

All this would end. Humankind was about to learn the massive quantities of water surrounding them didn't passively sit behind boundaries for no reason. The waters remained in place because they were subject to the control of their infinite Maker. The Maker who commanded the water to remain in its place could just as easily command it to spring forth if He desired.

God's Justice

Up to this point, we've given significant attention to God's mercy. Now, we must discuss God's *justice*.

Again, values come into play. Everything God created reflects His values. Everything was created the way He wanted and placed where He wanted it. In some cases, He placed things in ways we'll call "flexible". Stones can lie buried in the ground, but there's no rule saying they must remain there. People can dig them up and carve them into statues or place them one upon another to make buildings. In this case, the perfect, original location for a stone was a place it could be discovered. Here, God's values are expressed in giving someone the opportunity to share in the part of God's image that makes them want to create.

When the creatures God placed on earth rebelled against Him, however, they began to act in ways God calls evil. They began to destroy rather than create and kill rather than cultivate. The act of being creators resulted in offense, when statues became monuments to self and buildings were constructed with the intention of locking God out. When humans act in rebellious and evil ways, something is touched off inside God, compelling Him to respond: to call into account evil and the damage it creates. That is God's justice.

Being created in His image, we understand justice. We have created earthly courts with complex systems of judges, juries, prosecutors, and advocates because we can't help but create on earth a reflection of the heavenly justice system surrounding us.

God's personal sense of justice has been reflected in His creation. Remember God's words when Cain murdered Abel: "Your brother's blood cries out to me from the ground" (Gen. 4:10). In a mystical way, God's creation records the effects of evil. We said earlier God humbled Himself by committing to serve and maintain the creation. Sometimes the act of serving means responding to the cries for justice reverberating from the ground when a murder is committed upon it. Here, humans are limited. People can't see or hear the sympathetic recoil of nature when sins are committed in its midst, but God both sees and hears—and He is compelled to act.

Fortunately for us, God's justice is often restrained by His mercy. Acts of rebellion aren't always met with immediate, forceful replies. Sadly, this can cause a false sense of security, causing some to mock the idea of godly justice. The famous atheist Madeleine Murray O'Hare once went out during a thunderstorm and challenged God to strike her down. There were no lightning bolts hurled at her that night. She took this to be proof that God didn't exist (Murray 1982, 8). In response to this kind of reasoning, the apostle Paul wrote, "Do not be deceived: God cannot be mocked." (Gal. 6:7)

Until this time, God showed abundant mercy to the rebellious of earth. Sometimes, it was due to His kindness. At other times, though, the presence of multitudes from the godly line of Seth who called upon His name no doubt added to God's restraint. Now though, the number of people who followed Him had diminished. There was only a growing body of people whose desire and ability to create evil was growing ever more reproachful with each passing day. Justice would come, and it would be seen by all.

This wasn't to be the end of all life. God would take the one man on earth who still remained faithful and save him, along with his family. God would also call upon the man to take with him the seeds of a new age on earth: the animals needed to repopulate the planet.

This is one of the best-known stories of the Bible, so I don't need to describe it at length here. Suffice it to say Noah built the ship as God instructed, filled it as instructed, and was saved as God promised. Life on earth could begin anew. The people who chose evil over God learned in an epic disaster their Creator was to be taken seriously. The oceans of mercy that well up in God's heart often overcome the volcanoes of justice, but as we said, sometimes there are limits.

What about Science?

We need to take a quick break to discuss science and the Bible.

At one time, the Western world was governed by people who believed the biblical account of the flood. So, inhabitants of the last millennium assumed the flood to be real history. Then came "the Enlightenment" with more "rational" thinking. Some people began to question this story. One point of contention concerned the amount of water needed to cover the whole earth. The biblical account states water came down for forty days, so the oceans "rose and covered the mountains" (Gen. 7:20). We're told, "All the high mountains under the entire heavens were covered" (7:19).

"Forty days of rain? When did anyone ever see that?" moaned the skeptics. Then, someone calculated the water in the oceans, polar ice caps, and the atmosphere. "Not enough," they said. "The flood is impossible. Case closed. 'Rational thought' has won the day."

These charges are serious. How to answer? Before proceeding, there's the matter of biblical interpretation. Some suggest the word *all* is a figurative word rather than fully descriptive. Often, people in Hollywood throw a big party and later say, "Everyone was there!" Well, of course, everyone wasn't there. Perhaps there were lots of significant people, but there were at least a few

Eskimos from Alaska who didn't bother to come, along with others throughout the inhabited planet. It's not unusual for "all" to mean "lots" rather than "every last one". Did a few mountaintops here and there escape a total, lengthy submersion during the flood? Some very dedicated believers would say this is possibly the case. Others feel stricter about a literal interpretation of the word *all*.

People with advanced degrees from all disciplines have weighed in. I've seen debates where all participants have PhDs in science from major universities, and all sides have compelling arguments concerning where all that water could come from.

One Possibility: The Comet Theory

For those who want to do some reading, theories of the flood abound. Let's consider just one; it involves speculation of what would happen if large objects hit the earth.

One theory notes that ancient cultures on every continent record some sort of flood story. In one story, a gigantic fish-like creature is recorded in the sky. How do fish get into the sky? They don't, of course, but there are several phenomena that might look similar. To ancient minds, a comet could look something like a great fish.

In July of 1994, scientists recorded the impact of a comet called Shoemaker-Levy 9 into Jupiter. (Levy) The comet broke into pieces and impacted the "gas giant" over a period of six days. This caused catastrophic explosions on the surface of the planet. What if something similar happened on earth? The collisions of comet pieces into oceans would create tidal waves. The explosive impacts would send water vapor outside our atmosphere where it would orbit for days. That water would eventually reenter. The atmosphere of the planet would spend weeks stabilizing while hurricanes buffeted every continent. That sounds like plenty of water to me.

This is only one theory. It has supporters and critics. Again, I'll stress that highly intelligent and educated people have argued both sides of the flood issue. The average university student is accustomed to hearing arguments claiming to prove the *con* side of the discussion. We'll talk more about the relationship of science and faith later. For now, I suggest students would be surprised at the amount of scientific evidence for the *pro* side should they do some reading on their own.

What if both sides argue each other to a stalemate? The question becomes: how big is your view of the universe? When I peer into the skies, I see the works of a Being so powerful I can't imagine what He's capable of doing. In the heavens, He created titanic forces somehow kept in balance by means only He understands. Our sun, relatively small in comparison to the gigantic balls of fire populating our galaxy, has mass so great it can afford to turn four million tons of matter into energy every second and keep burning for billions of years. God tossed that celestial body into the center of our solar system as easily as a child can toss a marble onto the playroom floor. Would it be all that hard for Him to take a few "handfuls" of water and toss them across the face of the planet, apart from any force we have yet to discover? Would it be hard for Him to clean up the excess afterward, throwing it back into space as easily as leftover liquids from dinner are tossed into a kitchen sink?

I say all of this not because I think we'll never find a satisfactory explanation, but rather to make the following point: When many of our modern scientists look into the skies, they see something large but not ultimately mysterious. If they can't explain it all now, they will someday; or so they believe. They'll admit they don't know everything in the universe, but they'll say with incredible confidence what isn't there: God. God just can't be. He can't exist in the minds of many scientists because He can't be seen with one of their instruments or contained in a test tube. Therefore, any explanations of events in the universe which include Him are considered out of bounds for thinkers who wish to occupy the tenured seats of major universities.

Why bother with God? Someday we'll have enough knowledge to explain anything in the universe we might care about. Science fiction is full of stories about what humans will accomplish as their knowledge grows. They'll wipe out disease and suffering. They'll build marvelous ships powered by engines yet to be invented, allowing them to travel to the farthest reaches of the universe. They'll harness its massive forces, eventually mastering time and space. Ultimately, they'll develop controls for their machines that bypass hands and require only pure thought, some predict. Why do you need God when you're sure you'll be just like Him someday?

Why does 'being like God' sound so familiar? As I said in our discussion of the Garden of Eden, some of the things that happened there aren't limited to its generation.

Back to the Story

God stated at the end of the flood there would be no more events like it.

> Never again will I curse the ground because of man, even
> though every inclination of his heart is evil from childhood.
> And never again will I destroy all living creatures, as I have
> done. As long as the earth endures, seedtime and harvest, cold
> and heat, summer and winter, day and night will never cease.
> (Gen. 8:21–22)

> I establish my covenant with you: Never again will all life be
> cut off by the waters of a flood; never again will there be a
> flood to destroy the earth. (Gen. 9:11)

This statement contains a wonderful expression of God's mercy. It affirms His commitment to stand behind the gears of the universe and make them turn for the benefit of His creation. Something like a terrible fire was started when Adam and Eve decided to "play with matches" in the Garden. A lot of the damage caused by this fire was extinguished by the waters of the flood, eliminating the need for another judgment like it.

Unfortunately, sin itself wasn't washed away. Sin still existed in the hearts of humans, infecting them from the day of their birth like a deadly virus, for which there is no earthly medicine. After the flood was over, God said, "…every inclination of the human heart is evil from childhood." (Gen. 8:21)

I once heard a comedian ask, "Who teaches children to lie?" The answer is that no one teaches children to lie. They figure it out by themselves. We could also ask, "Who teaches children to bully each other and make fun of each other's small imperfections"? Can you picture a mother leaving a small child to play with others and saying, "I want you to find another child who has something different about them — say, big ears. I want you to point it out incessantly to all the other children and taunt the child who's different until they cry." No. No one needs to teach children any of this. No one has to teach them how to throw a tantrum, either. I once heard it said that one of the greatest acts of mercy given to humanity is that children are born small and uncoordinated. If children came out full-sized, few parents would survive the act of raising them. Children come out of the womb with the ability to lie, bully, and throw tantrums. They need adults to teach them how to *avoid* doing these things. Even Noah, the best man alive before the flood, was stained with sin. As a result, he passed it along to all the children who would follow.

A New Responsibility: Earthly Justice

Because of this, humanity received a new responsibility: the administration of earthly justice. "Whoever sheds the blood of man, by man shall his blood be shed; for in the image of God has God made man" (Gen. 9:6).

God gave humans a profound responsibility for a profound reason. People were to value all human life because humans are created in God's image; that makes each individual human incredibly valuable. If any person wantonly takes the life of another, his/her own life is to be taken by those who administer justice. Not because doing so always deters further crime, and not because it makes sense to our earthly minds, but because God ordered it.

God also draws a distinction between humans and animals:

> The fear and dread of you will fall upon all the beasts of the earth and all the birds of the air, upon every creature that moves along the ground, and upon all the fish of the sea; they are given into your hands. Everything that lives and moves will be food for you. Just as I gave you the green plants, I now give you everything. (Gen. 9:2–3)

Once again, God states His values. Humans are the highest creation on earth. They're on a different plane than animals. This doesn't mean humans should abuse animals. This isn't an excuse to kick the dog when you're angry. Nevertheless, humans can eat meat without guilt, because the animals were given to us to be used in this way.

Yes, humans are different than animals, and because humans are created in God's image, they're highly valuable. However, because they're sinful, a distinction is required. There is innocent life, and there is life possessed by those who choose to use violence against the innocent. This is an important distinction.

Later in the Scriptures, Moses would give several important principles concerning capital punishment. It was not to be a matter of personal revenge. The death penalty was only to be applied after a proper hearing by government representatives, with at least two witnesses testifying to the crime. (Deuteronomy 19.15) That's a very strict standard. No amount of circumstantial evidence could be used when determining the judgment of death.

Moses also made provision for those who use force to protect themselves and others against marauders (Exodus 22:2). On a higher level, there are times when governments may engage in "just wars" against aggressors. Unfortunately, it's not within the scope of this book to delve more deeply into this important topic. The main point is the value of individual human life. Each individual is to be protected against harm. Punishment is to be brought on those who choose to defy God's commands on this issue.

The battle continues. Because of sin, there are still terrible events waiting in the future for mankind. We'll continue to experience the results of our forebearers' decision to learn of good and evil apart from God, but we'll also see wonderful displays of mercy as well.

Chapter 8

What People Can Do When They All Work Together, Part I

More on Conflicting Values

Let me be candid: there was a time in my life when I wouldn't have believed anything I've written in this book. I'm not sure which point would have been most improbable to me or to other modern minds:

- A Creator God who made the universe with a master plan;
- Satan tempting the first humans in the Garden; and
- Destruction of the world in a great flood.

Thinking people of the twenty-first century differ in their acceptance of these points, but there's one idea, which seems most incomprehensible:

Mankind has a very big problem with sin.

This is hard for two reasons: first, modern culture dislikes the idea of one value system being better than another; this is sometimes understandable. There are lots of value systems. People who believe their values to be better than others have often treated others badly.

Although that's sad, we must ask a question: "With all these different values in the world, doesn't *someone* have to be right?"

Oddly, some answer, "No, no one has to be right." Many believe there's no such thing as "absolute truth". As such, there's no one who can state with confidence their views are better than others.

Those people might cite an idea like *synthesis*. The classic illustration of this concept involves several blind men and an elephant. One blind man encounters the elephant's trunk and thinks the elephant is like a snake.

Another feels the tusks and thinks the elephant resembles a rock. Another feels the ear and thinks the elephant is like a leaf. All perceptions are technically correct but incomplete. To have a fuller understanding of an elephant, these observers must combine, or synthesize, their observations.

So, some would say the universe is a gigantic object, which all people approach from different perspectives. Therefore, many have some truth, but none have all truth. As such, we all need to respect each other's views. Perhaps we can even work together to discover higher truths by synthesizing all our viewpoints. Those who deny absolute truth consider themselves to be among the most sophisticated thinkers of our age.

This concept is very clever and appealing. In some ways, it correctly describes how we often learn about our world. However, synthesis has two big problems.

First, what happens when someone has bad information? Let's say a fourth blind man attempts to examine the elephant, only he slips and falls into a creek. He comes out holding a fish. This blind man thinks an elephant is like a fish. If we include his observations, our quest for reality is hurt.

The second problem is even bigger. Often, people need something I'll call "*practical truth*". Practical truth occurs when there are *costs* involved with our perceptions of the world.

Imagine you're driving down a street in the United States, and you see a red sign with eight sides. Written on the sign is one word: STOP. You're approaching a well-known sign. It commands drivers to stop completely before proceeding into an intersection. However, this seemingly obvious sign has problems from the synthesis perspective. If someone came from a different direction, they'd see something different. Most stop signs only have STOP on one side — the side facing oncoming traffic. The other side is blank metal. So, someone coming the other way would have a different experience. If you asked two people who looked at the same sign from opposite sides to describe what they saw, they'd describe two different things. One would describe a STOP sign. The other would describe a blank piece of metal. Both descriptions would include commonalities, such as the object having eight sides. Both would also contain elements that appear to conflict. Both descriptions would be technically correct.

Here's where practical truth matters. In America, if I want a driver's license, I'm required to learn about road signs. It's easy to do. Most residents know exactly how they work. If I drive past a stop sign without stopping, I may discover a police vehicle following me. Having learned about driving laws, I know when I see bright flashing lights, I should pull over and stop.

In this case, someone in a police uniform will soon walk up to my automobile and say something like, "Do you know you just drove past a stop sign?"

Let's say I respond with the following statement: "You know, officer, this is very interesting. I know one side of the sign has the word STOP, but did you know the other side has no such word? It's possible for two people to view that sign differently. Isn't that fascinating? We should respect each other's viewpoints and work together to learn the ultimate truth."

Somehow, I don't think the police officer would be impressed by my remarks. If I caught an insightful police officer on a good day, he might respond with something like this: "That really is a very interesting observation. Thank you for helping me to have a wider perspective on truth. Now, I'm going to give you a piece of paper. In your reality, you can call it whatever you like. However, in our reality we call it a 'traffic ticket'. There's no writing on one side so I suppose two people could view it differently, believing there is 'truth' in the blank side as well as the written side. However, I would encourage you to pay special attention to the 'truth' found on the side with the writing. It's going to tell you important things, like the fine you'll have to pay for disregarding a stop sign. If you don't pay attention to the side with the writing, I must warn you you'll likely meet more people like me. They won't esteem you like your current friends. They won't find your reflections on 'truth' to be signs of sophistication. Rather, they'll likely regard you with low esteem and treat you in ways you consider to be uncivil. Have a nice day."

When I drive in America, I'm expected to learn driving laws. If I break the laws, I'm held responsible. In fact, I'm held responsible even if I don't understand the law.

In this example, we had some fun, but can I be more serious? Imagine we used the same example and added a woman pushing a baby stroller across the intersection. If someone disregards the stop sign, the results aren't funny; they're devastating. If someone tried to explain their actions in that case by talking about multiple perspectives on stop signs, the word *sophisticated* would be the last word applied to them.

The point? Although there are many ways to view the world we live in, some views are in fact better than others. At least, they're better from a practical perspective. If I visit a country, I'm required to learn its laws, so I won't break any. I'm not permitted when visiting another land to make up my own code of conduct. If I want to learn, all I need do is visit government officials. Usually they're happy to answer questions regarding their laws. On the other hand, let's say I do the following: I visit another country without bothering to learn their ways. One day, I break a law. When taken to court, I tell the court officers that I like their country and I want to live there, but I don't like its laws. I want to make up my own. I want to encourage others to follow the laws I create. In fact, I'm not interested in anything the government says concerning my conduct. The result of these statements will be one of three things:

1. Imprisonment;
2. Expulsion from the country; or
3. Number one (see above) followed by number two (see above).

Believers contend we live in a universe created by God. He allows us to use His creation, but we must understand the rules. It's our task to discover His laws, not make up our own.

Unfortunately, we're sinful; we're disconnected from God. We're self-standardizing rather than God-standardizing. As such, we make up our own rules in disregard of the Creator. We want to be gods ourselves. We want God's power and possessions, *but we don't want Him.* We break His laws. We take His things; doing so has consequences. Because God is merciful, we don't always see the immediate impact of our transgressions. In fact, we can never fully understand the ramifications of our sinful actions.

The Tower of Babel

Understanding this explains a lot of history—at least biblical history. One powerful example occurred in the city called Babel.

> Now the whole world had one language and a common speech. As men moved eastward, they found a plain in Shinar and settled there. They said to each other, "Come, let's make bricks and bake them thoroughly." They used brick instead of stone, and tar for mortar. Then they said, "Come, let us build ourselves a city, with a tower that reaches to the heavens, so that we may make a name for ourselves and not be scattered over the face of the whole earth."
>
> But the LORD came down to see the city and the tower that the men were building. The LORD said, "If as one people speaking the same language they have begun to do this, then nothing they plan to do will be impossible for them. Come, let us go down and confuse their language so they will not understand each other."

> So the LORD scattered them from there over all the earth,
> and they stopped building the city. That is why it was called
> Babel — because there the LORD confused the language of
> the whole world. From there the LORD scattered them over
> the face of the whole earth. (Genesis 11:1–8)

As I've said, there are lots of perspectives about the world and its work-ings. The idea of sin troubles many. If sin exists, it's a small problem. It's thought that humans are basically good. All we need do is create a good envi-ronment, encouraging humans to reach their potential. Problems in human behavior are the results of bad environments, not bad people.

If you follow this thinking, the story of Babel makes no sense.

In the story, we're told of a time when all people spoke one language. Life was good. The only problem was location. Noah's ark landed on a mountain. Mountains can be beautiful, but they're difficult places to live. It's hard get-ting things done when you're constantly climbing up and down. So, Noah's descendants traveled downhill and east. Eventually, everyone found what they considered an ideal place: a vast plain in ancient Mesopotamia named Shinar. The receding waters of the flood left a fertile, well-watered region where farmers and herdsmen could settle. Everything people needed was there. They had all the food they could eat, and they had each other. Everyone got along, speaking the same language. What a world!

So, people of the post-flood world should have been thankful to God, don't you think? They probably said, "Let's tell God how much He's appre-ciated for allowing us to survive after the flood and for letting us live in this wonderful place," right?

Well, no. That's not what they did.

Remember Adam and Eve? They lived in a perfect garden paradise. Did they say, "Thank you"? No, they let themselves believe God was evil and that He was withholding good things from them. They decided to steal from God what they believed He was withholding. How about Cain? He committed a horrific crime, yet he was granted mercy instead of the justice he deserved. Did he return later to thank God? No, he went away and built a city. Did he name the city after his parents, or did he name it in honor of some aspect of the God who treated him with kindness? No, he named it after his son and created a legacy of people who rebelled against God with greater intensity each passing generation.

So, God destroyed all of that. We now have people who benefitted from God's mercy once again. They lived in a beautiful, fertile place. What did they do? They built a city. That's sounding familiar, somehow. Now, cities aren't bad by themselves, but, this city had problems. The main problem was the reason it was built: "Come, let us build ourselves a city, with a tower that reaches to the heavens, so that we may make a name for ourselves and not be scattered over the face of the whole earth." (Gen. 11:4)

This city had three goals. Let's explain them in reverse order of the statement above.

The city was built so this early civilization wouldn't "be scattered over the face of the earth." What's so bad about that? These people liked each other. They got along. They worked well together. They liked their new location. What's wrong with wanting to hang around together? The problem involved the first responsibility given to Adam and Eve in the Garden. Immediately after their creation, God did the following:

> God blessed them and said to them, "Be fruitful and increase in number; *fill the earth and subdue it*. Rule over the fish of the sea and the birds of the air and over every living creature that moves on the ground." (Gen. 1:27; emphasis added)

So, God gave humanity a long-standing command to *spread out*. People were to "go where no man had gone before" to quote a famous line from science fiction. The response of the new plain dwellers? "Sorry, God. We like it here. Right here. We're not going anywhere."

Why would God give a command like this? Actually, a command shouldn't have been needed. The earth was an exciting place, full of opportunities to learn about God's creative wonders; but leaving the comforts of home would require something called "faith". People would need faith in God—faith that He would provide for them, protect them, and guide them. Faith would have led this early civilization to believe God had something even better for them than their current location. Unfortunately, they had no faith, so they decided to disobey. The city was an act of rebellion against a "prime directive" given by God.

The second goal of the city was to "make a name" for its builders. Again, what's wrong with that? Isn't every young person told to "go out and make a name" for him/herself? Because this is so common, it seems odd to question it. Nevertheless, this motivation was deemed wrong by God. To understand why, let's consider the events before this. God showed remarkable kindness to this group. Maybe their first official act could be to honor *His* name. Many people who followed later, and who were considered righteous, built monuments that caused them to remember God's kindness in their lives; with the hope that later generations would also be reminded to follow God. Not so, here; these people wanted *their* names to be remembered, not God's.

Not only that, the way one pursues a great name is important. Some seek to be great at any cost; the method doesn't matter. On a small scale, I remember a friend in college who told me of a day when he and his friends were eating in the dormitory cafeteria. It was an old building, and high over the students' heads was a beautiful mural painted by a famous artist. This mural was thought to be out of reach. However, on this day, one bored student decided to shoot a potato at the mural, using his fork as a catapult. He succeeded in getting the potato to stick to the nose of one of the figures in the mural. At the time my friend told the story, it had been a long time since any of the maintenance people who went through that building looked up at the mural. So, the potato was still there. Who knows? It may still be there today. My friend told me that any time this aspiring student made new friends, he initiated them into his circle by sharing the secret of the figure up over their heads who had a potato for a nose—and how it got there. In this case, a little "artistic vandalism" bought some small renown to an otherwise unexceptional student.

Sometimes, we hear much worse. We see news broadcasts created when someone takes a gun and shoots into a crowded place, thinking they'll appear on the evening news. Sadly, they often succeed. Here is the reason the method used by the city builders becomes the focal point.

The path to a great name was a great structure. It was to be a tower that reached "to the heavens". Once again, we find ourselves asking, "What's bad about that? Doesn't every city want to have the tallest building?" I live very close to New York City. New Yorkers possessed the tallest buildings in the world for much of the twentieth century. In 1931, they built the Empire State Building. At 1,250 feet, it was the tallest building in the world for decades. It was later surpassed by the first World Trade Center at 1,368 feet. Later, other countries entered the "world's biggest building" contest and surpassed these figures.

In the days of Babel, though, things were different. They had a wholly different view of how the universe runs than we have today. If we stand at the foot of a skyscraper and comment that it "reaches the heavens", we're speaking in purely figurative language. We know our atmosphere ends at a certain point, and space starts. We have no thought of actually climbing to the place where God lives when we build. The earliest inhabitants of the planet didn't know all of this. They may have thought they could build something that would allow them to enter heaven on foot. They had just invented a new method of construction, known as *bricks*, making it much easier to build big things. Previously, they had to carve stone out of the ground. Now they could take mud and clay right off the surface of the ground, apply a little heat, and voila! Start building skyward. Being very impressed with themselves and their technology, they started right away.

Again, what's so bad here? Isn't God a kindly, welcoming figure? Why would He be troubled by this? Shouldn't He react by commanding the angels to have lemonade ready when the newcomers arrive? If humans are basically good, and they just need to work together to reach their potential, then God would have welcomed all this.

However, if people are desperately flawed, God's reaction makes perfect sense. The first man and woman decided to steal from Him while they thought He wasn't looking. Now, there are thousands of humans working together. Some complain the forbidden fruit should have been kept high out of reach. "Out of reach" didn't stop these people; they attempted to build a huge ladder, which they thought would allow them to climb to the gates of heaven. Once there, *they could storm those gates and steal treasures from vaults hidden in the clouds*. In their minds, this was how to "make a name for themselves". This was their way to be remembered by their descendants forever. The titanic battle between good and rebellion was being taken (or so it was thought) to the throne room of God. This is the reason God intervened.

What did He do? Whenever we discuss God's actions, we should always mention what He could have done, or even what He should have done. God could have brought yet another calamity on the rebellious humans. Perhaps He could wait until all of them were inside the tower and knock it down on them. Once again, the judgment of death wasn't God's choice; instead, He chose to make it hard for the humans to work together the way they previously had. Until that time, God protected humanity from a normal tendency: changes in language. It's easy when two groups become separated to create new words and expressions. This is especially true if the two groups discover different things in their environments.

Let's say two friends walk down a path. They come to a fork, and they disagree on the direction to take. So, they decide to part and come back together later. After traveling a little way, one of them discovers a strange little plant. Today, we'd call it a mushroom. It's growing near some moss, so the first traveler names it a "mosser". The other discovers a similar little plant on his path, but decides it should be called a "dark button" because it looks like a little button growing in a dark area. If they never find each other, they each have the beginning of a new language. Should they meet again, they may have a worse problem, deciding which phrase is better for the little plant. Perhaps they'll never agree.

Until now God protected mankind from this tendency, but now He chooses to accelerate it. We don't know how long it took. It may have been an instant; perhaps it took years. Eventually, certain groups could communicate with themselves but not others. They likely began to dislike and distrust each other. Maybe they had some conversations like this:

Person 1: It's a mosser!
Person 2: No it's not, it's a dark button!
Person 1: Anyone with half a brain can tell it ought to be called a mosser!
Person 2: Oh yeah? And a half a brain is all you've got!

(Fists fly.)

Person 1: Hey, we need to stop this fighting!
Person 2: That's right—we need to work together at our new building.
Person 1: Agreed—let's get started. Would you hand me a brick?
Person 2: It's not a brick; it's a building block.
Person 1: (mutters something about blockhead)

(Fists fly.)

Eventually, construction stopped, and the people of earth were forced to move apart. The tower meant to reach into heaven became a pile of decaying brick slowly disappearing under the shifting sands of time. The people of earth were commanded to move out into the earth, and this is what they did, despite their contrary desires.

Chapter 9

What People Can Do When They All Work Together, Part II

The Towers of Today

What should we take from the Babel story? Two things are important. First, when God commands people to do something, they often wind up doing it, whether happily or otherwise. If we obey God and cooperate with Him, we enjoy the benefits of His promises, which always lie at the end of His commands.

In this case, imagine the joyful world we'd have if every person could travel anywhere in safety and easily share his/her experiences. What advances in science and technology would have occurred if humanity had worked together with one language to experience God's creation? We could live anywhere in peace. Bad weather? People would learn to build comfortable structures to shelter themselves from the most inhospitable climates. Some people experience a fraction of this today, but the whole human race could have experienced this millennia ago if humans chose to obey God and step out in faith to unknown lands.

Instead, we have competing nations with their tragic history of paranoia and hatred. History has seen wars so devastating they caused the extinction of whole civilizations. We have filled the earth, but we have often filled it with misery. The people of the Shinar plain had the privilege of a common language and a common experience. They used it to attempt an invasion into God's realm. The fate that they planned for God, invasion and ransack, was returned upon their own heads and repeated numerous times through the history of their descendants.

The second point grows out of the first. To understand it, we'll look back to the Garden of Eden. After their sin, Adam and Eve were forced out. We're told God left an angel with a flaming sword guarding the gate, so none could ever reenter. I sometimes wonder if anyone tried. People often attempt to revisit earlier times. They dream of a place where things will be simpler, easier, and, in general, better; they dream of such places because they were created to live in such places. As beautiful as our current world can be, it's a dark shadow of the one God intended for us. Deep in our psyches, we realize something better is waiting "out there". Because of this, different people have tried to facilitate a world where all people can once again live in unity.

For some, this is a magical event. Astrologers talk about the "Age of Aquarius", one of the twelve ages their system envisions. In the song "Aquarius" from the Broadway musical *Hair*, actors sing about a time when the planets will align because "love will steer the stars" (MacDermot, et al.). Everyone in the world will enjoy a harmonious and happy world of peace.

Others have been more pragmatic. Armies can be great unifiers. Every leader of a great civilization imagined their forces would conquer the world and cause it to unite under their reign. Names like Alexander the Great come to mind, as we envision men of military genius who led their armies to conquest after conquest. He failed to take over the world, but he succeeded in leaving behind a massive piece of real estate filled with people who spoke one common language (Greek) and who were greatly influenced by his people's culture. Later, the territories subdued by Alexander would succumb to the legions of Rome as great emperors sought to enforce Pax Romana (Roman peace) over the known world of their day. Again, though the Romans came far short of conquering the world, they succeeded in unifying a great expanse. Greek was still spoken by many, but Latin came close to becoming the common language of the West. Latin was (and is) used as the language of international science and scholarship in the Western world long after the Roman Empire fell.

The most recent attempt at such a military unification came from Adolf Hitler, when he marched his armies through Europe. The Third Reich (third reign or kingdom) would attempt the recreation of Charlemagne's Holy Roman Empire—only with a not-so-holy leader. Hitler envisioned a united Europe speaking German with himself as the emperor. He had grand ideas of prosperity spreading through the advancement of science and philosophy. Unfortunately, his grand scheme also involved the idea of a genetically superior Aryan race subduing or eliminating "lesser-evolved" races. Had his armies not fallen to the combined efforts of the Allied Nations, all of Europe (and possibly more) would be speaking German to this day.

Other attempts to unite the world centered on a philosophy rather than an army. With communism, Karl Marx foresaw a world where the workers would unite and throw off the shackles of upper-class elites. Under his plan, a worker's paradise would envelope the world. Marx proclaimed his paradise wouldn't include the Being who created the first paradise. Religion was the "opiate of the people". In the world of Marx, no Tower of Babel was needed; God had long been tossed from the throne.

In the twentieth century, another attempt to unite the world arose after the First World War. World leaders, horrified at the devastation created by the great conflict, created the League of Nations. The League was meant to be a cooperative effort of participating nations. It would prevent future wars and improve the living standard of the world. I stress the word *cooperative*, as opposed to *subordinating*. The League had no standing army and couldn't enforce any of its provisions without cooperation from participating nations. A subordinating organization would be a form of government and would have the power to enforce its decisions upon effected parties through use of the military. Because it had no internal, integrated enforcement mechanism, the League failed to stop the growth of belligerent powers like Germany in the 1930s. The result of this failure was the Second World War.

After World War II, the next stage in this movement's evolution was an organization with more resources and more power, the United Nations. The UN had more participating nations (193 at this writing, as opposed to 58 at the height of the League) and added an official force of "peacekeepers". The peacekeepers can be sent to troubled areas to enforce agreements created after hostilities have stopped. Then, involved parties can negotiate long-term peace. The problem of languages has been streamlined by establishing six official languages to conduct business (Arabic, Chinese, English, French, Russian, and Spanish). The UN has been more effective than its predecessor, but conflicts still occur throughout the world. In its current state, it's a cooperative effort like the League rather than a subordinating governmental body.

It's this last quality of the UN that concerns those who read and understand the story of Babel. There are those in the modern intelligentsia who believe we need a central organization with more power to enforce its decisions. That might mean giving more power to the UN or creating another organization like it to assume preeminent authority over all the nations of the world. This leaves believers in a bad position. No one can argue the value of a neutral place, where nations can negotiate settlements when problems arise. However, many are nervous about the idea of a preeminent organization that would either tacitly or officially create a one-world government.

Let's look again at our philosophical foundations. If people are basically good, we only need to learn to work together. Then we'll overcome our flaws and reach our potential. If this is the case, give the UN all the power it needs to enforce the decisions made by the noble residents of the planet; but if all the people of earth are stained with sin, it's only a matter of time before we start getting into big, big trouble.

What kind of trouble? The people of Shinar found a goal worthy of unification—dethroning God. Later, the communists adopted this goal. People who insist on belief in God are brutally oppressed under communist regimes. Joseph Stalin is credited with deaths in the millions, with many of the victims being church leaders and other faithful believers. Under the rule of Chairman Mao and the Chinese communists of the mid-twentieth century, millions more died. Again, the victims included many who insisted on worshipping the Creator.

How about the UN or an organization like it? Doesn't it respect world religions? Of course, it does, so long as religion doesn't stand in the way, but what would happen if the earth entered a period of worldwide catastrophe? A menacing war perhaps? A global epidemic? How about an economic collapse threatening multiple nations? Terrorists inciting anarchy? A potential global environmental failure? Perhaps more than one of these events happening simultaneously? What if earth's population becomes convinced the only solution is to grant power to a central organization able to solve our problems?

Now, what would that organization do with people who stood in the way, such as people thought to be superstitious and ignorant; people who reference "fairy tales" of places like Babel, and who foolishly impede "progress". Wouldn't it be logical to relieve the world of such people? They don't have to be killed, of course. Some maybe, but more would just be relieved of responsibilities. You can't have such people holding prominent positions in government, industry, or education. Some could be sent to "re-education" camps to be "straightened out" with the tools of modern behavioral sciences. They would need it for their own good, of course, and much more, the good of the world.

That sounds impossible to modern sophisticates, but it's already happened on a smaller scale. When Adolf Hitler took power in Germany, he decided Jews were bothersome. Original solutions involved merely moving the Jews someplace outside of the Fatherland. When this was found to be unworkable, other "solutions" were substituted eventually resulting in the deaths of seven million people.

Imagine what would happen if the world were to create one central government, give it ultimate power, and a madman like Adolf Hitler took over. During World War II, there were multiple, independent nations. Those who saw the disaster coming could become allies, uniting to defeat this monster. Please understand this vital point: *In a one-world government, there would be no one to stop such evil.*

When God performs acts like the confusion of languages at Babel, many regard those acts as unfair. However, the confusion of languages, which caused the establishment of multiple nations on the earth, was in fact another act of God's mercy. Images of nations at war aren't pretty. However, some of the greatest atrocities committed in world history have been committed against citizens of united governments. Many of the seven million Jews killed by Hitler were citizens of Germany; others were residents of nations like Poland that Hitler "united" through conquest. The millions killed by the communists in the former Soviet Union and in China likewise perished at the hands of unified governmental systems.

To many, the picture being painted here is too fantastic to be possible. Suggestions like this are met with cries of "That just wouldn't happen in *our* time", but why not? I once had dinner with a young communist. He was very dedicated to his worldview. I asked him, "So, how do you account for the fact that communist societies tend to be taken over by horrible dictators like Joseph Stalin in Russia?" His response, "That wouldn't happen to *us*." In other words, what my young friend was saying is "We're so smart and superior, failure of that kind is impossible—just because of who we are." Those sympathetic with communism and socialistic principles are oblivious to the idea they could be ushering in a world much like Stalinist Russia. Supporters of more peaceful sounding approaches to one-world governments are likewise blind to the possibility their attempts at utopian world peace could instead result in a "Fourth Reich".

We have labored long on this point, but allow me just a few more paragraphs. There are two reasons why such horrific nightmares are altogether too possible. The first we discussed above is the belief of many that it can't happen. People who think this way have ultimate faith in the goodness of humankind rather than caution concerning its flaws. Such people are simply naïve; their naiveté makes them easy prey when the darkness comes.

Second, such worlds are often created incrementally rather than quickly, and the incremental changes are made under the auspices of noble-sounding motives. The only thing needed to end up with an oppressive master government is to have lots of people believing in the power of numbers to solve all problems.

Let me give an example: let's say my next-door neighbor is out of work and needs money. I might choose to reach into my wallet and give him a loan or an all-out gift. That's an efficient way to help people with problems. Now, let's say someone tells me there is a person across town, who needs help. The individual who informed me of the problem is collecting money. I might choose to donate. Let's say this individual keeps discovering people in need and decides to quit his job to help troubled people full time. This is very noble, but also less efficient. That's because now he needs to keep some of the donated money to pay his living expenses. Still, it's not a bad idea. As his work grows, he requires more workers who also need expenses. This good idea can eventually become an organization of workers who benefit more from donated funds than some of the intended recipients. Even worse, the larger an organization grows, the more vulnerable it becomes to waste and exploitation from dishonest people. I don't want to diminish the work of large charitable institutions; many work well. I just want to mention that sometimes things go wrong.

Here's why that's important. Let's say I discover problems in one of these organizations. If I contribute to the organization, I can do something very significant. I can *choose* to *stop giving*. I can reconsider my charitable actions and send funds to other, more worthy causes. If enough people did that, the organization would be forced to consider changing or risk closing its doors.

Now, what if the government takes over these functions? This is the case as more and more countries move toward socialism. You get an organization that becomes more inefficient and trouble-prone as it grows. Here's the big problem: when its flaws are discovered, *I can no longer choose to withdraw my funds*. I can complain, but historically the more control a government has, the harder it is to reform; and corruption occurs in even the best-run governments. So, the government grows and grows, and takes up more and more of the resources of its people. This happens over a period of time, as the individuals in a society give up more and more control to their government. This last stage is the worst concern.

What could be a bigger concern than corruption and waste in government? What could be a bigger problem than an overbearing governmental body abusing its citizens? Think back to what we've said about *choice*; it's one of the greatest gifts ever given to humanity. God has gone to great lengths to allow people to make free choices. It's one of His goals for us. *Any system that removes choice removes the main tool God uses to help us reach our destinies*. If I see someone in need, I can choose to help him. I can choose to partake in God's divine nature by cultivating the potential for virtue He has placed inside me. I can also make bad choices. I can choose to hoard my money, keeping every penny for myself. If the government takes my money through taxes and distributes it to people of its choosing, then *I no longer have a choice*. My only choices are paying my taxes or being punished for noncompliance. As the tax burden grows, the concept of individual ownership of property is eroded. We stop talking about our money. We talk about government funds. With communism, the goal is the lofty-sounding creation of a utopian world where all needs are met, but the result is the removal of all rights to property; and along with that removal is the removal of much in the way of true choice.

This is the curse of growing government. The more powerful governments become, the more they remove our choices. Even when the results are noble sounding, like fighting poverty and relieving suffering, the effect on the souls is clear. We end up living in a more comfortable and sterile world, but our souls are impoverished. With God pushed to the side, a new god is created: *the government becomes the god*.

Normally, when people think of God, they think of an infinite being who protects us, heals us, and watches over us. When the government becomes our god, it takes over the role of protector, healer, and provider. It becomes government's role to give its people jobs, homes, healthcare, and education at all levels. In today's world, government adds a bonus: in the minds of some, it's the task of government to give people dignity, while maintaining its role in everything else.

This puts believers in a bad position. Wouldn't it be nice if no one was ever hungry? Wouldn't it be great if everyone had access to education and healthcare and a whole host of good things? The problem, though, is the growing number of people who suggest these things be provided by governmental organizations. This places us on the downhill path to growing government that gets alarmingly more powerful with each new acquisition of activities previously handled by private, charitable groups. So, believers wind up looking like stingy people who want to block a better world. In some cases, even believers miss the story of Babel and happily join the new order. There, they enjoy a sense of unity with the self-proclaimed emissaries of world peace and prosperity, but they're oblivious to what they're really creating: a world where the Creator God is cast off His throne and made to sit quietly in the corner, while the inhabitants of earth march past Him into their own kingdoms. In this new kingdom, humanity doesn't create a tower to reach God—they create a god of their own called "government".

Believers want a better world, too, but we want a world where freedom to choose is as valuable as a comfortable world, if not more valuable. We want a world where we don't fear ever-growing governments, where more and more power is given to higher and higher authorities until even nations are viewed as insufficient to solve our problems. A one-world government becomes the final goal to bring utopia. Sadly, our voices are drowned out by those calling for the creation of increasingly powerful government.

So, do believers have a better idea? Certainly! We'll pursue it by getting back to the story of Genesis.

Chapter 10

A New Direction

At this point in the Genesis story, mankind is now scattered over a wide area of the earth. They're probably unhappy about it; people like to stay where it's safe and easy. The population density of the planet is low. If you leave the safety of your family and your people, it wouldn't be long before the roads end and wilderness starts. One minute you've got the sneaking suspicion there may be something lurking around the next bend. The next minute you're getting thirsty and realize you have no idea where to find clean water. There are no fast-food restaurants, no convenience stores, and not even lights by the road. Without lights, when it gets dark, it gets *dark*. On a moonless night, you can only see a few feet. With moon and stars, you can see a little further, but those shadows in the distance could be anything. The world is a scary place.

Abram

Enter a man named Abram. One day, he had a surprise conversation with God:

> The LORD had said to Abram, "Leave your country, your
> people and your father's household and go to the land I
> will show you.
>
> I will make you into a great nation
> and I will bless you;
> I will make your name great,
> and you will be a blessing.
>
> I will bless those who bless you,
> and whoever curses you I will curse;
> and all peoples on earth
> will be blessed through you." (Genesis 12:1–3)

There are two ways to respond to the words God spoke to Abram that day. Abram could have answered much like people before him: "Oh no—It's that pesky God-character again. What? Leave here? I know everybody here. I've got a job. It's safe. Do you know what it's like out there? I heard that someone wandered out of town the other day and was eaten by a lion before he got ten cubits! Forget it, God. I'm staying here!"

Or, Abram could obey God. The command involved risk: Leave safety. Leave the familiar. Go—out there. Go someplace far, far away. Anyone living in that day knew the challenges. It was going to be a long, dangerous journey, but God also promised a grand reward. Abram would become a great nation. Most important, if he obeyed, all people on earth would be blessed. God said He'd keep Abram safe; anyone who tried to hurt Abram would answer to God.

How did Abram respond?

> So Abram left, as the LORD had told him; and Lot went with him. Abram was seventy-five years old when he set out from Haran. He took his wife Sarai, his nephew Lot, all the possessions they had accumulated and the people they had acquired in Haran, and they set out for the land of Canaan, and they arrived there. (vs. 4–5)

We've met a lot of people so far who were stumped when it came to the things of God. Finally, someone understands. He's given a very challenging command from God, *and he obeys*. The great battle for the hearts of mankind has taken a new direction. Abram left the comfort and security of his home and traveled to a distant land named Canaan. There were no street maps, no service stations for the car and, of course, no car.

The distance from Haran, Abram's starting point, to Shechem, his first stop in the land of Canaan, is over five hundred miles. That's not much by today's standards, but in those days, it was like a trip to another planet. After a trip probably taking over a month, Abram arrives:

> Abram traveled through the land as far as the site of the great tree of Moreh at Shechem. At that time the Canaanites were in the land. The LORD appeared to Abram and said, "To your offspring I will give this land." So he built an altar there to the LORD, who had appeared to him. (vs. 6–7)

What does Abram do when he reaches his destination? He builds an altar, not a city and not a monument to himself or his son or anyone else. He doesn't get into trouble. He doesn't complain about the long, hard trip. He says, "Thank you, Lord."

Abram marked a turning point in the history of mankind. Humans and God were entering a new era. Now, people lived all over the world, so the "go" part of God's earlier command was sufficiently met. Now, God gave a piece of real estate to this man Abram.

Sometimes, God's commands relate to a specific time. With the "Go and fill the earth" command, God was serious about mankind moving out. The people of Babel were disobedient. The problem with Babel wasn't that God was against humans building cities and nations; it just wasn't the right time.

Abram showed he was willing to leave comfort and security to follow God's commands. That made him a worthy man to introduce the new era; one in which many of God's followers would be associated with a *country*. The country had a strategic location; the land that later became known as Israel sat in the middle of the world at that time. Land travelers from Europe heading to Africa had to go through the crossroads of Israel. Anyone in Africa wanting to visit the Orient likewise had to travel through this land. This was going to be a prominent location in world history.

There's a lot to say about Abram. For now, three things stand out.

Abram Wasn't Perfect

Shortly after this monumental undertaking, Abram found himself in Egypt. For some reason, he forgot about God's protection and got himself into trouble by lying to the Pharaoh (Gen. 12:10–20). Fortunately, God worked in the Pharaoh's heart so that he was content to merely send Abram away. We learn from this that God doesn't require perfection from His followers. In a broken world filled with broken people, there's no one who performs perfectly. A psalmist later wrote:

> As a father has compassion on his children, so the LORD has compassion on those who fear him; for he knows how we are formed, he remembers that we are dust (Psalm 103:13–14).

Abram grew a lot over the years he followed God. He became a better man than when he started, but he never attained perfection. God doesn't demand perfection from His followers; He asks that they have faith in Him.

Abram Was a Man of Faith

This is the second thing about Abram we must understand. God promised Abram he'd become a great nation; the name *Abram* means "father of many". That was hard for Abram to understand, since he had no children and was growing old. Worse, his wife Sarai had what we would today call "fertility problems". Childbearing looked difficult for this couple. There may have been a few snickers when this elderly gentleman shared his name. How can you be a "father of many" when you don't have children? Although Abram sometimes had questions, he ultimately believed God's promises. His faith was rewarded. At a much later time, when both Abram and Sarai were very old, they had a child. The child's name was Isaac.

This leads to an important statement in the Bible: "Abram believed the LORD, and he credited it to him as righteousness." (Gen. 15:6)

The apostle Paul later quoted this statement as a core principle for believers (Romans 4:3). It's important to understand this because it goes counter to what many believe about God. Most people think of righteousness purely as performing good deeds. They believe that doing good deeds results in God liking you; in essence, you earn God's favor through your actions.

In the Bible, though, good works don't produce righteousness. Righteousness produces good works. When you have faith in God, you do what He says. You obey His commands; you observe His prohibitions. Faith comes first; good actions follow. When God saw Abram's *faith*, "he credited it to Abram as righteousness." (Gen.15:6)

What did Abram believe? Remember the temptation in the Garden. We said the serpent wanted Adam and Eve to doubt some things about God. They were to doubt God's willingness and ability to speak to us (God's word). They were to doubt God's ability to make His statements come to pass (His power). Finally, they were to doubt God's intentions (His character). The result of their doubt was bad actions.

God's statement about Abram was preceded by the following promise: "Do not be afraid, Abram. I am your shield, your very great reward" (Gen. 15:1b). God went on to confirm He was going to fulfill every promise He made to Abram. Abram heard these words from God and took them seriously. He had faith God would accomplish everything He said. He believed God was good and wise; it was this faith that made him obey God's commands. Abram's name was changed from that point to *Abraham* ("father of nations").

Abraham is a model of faith. When people have faith in God, it profoundly affects their decisions. Faith means choosing to listen when God speaks. Faith results in choosing obedience to God's commands. Faith means choosing to rely upon the promises God makes. Faith means choosing to assume God is good and wise rather than anything otherwise. With this kind of faith, the results can be summarized as good works.

Some years later, when Isaac grew into a young man, God put Abram through a terrifying test:

> Some time later God tested Abraham. He said to him, "Abraham!"
>
> "Here I am," he replied.
>
> Then God said, "Take your son, your only son, Isaac, whom you love, and go to the region of Moriah. Sacrifice him there as a burnt offering on one of the mountains I will tell you about." (Gen. 22:1–2)

If there were a time to say, "Maybe not, God," this would have been it. Abraham waited years for this child. This command was deeply troubling. Take your only child and kill him? Besides the obvious emotional trauma, what could be the sense in this? This fit no logical picture of how the world should work. How did Abraham respond?

> Early the next morning Abraham got up and saddled his donkey. He took with him two of his servants and his son Isaac. When he had cut enough wood for the burnt offering, he set out for the place God had told him about. On the third day Abraham looked up and saw the place in the distance. (Gen. 22:3–4)

As if all this wasn't hard enough, Abraham had three days to think about what he was going to do. People often start well, only to lose heart along the way. Would this be the breaking point for this otherwise faithful man? Perhaps actually standing at the foot of the mountain and looking up would be the point of turning back?

No. Abraham goes on, climbing up the mountain with his son. He actually gets to the point of building an altar, tying his son to it, and raising the knife when finally God stops him.

> But the angel of the LORD called out to him from heaven, "Abraham! Abraham!"

"Here I am," he replied.

"Do not lay a hand on the boy," he said. "Do not do anything to him. Now I know that you fear God, because you have not withheld from me your son, your only son." (Gen. 22:11–12)

So, what was faith to Abraham? Faith meant believing God could speak to him. What God said was taken seriously, even though it sometimes made no earthly sense. Faith meant believing God would accomplish what He said; and faith meant believing God was wise and good. He could be trusted with the most valuable things Abraham had.

Most important is the story's ending:

> Abraham looked up and there in a thicket he saw a ram caught by its horns. He went over and took the ram and sacrificed it as a burnt offering instead of his son. So Abraham called that place The LORD Will Provide. And to this day it is said, "On the mountain of the LORD it will be provided. (Gen.22:13–14)

One aspect of Abraham's faith was his utmost confidence that *God would provide what he needed*. Earlier in this story, Abraham made a prediction:

> As the two of them went on together, Isaac spoke up and said to his father Abraham, "Father?" "Yes, my son?" Abraham replied. "The fire and wood are here," Isaac said, "but where is the lamb for the burnt offering? Abraham answered, "God himself will provide the lamb for the burnt offering, my son." (Gen. 22:6b–8a)

Abraham believed no matter how dark things appeared, God would provide. This is important not only from the standpoint of history, but because of the last thing we must note about this man.

Abraham Served a Different God

Earlier, Abraham's faith made him follow God's command to go *to* a place. The command involved a second part; it also involved *leaving* a place. This isn't emphasized in Genesis, but it's proclaimed loudly by Joshua when he gave the great oration which inspired this book:

> Joshua said to all the people, "This is what the LORD, the God
> of Israel, says: 'Long ago your forefathers, including Terah
> the father of Abraham and Nahor, lived beyond the River and
> worshiped other gods. But I took your father Abraham from
> the land beyond the River and led him throughout Canaan
> and gave him many descendants." (Joshua 24:2–3a)

This is extremely important. Abraham's initial challenge wasn't just leaving a comfortable, safe place to go somewhere harder. The challenge involved leaving a land steeped in the worship and service of the "other gods". Originally, Abraham's family came from a place called Ur; this was in what today is southeastern Iraq. At one time, Ur was a coastal city near the mouth of the Euphrates River, but after centuries of sediment deposits, its location is well inland. One of the main things left standing from that ancient city is a ziggurat; a temple built by the ancient Sumerians to worship Nanna, the moon deity. Joshua tells us that Abraham's father Terah worshipped other gods, perhaps including this one. Originally, Terah left Ur and started a move to Canaan. However, he stopped far short in a place called Harran, the city where God spoke to Abraham. (Gen. 11:31) God may have spoken to Abraham's father as well. If this was the case, the father didn't obey completely—he didn't finish the journey. Perhaps Haran looked good enough.

At any rate, Abraham's journey involved a fresh start. It wasn't that Canaan lacked "other gods". It was the symbol of leaving the false gods behind and beginning anew that formed a major foundation of God's challenge to Abraham.

Here's why this is vital: when discussing modern views of religion, one question is asked repeatedly: "Aren't all religions the same? Don't we all worship the same god in one form or another?" To this question, Abraham would give a resounding "*no*." This is not a quiet, polite "no"; this is not an intellectual "no." Imagine someone asking this question and being met with a booming, room-shaking, "*No!*" That's the kind of answer Abraham would give. This is the whole point of Abraham's journey: the God who called him was very different from the gods of the land in which he lived. *Otherwise, he could have stayed home and lived a happy, safe, and prosperous life.*

Abraham set out on an amazing journey because he believed his God was *different*. He believed he *served* a different God. He believed he was *protected* and *provided for* by a different God. When he made a decision to sacrifice the most important things in his life, he believed he was offering them to a different God. The reason for this was his belief that he followed the *one true God;* in Abraham's mind, the other gods were false gods and weren't worthy of his faith.

Let's state it even more strongly: Abraham believed what he did was *right.* Following the other gods was *wrong. The kind of faith credited to Abraham as righteousness led him to turn from the "other gods" to the one true God.* This is a very unpopular statement in modern, polite society. It's crucially important, though, that we understand it.

Who were these other gods? Where did they come from? Why were they worshipped? We'll try to answer those questions in the next chapter.

Chapter 11

Who Were the "Other Gods", and What Made Them So Desirable?

Archeology — What It Tells Us about the Bible and the "Other Gods".

Years ago, I watched the movie, *Indiana Jones and the Temple of Doom*. In the opening scene, Indiana Jones (a.k.a "Indy"), enters an ancient temple in the jungles of Peru. He navigates through a long passageway strewn with deadly, well-concealed traps. We then see him stand before an ancient altar in a massive room filled with primitive stone carvings. There, he finds the object of his search, the Chachapoyan fertility idol (mysterious-sounding music plays). Unfortunately, removing the idol from its altar causes the temple to self-destruct. Indy must run at full tilt from the crumbling structure, tripping some traps he previously missed. Fortunately, the poison-tipped arrows flying from everywhere are meant for someone much slower than Indy. Will he make it out? Seeing as it's the start of the film, he'd better. We don't want the movie ending before we finish our popcorn!

Indy turns out to be a bit of an idol himself. He's a brilliant, yet suave, professor of archeology during the week. On the weekends, he's a whip-yielding, gun-toting adventurer. There's always a beautiful woman at his side (a new one for each adventure, of course). You'd think archeology is a very exciting profession if this film was your only exposure.

In the real world, archeology's a quieter, more patient profession. Archeologists do more digging than running. They don't have to run because they get permission before digging. Their work involves collecting scores of things and carefully categorizing them. This is done so the things they find can be identified and placed like jigsaw pieces into massive puzzles, forming images of the world's past. Archeologists sometimes discover objects that are large, beautiful, and well preserved. That's exciting. More often, they find fragments of broken things, which must be painstakingly assembled into pots, dishes, and other common objects.

The work of archeologists is an immense help in understanding the people who inhabited the world before us. As such, they enable us to comprehend more fully men like Abraham and others who appear in the Bible. Archeologists help us understand the thoughts, philosophies, and religions of those people. Because of all this, we have a better idea of what people were thinking when they worshipped the other gods.

For example, we know much about the building where many of Abraham's friends, if not his family, worshipped. The Great Ziggurat of Ur has been almost fully excavated. It's a semi-pyramid standing 100 feet high, with a base stretching over 200 feet. You can still see the stairways where worshippers ascended to make offerings to Nanna, the moon goddess. The temple was completed in the twenty-first century BC by a King Shulgi, who proclaimed himself a god as well. Considering the size of this temple, you can ascertain one thing if nothing else: the worshippers of Nanna took her seriously. Further knowledge is limited; the temple was eventually sacked by a people called the Elamites, who stole its treasures. It's not unusual for the gods to be preeminent one day and forgotten the next.

Easy come, easy go.

Four Important "Gods"

For us, the most important gods are the ones mentioned in the Bible. There are many, but we'll limit our discussion to four. They are Dagon, Baal, Asherah, and Molech. They're important because they have commonalities with gods around the world. Also, they demonstrate why the "other gods" were abhorrent to Abraham and those who came after.

Dagon was a god of waters. He was often pictured with a fish's body and a man's head. Dagon was revered by the Philistines, a people with whom the descendants of Abraham often fought. You can understand why people wanted to get on the good side of the god who they thought provided water, often in the form of rain. No rain meant no harvest and no harvest, no food. From an earthly perspective, it makes sense.

The strong man Samson, as his final act in life, brought down a temple built for Dagon. He did this by pushing two great pillars supporting it. This caused the massive structure to come down on his own head, along with hundreds of this false god's worshippers. (Judges 16:23-31) Dagon was so abhorrent to Samson, he gave his own life to destroy that temple.

Baal was a common word for "master" or "lord". Many believed he was the son of Dagon. Baal was associated with abundance from the field, the flock, and the family. He accepted animal sacrifices, but on some occasions people offered something much more significant: their children. His worship was common among the Canaanites.

Asherah was the goddess of femininity and fertility. More bluntly, she was the goddess of sex. She was usually pictured as a naked woman carrying a lily in one hand and a serpent in the other. For an added sense of power, she is sometimes pictured riding a lion. Some believed she was the consort of Baal. As a goddess of sex, her shrines often had prostitutes in residence, both male and female, to assist "worshippers". An object often found in her shrines was the Asherah pole, a large rod that may have had phallic significance.

Finally, there was **Molech**. Followers of the true God considered the previous gods vile, but Molech was especially so. He was pictured with a bull's head and a man's body. Bulls were often associated with strength, so this form symbolized a powerful protector. Whereas people sacrificed children to Baal on occasion, they sacrificed children to Molech regularly. (Jeremiah 32:35) The sacrifice often involved fire. (2 Kings 23:10) There's no indication that the children were killed before burning, which may indicate one of the most hideous forms of sacrifice ever enacted. As horrible as this sounds, the act of sacrificing children was so common in the ancient world, some scholars suggest Molech was a concept spread across multiple pagan rites rather than an individual deity. Others believe him to be a god in his own right.

Why Were These "Gods" So Tempting?

The pictures I've just described seem very different at first, but they all have several things in common; things they share with the "other gods" spread throughout the world.

Fundamental to all of the other gods is this: *they give you things*. The things differ from deity to deity, but the reason you approach the gods and give them offerings is you want something in return. People believe the gods have access to things they want. The gods control invisible, elemental forces humans can't touch. You want rain for the harvest? Visit Dagon and his friends and make an offering. You want your herds, flocks, and family to grow? Go to the fertility goddess.

The things you get from the gods can be grouped into five categories I'll call "The Five P's": prosperity, protection, pleasure, popularity, and power.

Prosperity

In the year 2000, we entered a new millennium. Articles about the significance of this event abounded. I saw lots of titles like, "What was the best thing to happen in the last century?" Some articles extended the time to the last millennium or even all human history.

One article asked the question of "the best" concerning inventions. Was it the light bulb? Powered flight? Going far back in history to the beginnings of invention, was it fire or the wheel? One suggestion for best invention of all time surprised me: the invention of the basket. The basket was an important invention, because it marked the time when people started to store things away. Prior to that, people wandered and gathered what they could hold in their hands. The basket allowed people to gather more food than they needed for a given moment. Add the invention of jars, and you could store food like grain and juice for a long time. Throw in barns and silos and the results are limitless. With this much food stored away, maybe you don't need to spend all your time growing and gathering and hunting. You can have a little fun. Let the good times roll. Prosperity is a happy thing.

Then, you experience a drought. All advancements were erased when the ground dried up. For early man, it was scary. Did I say early man? We still experience droughts today. In America, we still hear about the dustbowls of the 1930s where millions of acres produced no food, causing mass poverty. Today, the average person living in the Western world doesn't fear starvation. However, there are still areas of the world where people make only enough each day to carry them to the next. The prosperity enjoyed by much of the modern world was unknown in earlier days. Those who enjoy abundance have little comprehension of a day when one basket of food was a triumph. If your prosperity was threatened by uncertainty, however, there was a place to go. The gods were there to help.

Protection

Droughts and other natural disasters are impediments to prosperity. Another is attack; in a broken world, some prefer to gather other people's food rather than work for their own. Today, in America and other Western nations, many live in safety previously unknown. People can do things like go for a walk in the afternoon without any concern of attack. We have police to prevent that kind of thing. Police are backed up with prisons and other tools of justice; and we certainly don't worry about the next community forming a small army and coming to take our things.

The ancient world was a different place. You never knew when a marauding band would appear to take the food you worked so hard to grow. After attacking, maybe the thugs would burn down your barn just for the fun of it. Maybe they would kill you just because they enjoyed a good show; or, maybe they would carry away you and your family to serve as slaves for the rest of your lives. You'd appreciate a little protection.

Enter the gods. Let one live in your area, and they would take care of you. If they didn't scare away the bad guys themselves, they could strengthen you, so you would be assured of victory in a fight. Just build them a shrine, give them what they ask, and the gods will protect you.

Pleasure

All work and no play makes Jack a dull boy, right? Perhaps the day comes when your barns are full. You feel safe and secure. What then? There's nothing wrong with a little fun. Sometimes, though, people want more. Sometimes, the more free time people have, the more pleasure they want; and talk about inventions—it didn't take long for ancient people to figure out that fruit juice develops a kick when left around for a while. Likewise, with a little work, grain can be made into drinks providing bubbles, along with good feelings. If you're clever, you can enhance the kick, but the kind of kick some people want in their drinks requires more fruit and grain than the minimum people need to survive. You'd better get those harvest gods and rain gods working!

Of course, there's the other gender. Now, there is good, legitimate fun for those willing to marry, but sometimes, your spouse isn't up to the fun. Maybe he/she's getting older? Maybe his/her back is getting bad? Maybe he/she doesn't look as good as the younger ones across the way? In agricultural societies, prosperity requires children. You need them to work the farm and carry on the family name.

Once again, the gods step in to help. In a good fertility cult, you get all the pleasure you want provided by professionals: all you need is the proper offering.

Popularity

Most people want to be liked. Psychologists speculate at the motivations for this; some call this the desire to be valuable. Others call it the quest for significance. In purer form, people want to be loved. When you can't get love, though, being liked can run a close second. Maybe you're not sure what those gods in the shrine on the hill do, but there are lots of other people going there to spend time. Why not join the party? Sincere followers are always preferred members of the worship team, but people who go through the motions to gain good standing in the community are sometimes equally useful. Following the right gods can help in the popularity polls, so many follow for this reason alone.

Power

Finally, when you can't be loved or liked, sometimes being feared works. As we said earlier, humans are like their Creator because they like to create. They like to move things around and shape them, but sometimes this gets out of hand. Sometimes the quest for significance deteriorates into the quest for power, for power's sake. If two people have conflicting ideas about where to move something, someone must win. I remember watching some dinner preparations once. Two people argued about proper placement of the silverware. I don't recall who won, but the act of deciding wasn't pretty. Sometimes it doesn't matter where the utensils go, just that the winner got to make the decision.

Power is desirable, and the gods are happy to promise it.

Summary of "The Five Ps"

If you have trouble remembering the list, it can be summed up with just two "Ps": *provision and protection.* If we want or need something, where do we go for it? Who will provide? If someone tries to take that something away, who will protect us?

Problems with the "Gods"

The gods bring good news and bad news. The good news is they start out as simple business relationships. You bring an offering; they give you things. Whatever their specialty, you get it. Here's the bad news: the gods can also take away. If good times come from the gods, maybe bad times do, too. So if it doesn't rain for a while, maybe it's because you haven't done enough to please the rain god. You'd better grab an offering and get to the shrine, pronto. Maybe you've done something to offend the gods. Better run off to the altar with the little statue on it and find out from the priest or priestess what you did. At some point, it seems you're never quite sure what to do; and whatever it is you need to do, you're never doing enough.

Your simple business relationships have gradually become something more demanding. The offerings get larger and larger, and the time involved gets greater and greater. It's like the proverbial rodent on the treadmill; and what if you encounter a *really* big problem? What if there's an invading army on the horizon? You don't have the manpower to take them on. Measuring out some grain from your barn or grabbing an animal from the flock is no longer sufficient for this kind of problem. No, for this you need a professional-strength offering. What to give? Perhaps offering a *human being* will give the gods what they want. It's scary at first, but after a while it's not so bad, really. Don't the needs of the many outweigh the needs of the few? What's one child more or less? You can always run to the fertility goddess if you want more.

So, what starts as a little dabbling with the gods becomes a lifetime of slavery and vile superstition. Could there be a sadder picture? The answer is yes. You see, *the gods aren't real.*

The prophet Isaiah says it well:

> The carpenter measures with a line
> and makes an outline with a marker;
> he roughs it out with chisels
> and marks it with compasses.
> He shapes it in the form of man,
> of man in all his glory,
> that it may dwell in a shrine.
> He cut down cedars,
> or perhaps took a cypress or oak.
> He let it grow among the trees of the forest,
> or planted a pine, and the rain made it grow.
> It is man's fuel for burning;
> some of it he takes and warms himself,
> he kindles a fire and bakes bread.
> But he also fashions a god and worships it;
> he makes an idol and bows down to it.
> Half of the wood he burns in the fire;
> over it he prepares his meal,
> he roasts his meat and eats his fill.
> He also warms himself and says,
> "Ah! I am warm; I see the fire."
> From the rest he makes a god, his idol;
> he bows down to it and worships.

He prays to it and says,
"Save me; you are my god."
They know nothing, they understand nothing;
their eyes are plastered over so they cannot see,
and their minds closed so they cannot understand.
No one stops to think,
no one has the knowledge or understanding to say,
"Half of it I used for fuel;
I even baked bread over its coals,
I roasted meat and I ate.
Shall I make a detestable thing from what is left?
Shall I bow down to a block of wood?" (Isaiah 44:10–19)

To those who believe everyone worships the same god, Isaiah joins the chorus of those who proclaim, "*No!*" Some people worship false gods, and it's painfully obvious.

Some ask a related question: "But don't these figures represent something real in the heavenly realms?" Isaiah again answers, "No." The other gods he describes are fabrications dreamed up in the minds of the superstitious. People want something, so they imagine they can get it by making a statue representing a higher reality; but there is nothing there other than the base materials they used for their sculpturing. They're just wood and stone—no higher reality. They're just fantasy and wishful thinking.

A side note: this may seem surprising. "Didn't you tell us earlier you believed in Satan and demons?" Yes, that's exactly what I said. "So, shouldn't you be telling us that some of these statues have magical, demonic qualities?" Sadly, we don't have room to go into a full discussion of all the ways invisible forces of the universe manifest themselves. The gospels record several times when Jesus had dealings with either Satan himself or individuals possessed by demons. However, there are no recorded instances of Him doing battle with statues. As you read the ancient stories of Hebrew scripture, the writers appear to be more concerned with what the statues meant to people than whether the statues had any true magical values. That was Isaiah's point. If you go back to the Garden of Eden, the problem wasn't supernatural, demonic manifestations per se. The problem was *words and ideas*. There, Satan created one of the greatest acts of evil in history, using only words and ideas. He used no magical spells. As such, this book is concerned with ideas and meaning, because that's where the greatest battles for the hearts of mankind are fought.

What about the Real God?

There are a number of distinctions between the real God and the false ones. From a practical standpoint, here's one of the biggest: the real God desires to give us all of the things we really need and more. God wants to give it to us *for free*.

"Wait a minute!" some say. "God wants things, too—He wants us to go to a place of worship and give money and do good deeds, doesn't He?" The answer is, "Yes, He does." However, the dynamic is totally different. The real God doesn't want a business relationship with us. We don't purchase things from God by our actions or offerings. When you think about it, why would anyone even try? What does God need from us? If God wanted anything, He could make it Himself. If God needed anything done, He could do it Himself or have an angel do it. If He did it, it would be much better than anything we could do.

No, God doesn't need anything from us; instead, *He wants to give things to us*. This is the God who created the heavens and the earth, and then created Adam and Eve in the midst of it, giving it all to them *for free*. That's what a loving father does for His children. I once heard a father describe how he looked in on his children while they slept one night. They looked safe and warm wrapped up in their blankets. To the extent you can look happy while you sleep; that's how they looked. The man who told the story said he felt an incredible sense of inner happiness and contentment, looking at his children while they slept. They didn't have to do a single thing to make him happy. They didn't have to give him anything.

God wants to give us all the categories of things people long for. How about prosperity? The land which God gave to the descendants of Abraham is described numerous times in the Bible as a land "flowing with milk and honey". Those were symbols of prosperity back then. To have milk meant you had good food to eat. To have honey meant you had the extra things, making life more than just nutrition.

What about protection? Abraham's great faith was recognized when he believed God's statement, "I am your shield" (Gen. 15:1). What army can stand against the Being who created the ground on which the army marches? Abraham's descendants later saw scores of times when God protected them against seemingly overwhelming odds.

Consider pleasure. With the contentment accompanying God's abundant provision and the security coming from God's protection, there would be plenty of time to enjoy the wonders of God's creation. People would savor the taste of honey and other wonderful foods. They could run through the fresh dew on green, grassy meadows each morning. They could enjoy these things, while hand in hand with the special someone God sent as a spouse. Yes, there would be plenty of real pleasure for all. The psalmist David later penned some of the most famous words in the Bible:

> The LORD is my shepherd, I shall not be in want.
> He makes me lie down in green pastures,
> he leads me beside quiet waters,
> he restores my soul.
> He guides me in paths of righteousness
> for his name's sake.
> Even though I walk
> through the valley of the shadow of death,
> I will fear no evil,
> for you are with me;
> your rod and your staff,
> they comfort me.
> You prepare a table before me
> in the presence of my enemies.
> You anoint my head with oil;
> my cup overflows.
> Surely goodness and love will follow me
> all the days of my life,
> and I will dwell in the house of the LORD
> forever. (Psalm 23)

I haven't mentioned the other two items yet; popularity and power lose significance when you understand God offers us something of much greater value. He offers us His love. He loves us dearly. If we long for significance, we find it in His love. If we want to be important, we can find satisfaction in the knowledge that we're important to Him; and His love is forever. It's nothing like the fleeting popularity of telling a good joke at a party. It's not like the short, selfish feeling of satisfaction you get from winning an argument. His love is the real thing.

The Challenge

"All right, Pollyanna," shouts someone from the back row. "Enough of this! I have plenty of times I don't feel safe or secure or full or much of anything else good. What gives?"

Yes, there's a problem in all this, at least from our human perspective; it started in the Garden. Two people were plopped down in a truly wonderful place. It had all the abundance you could dream of, with no attackers anywhere. They had each other; naked and unashamed, with plenty of pleasure on the horizon.

We think having prosperity, protection, pleasure, popularity, and power is all anyone should want in life; but because of His deep love for Adam and Eve, God wanted them to have something more. You remember what it was. God wanted them to have Himself. God wanted them to become like Him. He wanted them to be beings who made decisions based on godly virtues as He does. He wanted them to participate in His divine nature. All that was more valuable than all the earthly things He gave them.

That's His desire for us, too. He wants us to grow in humility—to remember God is God, and we are the creation. God created a universe and then committed Himself to serve it, maintaining it for all the eons of its existence; and so, we likewise are to serve. God is wise and wants to share that wisdom with us. We must learn to receive God's wisdom. God wants us to have faith and trust Him, believing in the words He gives us; words expressing His power and character. Finally, He loves us; and He wants us to love Him and our fellow humans, who are made in God's image.

Adam and Eve had one choice, and they chose badly. They chose to learn of evil by experiencing it. The result is a broken world, filled with sinful, broken people; but the world didn't end at the Fall. God still wants us to have what He offered to Adam and Eve. Only now, it will be a series of choices, not just one. We will need to choose well over and over again if we are to gain the rewards God wants to give us.

The wedge the serpent drove between the first people and God involved an attack on faith. That's why it was so important for Abraham to start right there. Adam and Eve chose to doubt God's word, His power, and His character, even though they were immersed in evidence indicating they should do the opposite. So, the development of faith involves traveling through a world where evidence is much less prevalent than it was in the Garden. Humans must learn to trust their Creator, even when their senses return contradictory feelings that seem to indicate God is nowhere to be found.

That's why God called to Abraham one day and told him to leave the safety, security, and abundance of his home. God told him not to fear attack because he would be Abraham's shield. God would provide; Abraham wouldn't lack anything he truly needed.

Abraham had faith in God, so he obeyed. That's the pattern our God lays before us. Sometimes, getting everything we think we need right when we want it isn't the best way to fulfill the plan God has for us. If we see an attacker coming over the hill, we want him stopped on the hill, not at our doorstep. If we feel hungry now, we don't want to wait until our cravings get intense—we want food now. Of course, we want to feel good; and now is when we want that, too.

That's why it can be hard to follow God. It doesn't always make sense. In one of the most unusual stories of the Bible, a man named Jacob, the grandson of Abraham, met God one night (Gen. 32). Jacob was in a tough place; he just fled a dangerous situation and was heading into something potentially worse. Just when he was about to arrive at "potentially worse", God appears. What followed? Did God simply give to Jacob everything Jacob wanted? No. Jacob and God got involved in a wrestling match; it lasted all night. It resulted in Jacob's hip being injured so badly he would never walk correctly again. Later, Jacob learned God had amply provided; Jacob and his family would be safe. After that event, Jacob's name was changed to Israel. The name means "God struggles" or "God contends". Even though Jacob wrestled with God, God was faithful. That name has been taken by his descendants, the children of Israel.

We, too, sometimes struggle with God. It can be hard trusting someone who places our character above the immediate fulfillment of our desires. It can be harder to trust when waiting is stressed over quick results.

There's an old story about a man walking on a mountain path one day. He slips. He rolls off the path and starts to slide down a steep slope. As his speed increases, the terrified man starts to reach out, desperately grasping at anything he can. Unfortunately, his efforts are useless. In what seems only an instant, he falls off a steep cliff. Fortunately, there's a small tree growing out from a crack in the cliff just below the edge, and the man grabs it in the nick of time. When he gains his composure, he finds himself hanging precariously over a fog-filled abyss. He knows there's no one anywhere close, so he looks up to the sky and cries out, "Is anyone up there?" There's only silence. He's beginning to lose his grip so he cries out more loudly, "Is *anyone* up there?" More silence. Fearing he can't hold on much longer, he lets out one last call of distress: "*Is anyone up there?*" At this point, the clouds above part and a voice comes down from the skies. "What do you want me to do?" the voice asks. "Save me!" replies the terrified man. The voice answers back, "I have heard your pleas, and I will help you." The man sighs with relief. Then the voice says, "Now, let go of the branch." The man considers this for a minute. He then looks back up to heaven and cries out, "Is anyone *else* up there?"

I've heard that story told many times. In one telling, a wind blows away the fog below, revealing a ledge only a few inches below the man's feet. In another version, the story suggests God could catch the man supernaturally if the man would only trust. Some even go so far as to suggest a worst-case scenario involving the man plunging to his death, but awakening with God in eternal paradise. All cases, though, illustrate the same thing: we call to God for help, but we don't trust Him for the answer, *so we look elsewhere*.

Enter the "other gods": they become the symbols of all the opportunities we have to make bad choices. When we're afraid, they're the voices that say, "Why struggle? Don't listen to God; He can't be trusted. He's not going to take care of you—let *us* do it. We'll provide for you and give you everything you want. We'll protect you. And once we give you those things, just stick around. Pleasure, popularity, and power are on the way."

So, we must choose. Some at this point are convinced they need to listen to the one true God of the Bible. They want to know what to do in response. Others need more. Where should we start? Either way, the answer lies in a concept theologians call *revelation*.

Chapter 12

The Foundations of God's Revelation, Part I

A Confusing World with Confusing Voices

In the 1930s, America experienced the Great Depression; at its height, unemployment reached twenty-five percent. People were scared. Even worse, there were threats worldwide. The Nazis were rising in Europe. The Communists, who took over Russia in a bloody revolution, were spreading turmoil beyond their borders. Many still grieved over loved ones lost in World War One. Few people had interest in international conflicts, but things were getting dark out there.

What to do? To escape the tension of life, hordes of people ran into movie theaters to see the latest Hollywood offerings. Hunger for respite made millions for the movie industry. A moviegoer might see a Marx Brothers comedy or maybe a musical like Cole Porter's *Anything Goes*. The fantasy of film offered a break from the world's problems.

In 1939, moviegoers were enraptured by one of the first color films; a musical adaption of the popular children's book *The Wizard of Oz*, by Frank L. Baum. Audiences sat back and watched as a young Judy Garland played Dorothy, the little farm girl from Kansas who fell unconscious at one moment and woke up the next, lost in a mystical land. Dark forces were at work there, too. A wicked witch commanding an army of soldiers and filling the skies with winged monkeys threatened from her ancient castle. The beautiful Good Witch of the North helped when she could, but the forces of good fought to a stalemate with the forces of evil.

There was hope—a powerful wizard living in the land of Oz might be able to save the day. The mysterious ruler could be found only if Dorothy undertook a long and challenging journey on the meandering yellow-brick road.

She would discover, though, the road had some forks. At one intersection, Dorothy stands with her dog Toto puzzling over the correct path. She's shocked when a strange voice comes from a scarecrow. He points right and suggests she go there. A second later he points in the opposite direction saying it's a good way, too. The confounded Dorothy is still processing the idea that a scarecrow could give her directions, when the strawman confidently tells her that some people go both ways.

On a subconscious level, the world of the 1930s probably felt like Oz. People were scared and didn't know where to go. When they asked questions, they received confusing and conflicting answers.

How do you know which voice to listen to in a confusing world?

Centuries ago, a man named Abraham felt he had the answer. He sought to follow the Creator God. Here's a question, though: Why do we know anything about Abraham? He didn't write anything still existing today. The answer: We're taught about Abraham by one of the most influential men in history: a man named Moses.

The Story of Moses

Some years after Abraham's death, his great-grandchildren wandered into Egypt. The world suffered from a famine, but there was plenty of food in the land of the Nile. This prosperity was owed to a man named Joseph, one of the great-grandchildren. His jealous brothers sold him into slavery years before, but instead of dying in ignobility, he miraculously rose to be the prime minister of Egypt. (Gen. 37-41) How he did this is a topic for another book, but suffice it to say Egypt looked pretty good for the moment.

For some reason, the family stayed in Egypt too long. Famines don't normally last multiple generations, but the children of Abraham stayed for that long. Likely, they became comfortable with their surroundings. Perhaps Egypt appeared more civilized than the land promised to Abraham. Life was no doubt easier there. It may also have been more entertaining.

Then, Joseph and his generation died. Later, the pharaoh who called Joseph to his right hand also passed away. Then we're told, "A new king, who did not know about Joseph, came to power in Egypt" (Exodus. 1:8). The new king and his advisors foresaw a dilemma approaching with the people now known as the Hebrews. They were becoming numerous. God blessed them in everything they did, so they were profitable to have around. On the other hand, they were foreigners. The new Egyptian king grew concerned about whose side they would take should conflicts break out with neighboring nations. (Exod. 1:10)

The solution was to enslave the Hebrews. For the Egyptians, it was a great idea; they got cheap labor. For the cost of a few whips, the Pharaoh could begin construction on great monuments and whole cities. It was, of course, less exciting for the Hebrews. They learned the hard way that getting too comfortable in the wrong place can result in unpleasant surprises.

The Hebrews also learned something about the "other gods" the Egyptians worshipped. Those gods gave their worshippers no concept of the value of human life. It wasn't enough to enslave the Hebrews. The slaves were a fertile bunch, which presented a big problem. They were an ever-growing population quickly becoming unmanageable. However useful the new labor force was, if it got too big; things could get out of hand. In response to this, Pharaoh came up with the first official "solution" to the supposed problems presented by the Hebrew people. "Solutions" have plagued the children of Israel ever since. The pharaoh instructed the Hebrew midwives to kill any male children they encountered. (Exod. 1:15-16) By killing the males, the slaves could be bred like cattle when needed. In this action, the pharaoh showed his belief that his slaves were less than human. This has been true for slave owners throughout the ages. I will add the sad speculation that the females were left untouched because the younger and more attractive of them could be carried off and used as free prostitutes. Slave owners have a funny way of treating their slaves as less than human until it comes time for sex.

The midwives publicly assented, but privately refused to follow through. They made the excuse that their patients were so healthy and strong, children popped out before midwives could arrive. Next, callous Pharaoh commanded male Hebrew children be thrown into the river. (Exod. 1:17-22)

One Hebrew mother found a creative solution of her own. She hid her baby boy as long as possible, but when she could no longer conceal the child, she made a small boat out of a basket and set it on the surface of the Nile. If her child were to go into the river, he would go safely. Her gamble paid off. Shortly after being set on the water, the crying child was noticed by Pharaoh's daughter who, unlike her father, possessed some compassion. She took the child in. (Exod. 2:1-10) Like Joseph before him, a descendent of Abraham found miraculous access to Egypt's halls of power.

The young man Moses grew up in the court of Pharaoh. There, he was exposed to both the luxury and the sophistication of royalty. We know little about these years because the story fast-forwards to a very fateful day:

> One day, after Moses had grown up, he went out to where his own people were and watched them at their hard labor. He saw an Egyptian beating a Hebrew, one of his own people. Glancing this way and that and seeing no one, he killed the Egyptian and hid him in the sand. (Exod. 1:11–12)

There are many who live surrounded by oppression and injustice, who blithely overlook the scenes around them. This skill is usually developed strongest by those on the winning side of injustice; Moses, however, wasn't like that. One day, he decided to attempt an understanding of his people's lives. Doing so meant stepping outside the protected life of the royal court. As he watched, he observed some of the worst of the oppression. He became incensed after seeing an Egyptian slave master beating someone who didn't seem to deserve it.

Moses wasn't driven into senseless rage, though. He was angry enough to do something dangerous, but not driven beyond rationality. We're told he looked around to make sure "the coast was clear". (Exod. 2:12) It was only after feeling assured he could act with impunity that he killed the oppressor. Just to be on the safe side, Moses hid the body. I mention these details because, often, storytellers portray the event as an accident. Moses is often shown pushing the Egyptian or hitting him because of thoughtless impulse. The Egyptian falls off a high place or randomly strikes his head after hitting the ground. Moses is then pictured with a look that says, "Oops!"

No, the language of the text doesn't allow this. Moses' actions involved premeditation. We don't know exactly what Moses intended, but his actions suggest he mentally left the halls of Pharaoh and chose to side with his own people.

What was Moses to do? Would he try to foment a rebellion? Would he ride in on a white horse, leading his fellow countrymen to freedom? Would he be revered as the hero, liberating the struggling Hebrews after they were forced so ruthlessly into bondage?

Well, no. Whatever visions Moses had for his revolution, they were short lived:

> The next day he went out and saw two Hebrews fighting. He asked the one in the wrong, "Why are you hitting your fellow Hebrew?" The man said, "Who made you ruler and judge over us? Are you thinking of killing me as you killed the Egyptian?" Then Moses was afraid and thought, "What I did must have become known." (Exod. 2:13–14)

Oh, the best laid plans of mice and men.

Someone saw. Someone told. Within only a day, Moses' actions were headlining the newspapers of Egypt. What is particularly interesting is the reaction of the group Moses thought would be his fellow revolutionaries. Some people in bondage grow accustomed to it. Life stinks, but you can't take your anger out on your oppressors without paying a price. So, you fight with your fellow slaves. Picking someone smaller and weaker is usually the modus operandi at times like this. Of course, on a larger scale, slavery often involves stratification. Those who cooperate with the oppressors get along well with those in power. Slaves who do this can be put in charge of other slaves. Life for those individuals isn't perfect, but it's better than others around them. So hey, why fight it? Whatever the case, Moses spoke here with one of the beneficiaries of the status quo. The response of this slave? "Revolution? With you leading it? No thanks—I'm doing just fine the way things are. Now please excuse me while I get back to beating up someone who's lower in the pecking order than I am."

Pharaoh certainly understood what was going on. He may have always had his suspicions about this Hebrew child brought in by his strong-willed daughter. He may have been willing to go along with the game while there were other, more important battles to be fought; but now, things were getting out of hand. As we saw earlier, out of hand was something not tolerated by the Pharaoh: "When Pharaoh heard of this, he tried to kill Moses, but Moses fled from Pharaoh and went to live in Midian" (Exod. 2:15).

In fear of his life, Moses fled hundreds of miles to the east and eventually landed in a place called Midian. There, he was far enough away that his pursuers gave up. He knew he could never return, so he let himself be adopted by a local family. He became a shepherd; in an act of providence, Moses had returned to his roots and taken his ancestor's profession.

Shepherding is a hard life, but not intellectually challenging. Moses had lots of time to reflect on his past. Previously, he sat at the feet of the greatest scholars of the ancient world. Now, he spent his days chasing animals around the countryside. In his early life, he quite possibly allowed himself to be led into the great temples of Egypt, where the upper class worshipped the deities of that land—not as the ancient statues we see today in museums, but as mystical beings thought to have great power. Although he eventually became one of the greatest names in the vocabulary of those who seek the one true God, I find it hard to believe he would have been allowed to loudly challenge the belief system of the Egyptian royalty in whose palaces he lived. At any rate, those deities were now far away.

In another act of providence, the family Moses joined was led by Jethro, a "priest of Midian." (Exod. 2:16) Tradition states Jethro worshipped the one true God. So, Moses begins to have the beliefs of his royal youth challenged. Perhaps Moses noticed that the Egyptian sun god Ra was not worshipped by people outside of Egypt's borders; yet, somehow in the distant land in which he lived, the sun dependably rose and set each day. The moon god, thought to be powerful in Egypt, didn't seem to have the power to pursue this young man, who almost created a revolution against the deity's devoted followers. The animals elevated by the Egyptians to deity, cats, dogs, and bulls, were decidedly unintelligent when Moses met them in the pastures of Midian.

Whatever Moses wondered about, he had a long time to do it. For forty years, he lived a quiet life with his new family and their sheep. That's plenty of time for the courts of Egypt to become a distant memory. Moses would have silently slipped off the pages of history in this rural corner of the world, were it not for one thing: God had much bigger plans for him.

Moses Meets God

The new routine Moses learned in Midian eventually became old. After decades of the same mundane activities, on a day that seemed the same as any other, Moses set out for yet another day of tending sheep. Then, on that otherwise average day, Moses had one of the most fantastic and rare experiences ever given to a mortal. That day, God revealed himself directly to Moses. Moses later recorded that experience, along with many others. His writings became the foundation for the written revelation of God to man.

> Now Moses was tending the flock of Jethro his father-in-law, the priest of Midian, and he led the flock to the far side of the desert and came to Horeb, the mountain of God. There the angel of the LORD appeared to him in flames of fire from within a bush. Moses saw that though the bush was on fire it did not burn up. So Moses thought, "I will go over and see this strange sight—why the bush does not burn up." When the LORD saw that he had gone over to look, God called to him from within the bush, "Moses! Moses!" And Moses said, "Here I am." "Do not come any closer," God said. "Take off your sandals, for the place where you are standing is holy ground." Then he said, "I am the God of your father, the God of Abraham, the God of Isaac and the God of Jacob." At this, Moses hid his face, because he was afraid to look at God. (Exod. 3:1–6)

Moses had an encounter with what the Scriptures call "the Angel of the Lord". (Exod. 3:2) Note here that this is not "an angel", but rather "*the* angel of the LORD". What Moses saw was very special. This being appears in other places in Scriptures; in every instance, he talks to people and speaks authoritatively about God's will. Here, we see some distinct qualities of "the angel of the Lord".

The angel of the Lord appeared to Moses in "flames of fire", but this was no ordinary fire. Fire consumes combustible materials, like the wood found in a bush. Not so here; God made sure the manifestation wouldn't be mistaken for something commonplace.

We then read God called to Moses from within the bush. The "angel of the Lord" was in the bush. God was in the bush. From here forward, we're told any further communication comes from God Himself; "I am the God of your father, the God of Abraham." (Exod. 3:6a) The angel of the Lord and God are one and the same. If not, it was getting crowded in that little bush. Moses understood this—we're told he hid his face, because "he was afraid to look at God". (3:6b)

Something's happening here that's profound and awesome; and it's dangerous; Moses was warned he shouldn't come too close. God didn't say, "Hey Moses—come over here and give me a big hug!" No, Moses must keep his distance.

He was commanded to remove his sandals. Remember, Moses was a shepherd. The more prosperous shepherds got sandals because they had to walk in all the stuff the sheep left behind. This was a symbolic gesture. The earth is full of microbes and unpleasant organic matter. Moses spent his days with sheep, which are not the neatest of animals. It's not likely he had questionable stuff on his feet alone. Here, though, we need a *symbol*. It's important to introduce the image of a God who is *separate* from the unclean things of the world; uncleanness represents the corruption of evil and sin. Moses was told the ground he walked upon was *holy*. He was meeting with a Being who is free from evil, free from moral blemish. This is in addition to the fact that God is separate from His creation; He and the creation aren't the same.

Here's a vitally important point: In all this, God can create *points of contact* between Himself and His creation. He's created one here. He can do this because He's all-powerful. He can do anything He wants. He used this point of contact to communicate with Moses. Also important is the manner in which God communicated. The communication involved words of human language. Moses heard words. He spoke words back. There are several reasons this is important.

Language is specific. Moses wasn't experiencing warm, vague feelings about God. God was telling Moses exactly what was on His mind. Moses wouldn't have indistinct ideas of God that aren't any better than the thoughts and feelings of others. This has *authority*. Because language is specific, and because the words Moses was hearing were authoritative, Moses could record the words in writing. Those writings can be read and understood by others. This awesome moment was the germinal event for what later grew into *the Scriptures*, the writings that represent God's will for all humanity.

Finally, this method of communication demonstrates God is not just all-powerful; He's all-knowing and infinitely intelligent. His complexity in comparison to humans is like comparing humans to microbes. Yet, He can speak to us in our languages. Any biology student can fill a Petri dish with microbes, but he can't talk with them. The authority of these words comes from their source: the all-powerful and all-knowing Creator.

Lots of people have had experiences they interpreted as talking with God. Many of them wrote down what they experienced; and sadly, many of them disagree with Moses. Why are the writings of Moses different? Let's find out by looking further at his story.

The Call of Moses

> The LORD said, "I have indeed seen the misery of my people in Egypt. I have heard them crying out because of their slave drivers, and I am concerned about their suffering. So I have come down to rescue them from the hand of the Egyptians." (Exod. 3:7–8a)

God wasn't oblivious to His children's suffering; He never is. He had a plan for them, and the plan involved Moses. God said to him, "So now, go. I am sending you to Pharaoh to bring my people the Israelites out of Egypt" (vs. 10).

For Moses, this called up bad memories; he tried that years ago. The results weren't what we'd expect in a Hollywood action film. "But Moses said to God, 'Who am I, that I should go to Pharaoh and bring the Israelites out of Egypt?' And God said, 'I will be with you'" (vs. 11–12a).

Forty years in the wilderness did something to Moses. He was more *humble*. Forty years before, Moses was a one-man revolution ready to storm Pharaoh's palace. Now, he asked, "Who am I to do this?" God has a unique way of working in each person. Of all the things He can give someone, development of the four godly virtues is paramount. The development of humility in Moses took years, but now it was there. Something about the life Moses lived between the time he left Egypt until now caused him to reevaluate himself. He now had a more accurate view of who he was. He would soon develop a real appreciation for who God is.

If you remember the last time Moses tried to rescue his people, he was asked, "Who made you ruler and judge over us?" Although asked by someone whose attitude was less than noble, it was a good question. History is filled with stories of self-proclaimed saviors. No, actually that's not quite right; history isn't filled with them. History only tells us about the successes. Most revolutions are crushed before they get anywhere near the history books. Most revolutionaries die at the hands of oppressors, whether through execution or by languishing behind the walls of prisons. The evil slave who rebuked Moses may have had a point. "Why should we listen to you? What makes Moses so special that we should risk our lives for him?" Perhaps this question even occurred to Moses at some point over the last forty years. However, God said to him, "I will be with you." In other words, "Last time, you acted on your own from an impulsive spirit, but this time you'll be sent by Me. You'll act by My command. This time you'll have *My authority*."

At this point, the skeptic says, "Well, well. The story is developing nicely. We have the makings of an entertaining novel. But again, what makes this man different from others who believed they heard God's voice?"

Now, many haven't heard the story of Moses. If you have, imagine you're among those who missed this great narrative. Imagine you live under a repressive regime. You're sitting on the curb one day when someone jumps into the street and proclaims, "God has spoken to me! He'll free you all—just follow me!" How do you know this guy isn't drunk? Maybe he's crazy? Maybe it would be better just to ignore him.

Here's what's different with Moses: "And this will be the sign to you that it is I who have sent you: When you have brought the people out of Egypt, you will worship God on this mountain" (Exod. 3:12b).

According to the story, this is the God of the heavens and the earth speaking. He doesn't have to explain Himself. He doesn't have to prove anything; yet, He offers something special to Moses: *evidence*. The evidence involves a *prediction*. If the prediction comes true, Moses is following God. If not, Moses is experiencing a bad reaction to last night's lamb entree. Here's the prediction: after Moses does everything God tells him, a few hundred thousand people will accomplish the impossible. They'll escape one of the most powerful and oppressive regimes in history. After escaping, they'll live and worship in freedom. They'll end up at a specific location, the mountain where Moses has heard God's voice.

With all of this, God doesn't require Moses to leave his brain home. This is a big promise, with the fulfillment a long time off. So, God gives Moses a smaller demonstration of His power first.

> Then the LORD said to him, "What is that in your hand?" "A
> staff," he replied. The LORD said, "Throw it on the ground."
> Moses threw it on the ground and it became a snake, and he
> ran from it. Then the LORD said to him, "Reach out your
> hand and take it by the tail." So Moses reached out and took
> hold of the snake and it turned back into a staff in his hand.
> "This," said the LORD, "is so that they may believe that the
> LORD, the God of their fathers—the God of Abraham, the
> God of Isaac and the God of Jacob—has appeared to you."
> (Exod. 4:2–5)

Let's look at how God works here: He starts small and then moves on to
bigger things. Moses knew his staff. He carried it most days. It had no magical powers, but right before him, it became a dangerous serpent. Moses knew
what it was and ran. Then, God told Moses to pick up the snake by the tail.
Moses was experienced in field living. He's already reacted in the appropriate
manner for snakes. You run. You leave snakes alone; you don't pick them up
and play with them. God told Moses to pick it up. Moses did and saw God is
in control. Now he knows he can trust God with bigger things.

God often does this with average people. He introduces faith through
small things and moves on to larger tasks requiring greater levels of trust in
His providence and power. For most, though, it's not on such grand scale.
Most people will never see miracles of the kind shown to Moses, and later
the Hebrew people of his generation. *Such miracles are rare.*

However, there are special times when God needs to show that someone
has His authority. This is a unique and incredibly important event. Moses
later wrote the following words:

> You may say to yourselves, "How can we know when a mes-
> sage has not been spoken by the LORD?" If what a prophet
> proclaims in the name of the LORD does not take place or
> come true, that is a message the LORD has not spoken. That
> prophet has spoken presumptuously. Do not be afraid of him.
> (Deuteronomy 18:21–22)

A prophet is someone who speaks with the full authority of God. This is
the pattern: someone who speaks authoritatively for God will eventually be
given words that involve a prediction about things in the near future. Those
things will come to pass. If they don't, you don't have someone who speaks
authoritatively for God.

In the days when the Scriptures were being given, the penalty for false prophets was severe—death. (Deut. 18:20) In that environment, someone who claimed to speak for God had to be certain. Let's compare this to the modern day. Every time I go to the grocery store, I see magazine racks with tabloid newspapers. Often, they'll contain headlines something like, "Our Psychics Make Predictions for the Coming Year." They'll feature people who claim they can tell the future. Often, they'll be rated by the percentage of previous success they've had. Some have sixty percent success. Others have seventy or eighty percent, but none have a hundred percent. In the days of Moses, the only thing that mattered was a hundred percent. Anything less deserved the death penalty; that's how important authority was to Moses.

Armed with God's authority, Moses again set out to rescue his people.

Chapter 13

The Foundations of God's Revelation, Part II

God's Power Shown to the Egyptians and the Hebrews

God had more predictions for Moses:

> The elders of Israel will listen to you. Then you and the elders are to go to the king of Egypt and say to him, 'The LORD, the God of the Hebrews, has met with us. Let us take a three-day journey into the desert to offer sacrifices to the LORD our God.' But I know that the king of Egypt will not let you go unless a mighty hand compels him. So I will stretch out my hand and strike the Egyptians with all the wonders that I will perform among them. After that, he will let you go. (Exodus 3:18–20)

God tells Moses the leaders of the captive Hebrews will listen. The king, however, will be a tougher sell. The solution to the king's stubbornness will involve a display of God's awesome power. Moses will get first notice. Moses will then announce God's planned actions.

God's actions will be more than large-scale parlor tricks. They'll counter the belief system of Egypt, which was based on a pantheon of "other gods". Recall, people presume the gods give them things, such as prosperity, protection, pleasure, popularity, and power. The gods of Egypt claimed to provide them all, but now, the gods of Egypt would be challenged with forces summarized in a single word: *plague*.

The first plague involved the Nile. The bulk of Egypt is covered with the dry dust of the Sahara Desert. To have the good things of life, you want to live close to the Nile; the great river originating in the heart of Africa and bringing life to what would otherwise be a very inhospitable place. To make sure the waters of the Nile behave, the Egyptians worshipped the god of the Nile, Hapi.

After Moses left for Midian, a new king arose in Egypt. Moses went to him and told him what God said. The king responded by further oppressing the Hebrews (we're shortening a long story here). Since reason didn't work, Moses gave Pharaoh the following message:

> This is what the LORD says: By this you will know that I am the LORD: With the staff that is in my hand I will strike the water of the Nile, and it will be changed into blood. The fish in the Nile will die, and the river will stink; the Egyptians will not be able to drink its water. (Exod. 7:17–18)

God demonstrated He was greater than the Nile god. It was He who commanded the Nile to bring life, not Hapi. Unfortunately, the magicians of Pharaoh's court were able to do something similar. So, we're told, "Pharaoh's heart was hardened" (Exod. 7:22), but in modern language, this was only the warm-up act for God. More plagues would come, demonstrating that it's God alone who controls the forces of nature.

Next came frogs. The Egyptians, noting there were lots of frogs near the Nile, figured the frogs must be fertile little creatures. Hence, they revered the frog-goddess Heqet, a goddess of fertility and child-bearing. As a fertility goddess, we can guess what went on in her temple.

God caused frogs to leave the Nile and infest the city of the king. Frogs are one of those little critters that are somewhat cute, in spite of their unattractive profiles. One or two frogs can make a visit to the pond entertaining for the kids, but God caused *lots* of frogs to enter Egyptian dwellings, and they became annoying. The kind of pleasure people seek from fertility goddesses disappears fast if you have a dozen frogs croaking in your bed.

The frogs were followed by pesky gnats, and then flies; not just the occasional fly that distracts you when you're trying to read a book. We're told that "Dense swarms of flies poured into Pharaoh's palace and into the houses of his officials, and throughout Egypt the land was ruined by the flies" (Exod. 8:24b). To make the point even more clear, Moses informed the king none of these plagues would occur in the land of Goshen where the Hebrews lived. By this time, the king's magicians gave up. "The magicians said to Pharaoh, 'This is the finger of God.'" But that wasn't enough; "Pharaoh's heart was hard and he would not listen" (8:19).

Did I forget to mention the importance of flies in Egyptian mythology? They were supposed to bring health and good luck; so much for that.

They say stress isn't so bad if your health is good and you're feeling well. Some say, if you look good, you feel good. To answer that, the next plague was boils. God caused large, festering boils to break out on the skin of the Egyptians. Forget the pursuit of pleasure—the typical Egyptian, at this point, would settle for freedom from the painful eruptions covering their bodies.

If you're sick, you can at least enjoy a good meal, right? Next, God sent a plague of hail that killed livestock and decimated crops growing in the fields. When Pharaoh still resisted, massive swarms of locusts arose from the deserts, destroying any food that was left.

Some say the plagues had natural causes, making them easy to explain. Sometimes there are landslides of clay-filled soil upstream in the Nile that would give the water a red appearance. This would cause fish to die. Any creature able to leave the water would do so; hence the frogs. As the fish and frogs died, they attracted gnats and flies, which bring disease, hence the boils. See how easy this is?

The only problem with this explanation is timing. All this happened on schedule, as though it were a symphony conducted by a master musician. That's hard, and having all this happen to one group of people, when their neighbors up the road, remain unaffected is harder still. If events on the ground weren't hard enough, any semblance of easily explained causality evaporated when God sent hail on the Egyptians. It was "the worst storm in all the land of Egypt since it had become a nation" (Exod. 9:24b).

The gods of Egypt received a thorough thrashing here. The gods who promised the five "Ps" through the Nile, frogs, harvest, and a host of other things, all came up empty against the God who spoke through Moses. The man who predicted plagues and saw them come on schedule had authority unlike anything the Egyptians ever saw.

Perhaps the most powerful Egyptian god would fare better? Surely the great sun god, Ra, would prevail over this intruder from the east.

> Then the LORD said to Moses, "Stretch out your hand toward the sky so that darkness will spread over Egypt—darkness that can be felt." So Moses stretched out his hand toward the sky, and total darkness covered all Egypt for three days. No one could see anyone else or leave his place for three days. Yet all the Israelites had light in the places where they lived. (Exod. 10:21–23)

Not even the sun god could compete with the God of Moses. The sun was blackened for not one, not two, but three days. This wasn't a solar eclipse, which lasts only a few hours. This wasn't a few clouds turning a sunny day gray. This was total blackness, paralyzing all Egypt—all of course, except the Hebrews whose territory enjoyed sunshine worthy of the best beach vacation.

Even in all of this, Pharaoh would not relent:

> But the LORD hardened Pharaoh's heart, and he was not willing to let them go. Pharaoh said to Moses, "Get out of my sight! Make sure you do not appear before me again! The day you see my face you will die." "Just as you say," Moses replied, "I will never appear before you again." (Exod. 10:27–29)

Pharaoh was never moved toward God. In typical fashion, he believed kicking out God's representative would make God go away, too. One final salvo at the gods of Egypt was required to bring Pharaoh and the Egyptians to their knees.

Moses proclaims:

> This is what the LORD says: "About midnight I will go throughout Egypt. Every firstborn son in Egypt will die, from the firstborn son of Pharaoh, who sits on the throne, to the firstborn son of the slave girl, who is at her hand mill, and all the firstborn of the cattle as well. There will be loud wailing throughout Egypt—worse than there has ever been or ever will be again. But among the Israelites not a dog will bark at any man or animal.' Then you will know that the LORD makes a distinction between Egypt and Israel." (Exod. 11:4–7)

Next to the king, the most important person in any kingdom is the heir to the throne. The son of Pharaoh was groomed to take over one of the most powerful monarchies in the world. He was the link allowing the name of Pharaoh's family to continue forever. At points in Egyptian religion, the pharaoh was considered to be an embodiment of the sun god, Ra. A successful attack on Pharaoh's family was like killing one of the gods, and a chief god at that. As such, the prince was difficult to attack. Assassination would be a "mission impossible"; and if you were going to try it, you certainly wouldn't announce your plans.

Announce was exactly what Moses did. The Egyptians were given time to muster all available resources. The palace guard could be tripled. Altars in every temple could be loaded with sacrifices to rally the gods. Though beaten separately, perhaps the combined supernatural forces of the Egyptian gods could prevail over the one God served by Moses. Perhaps Anubis, guardian of the gates of hell, could be called to block the gates instead of ushering people in. Perhaps Osiris, god of the afterlife, could be petitioned to give a short holiday to death itself.

Another thought: Many believe prayer is a cosmic force generated when people concentrate on spiritual things. It doesn't matter to whom or to what people pray; it's the energy exerted by the participants that matters. If this were the case, surely that cosmic force would be multiplied thousands of times when all Egypt prayed to their gods. Pray they would, because Moses predicted the pain wouldn't stop at Pharaoh's household. Every family, every flock, and every herd in Egypt would be hit.

You might ask: "We can see how Pharaoh needed to be taught a lesson, but why the other Egyptians?" Because every family in Egypt profited from the suffering of God's people, the Hebrews. It was too easy to look the other way when Pharaoh took a nation of innocent people who came as friends and forced them into bondage. No one spoke out; rather, they accepted this new underclass. The slaves built palaces and monuments for the ruling class, of course, but everyone enjoyed the new roads and other works coming from the cheap labor made possible by the whips of ruthless Egyptian taskmasters. All were guilty, and all would be judged.

All would be shown convincing evidence that this was no trick. The prediction was specific; only the firstborns were affected. Everything would happen in one night, and the Hebrew people wouldn't be touched. This wasn't a random disease, and no one could claim it as such. It was a clear display of God's power and judgment.

This plague would be different for the Hebrews. Unlike the other plagues, there was something they needed to do. They were to slaughter a lamb and apply its blood to their doorposts. Then they were to remain in their homes where they would be protected by this sign.

God was about to use the liberation of the Hebrew people as a monumental symbol of something called "sanctification", being made holy. They were going to be removed from a land of people who worshipped other gods, a land where slavery characterized Hebrew lives. The Hebrews would *come out from among* the Egyptians and their idolatrous ways to become a people set apart for God.

When the final plague was finished, having come solemnly on schedule as Moses predicted, Pharaoh finally relented and freed the children of Israel. Though not noted at the time, the picture that followed was one of the most triumphant in history and yet, one of the saddest. Triumphant, because God displayed a very rare show of His awesome power and gave freedom to an oppressed people. Sad, because the people of Egypt chose to stay where they were. They came to believe in the Hebrew God in a certain sense, too; but in essence, they said, "Now we believe in your God, so please go away—and take Him with you! Tell Him to leave us alone, so we can go back to our old ways."

I have been confronted many times by people asking questions like, "Why doesn't this God of yours do something to let us know He's really there? Can't He show us some kind of miracle?" The answer to this question is no, because *miracles alone don't create faith*. The problem between humans and God isn't a lack of willingness on God's part to speak to us and show His power in our lives; it's our unwillingness to believe God. All the miracles shown to Pharaoh and to the Egyptians were insufficient to convince them to follow God.

So, How Do We Find Out What God Wants?

We started the chapter with an illustration from *The Wizard of Oz*. That book sends a surprisingly confusing message, considering it was a beloved children's classic for many years after its publication in 1901. Dorothy follows the yellow-brick road faithfully, and after finding the Wizard, she follows his instructions perfectly. When it comes time to claim the reward of her faithfulness, she discovers that the great and powerful wizard she trusted with her life was a total fake! He was just a circus performer who landed by accident one day in a strange place and managed to con the locals into believing he was something special. It was all a scam.

History is filled with people who claim to be in touch with higher powers, *but Moses was different*. He was empowered by God to give the ancient Hebrew people convincing evidence that he spoke with authority. Of him, God said:

> Listen to my words:
> "When a prophet of the LORD is among you,
> I reveal myself to him in visions,
> I speak to him in dreams.
> But this is not true of my servant Moses;
> he is faithful in all my house.
> With him I speak face to face,
> clearly and not in riddles;

he sees the form of the LORD. (Numbers 12:6b–8)

Eventually, God brought the Hebrews to the mountain where He promised Moses they would meet. God proved everything He told Moses. In doing
so, He established Moses' authority as the first great prophet of the Scriptures.
This is why Moses is honored by the three major religions of the Western
world: Judaism, Christianity, and Islam. Moses recorded his experiences and
the things God told him in a series of writings comprising the first five books
of the Bible: Genesis, Exodus, Leviticus, Numbers, and Deuteronomy.

Other prophets followed. As Moses instructed, their authority was based
on their ability to predict God's actions. Prophets appeared over the following
centuries, with names like Jeremiah, Ezekiel, Isaiah, and Daniel. The final
great prophet is referred to as "the Messiah". The Jews believe him to be an
individual yet to appear. Christians believe him to be Jesus Christ. We'll talk
more about that in a later chapter.

What does all this mean for us? Should we wait for miracles, so we
can understand what God wants? No. Moses, Jeremiah, Isaiah, Daniel, and
others wrote down what they learned from God. We rely on the writings, the
Scriptures, to understand what God wants. We read their writings rather than
waiting for more direct revelation.

Feelings, Names, Actions, and Words

As I stated earlier, humans have no innate ability to fully perceive ultimate truth. God didn't place Adam and Eve in the Garden and make them
guess about the Tree of the Knowledge of Good and Evil. He didn't tell them
to rely on their feelings. He told them about the Tree and many other things
in plain words. *The problems they encountered resulted from trusting too
much in their feelings and emotions, rather than listening to the words God
gave them.* From the first days of humanity in the Garden until now, we discover God's will for us from His revealed words. Those words are recorded
in the Bible.

Now, there are lots of words in the Bible. Why so many? Because there
is a lot to learn about our Creator: He's complex, and His actions in history
are complex. We see this in one of Moses' encounters with God:

> Moses said to God, "Suppose I go to the Israelites and say to
> them, 'The God of your fathers has sent me to you,' and they
> ask me, 'What is his name?' Then what shall I tell them?"

138

God said to Moses, "I am who I am. This is what you are to
say to the Israelites: 'I AM has sent me to you.'"

God also said to Moses, "Say to the Israelites, 'The LORD,
the God of your fathers—the God of Abraham, the God of
Isaac and the God of Jacob—has sent me to you.' This is my
name forever, the name by which I am to be remembered
from generation to generation." (Exod. 3:13–15)

The Egyptian gods all had names. If someone visited Egypt in the Moses'
day and expressed interest in the Egyptian religious system, they would be
taken from temple to temple and introduced to beings like Ra, god of the
sun, or Osiris, god of the dead. Each had one thing in common: their names
linked them to a piece of real estate in the cosmos. It was natural for Moses
to throw in the question, "By the way, what's *your* name?"

In his answer, God made something clear to Moses at the outset: He was
not to be compared with the gods of Egypt. He wasn't limited to even the
most powerful of celestial objects, much less their earth-bound representatives. His existence cannot be summarized in one easy word. Centuries later,
a man name Manoah, the father of Samson, met the angel of the Lord and
again asked for a name. The answer? "Why do you ask my name? It is beyond
understanding" (Judges 13:18).

There is no one word that summarizes God. There is only a place to start.
Moses is given the words for it. God simply starts with His existence.

Though God cannot be summarized in one word, we can learn about Him.
We do this through reading about His *actions* in the world. The first thing
He wanted the children of Israel to know was that He was the God of their
fathers: Abraham, Isaac, and Jacob. He hadn't forgotten the children of these
men. He returned to deliver them.

At other times in history, God allows the name He gave to Moses to be
used as a sort of placeholder for things people learned about Him. When
teaching His people about holiness, God refers to Himself as "the LORD who
sanctifies" (Lev. 20:8). Later, He's called "the LORD Almighty" (Ps. 46:7).
Gideon calls him "the LORD our peace" (Judg. 6:24).

With each sentence of each story in the Bible, we learn more about God.
We learn how God can support those who love Him when we read the story
of the young shepherd boy David. God empowered him to beat the mighty
giant Goliath in battle. We learn how God gives wisdom to those who seek
to rule well for Him when He made Solomon the wisest king ever to live.

We learn about what God approves. We learn about what God rejects. We learn God's *values*.

As we read the stories of the Bible, something utterly fantastic happens. *We meet God.* Although not as overtly as the way Moses met Him, meeting God in the Scriptures can be just as profound. As we read, we realize the meaning of God's words to the prophet Jeremiah:

> Let him who boasts boast about this:
> that he understands and knows me,
> that I am the LORD, who exercises kindness,
> justice and righteousness on earth,
> for in these I delight,"
> declares the LORD. (Jeremiah 9:24)

Chapter 14

Some Important Points in the History of the Hebrew People

Judges and Kings

Years later, Moses passed away, and the Hebrew people entered the Promised Land. The battle for the hearts of mankind now had a centralized theater: the land known as Israel. Over the centuries that followed, the children of Israel experienced God in a multitude of different ways. The events considered important during this time are found in the group of biblical books following the writings of Moses. In the Christian Bible, they stretch from the book of Joshua through the story of Esther (there is a different arrangement in the Hebrew Tanakh). Unfortunately, time only permits us to highlight a small group of facts from this history. In particular, we need to look at how the Hebrew people developed a government.

At first, the Hebrew government was sparse; the people were led by individuals known as *judges*. A judge does what the name implies: they decide issues. This was started by Moses. At first, when there was a dispute, people came to Moses, requesting he arbitrate. Growing numbers of requesters made this impractical at some point, so Moses accepted a suggestion: divide the people into groups and levels. Each level had a reliable person who was the appointed arbitrator. If something was too hard for them, litigants went up to the next level. After this, only the hardest problems came to Moses. (Exod. 18) This system continued after the people crossed into the Promised Land.

Judges didn't tax, they didn't draft citizens for armies, and they didn't build palaces. They allowed for a lean and economical government.

Three things are needed for this enviable system to work. The first is a sense of safety. When people don't feel threatened by neighboring nations, no standing army is required. Second is a populace who are committed to following law. When people are orderly, they don't need police or a complicated legal structure. This is one of the reasons why it's so important to stress the heart as the first arbiter of morality for any people. The third is trust in the individuals who act as judges. When a crime is committed, or a disagreement is large enough to need arbitration, people need to feel their judges will be wise and fair. Judges who accept bribes or who show any partiality break the whole system.

For generations, the Israelite judges spoke consistently: "Follow the one true God, and he will provide for you and protect you." With protection and provision taken care of, any remaining problems would be relegated to occasional disputes over property boundaries and clarifications of legal matters; such could be handled by the judges.

This system lasted for centuries. This isn't to say that it was followed perfectly. There were times when all or most of the people chose to follow God and honor His law. Along with this came prosperity and peace. At other times, the people fell into disobedience and worshipped other gods. During these times, the whole system broke down. The population became vulnerable to attack from neighboring nations and suffered oppression by cruel overlords.

During the time of Samuel, the last of Israel's judges, the people of Israel began to distrust this system. The world was as scary a place as ever. They had neighbors who looked threatening. The judge system appeared inadequate. The people forgot that there was a one-to-one correlation: obedience and faith led to peace and safety, while oppression followed on the heels of disobedience and idolatry.

They noticed the surrounding nations had kings, and these kings looked impressive. They could raise armies and quell disputes. So, Israel decided this was the ticket to safety and justice. It was time in their minds for Israel to follow the lead of their neighbors. They demanded Samuel appoint someone as king.

Samuel was a good and righteous judge. He recognized that the root of this request was a failure of faith. So, Samuel prayed. The Scriptures record God's response:

> But when they said, "Give us a king to lead us," this displeased Samuel; so he prayed to the LORD. And the LORD told him: "Listen to all that the people are saying to you; it is not you they have rejected, but they have rejected me as their king. As they have done from the day I brought them up out of Egypt until this day, forsaking me and serving other gods, so they are doing to you. Now listen to them; but warn

them solemnly and let them know what the king who will reign over them will do." (I Samuel 8:6–9)

Samuel did as God directed and gave the Israelites the following warning (vs. 10–18): They could have the king they demanded, but he would be costly and oppressive. In the end, they would regret their request; but once a dynasty was established, there was no taking it away. They responded as follows:

But the people refused to listen to Samuel. "No!" they said. "We want a king over us. Then we will be like all the other nations, with a king to lead us and to go out before us and fight our battles." (vs. 19–20)

Previously, God offered provision and protection to Israel. He offered to serve as their king, but they didn't believe in him. In the past, they might have chosen to directly worship the other gods of surrounding lands, but this always resulted in tragedy. Israel was getting cleverer by this time, so they chose something different: a king. This is an important concept: Israel thought a king would give them what the gods of the surrounding nations provided. At the same time, this would give the appearance of faith, because they asked God's representative Samuel to help them. This was an important development: *the concept of idolatry was becoming more complex.* In this case, the king became a kind of god. He would supply what the people thought was lacking in the true God, and, as such, this new god was intended to replace the real one.

Israel discovered that their cleverness in no way provided an escape from the clear message God had been giving for generations. Only God can ultimately provide for and protect His followers. To make a long story short, for the centuries following, kings ruled the Hebrew people. The results were mixed. The first king, Saul, started well but fell away from God at the end of his life. The second king, David, was a good king—so good he became the model for any king. His son, Solomon, was the wisest Hebrew king. Sadly, his wisdom didn't prevent him from falling into the grip of foreign gods late in life.

Under the reigns of David and Solomon, the children of Israel grew from a band of wandering nomads to one of the most powerful kingdoms in the ancient Middle East. Unfortunately, whereas Solomon was the wisest of kings, his son Rehoboam was an idiot. He ruled so poorly that within a short time, the northern Hebrew territories revolted and formed their own kingdom.

From that point, the Hebrews were divided into the northern kingdom of Israel and the southern kingdom of Judah.

The Cycles of Israel

From there, a tragic series of cycles began, which I mentioned in the opening pages of this book. When a king chose faithfulness to the true God, the nation under him experienced the blessings of safety and provision. When a king chose to disobey and worship other gods, failure, oppression, and bondage followed. There was faith one generation and spiritual rebellion the next, then faith, and then rebellion. The cycle took place repeatedly, only with widening distance between peaks and valleys in its gyrations.

The presence of a king, in no way, removed the responsibility of individuals and the nation as a group to follow God. In fact, the king often made things harder when his subjects chose to be faithful and the king did otherwise.

Here's where we meet the phrase that inspired this book's title. Prior to the reign of Solomon, the third king of Israel, the nation didn't have a central temple. So, oftentimes people worshipped on the "high places", including hilltops in the surrounding countryside. Sometimes they worshipped God; sometimes they worshipped other gods. After the first great temple was built by Solomon, worshippers of the true God went there. Worship at the high places often involved other gods, since worshippers of the true God had a better place to go. When a bad king arose, he tragically led the way in false worship. The "high places" became prominent when kings and their people chose rebellion. By the time of Jeroboam, the fourth king of Judah, we read the following:

> Judah did evil in the eyes of the LORD. By the sins they
> committed they stirred up his jealous anger more than their
> fathers had done. They also set up for themselves high places,
> sacred stones and Asherah poles on every high hill and under
> every spreading tree. (I Kings 14:22–23)

What was God's response? He allowed a devastating attack from a neighboring country that penetrated to the king's palace itself:

> In the fifth year of King Rehoboam, Shishak king of Egypt
> attacked Jerusalem. He carried off the treasures of the temple
> of the LORD and the treasures of the royal palace. He took

everything, including all the gold shields Solomon had made. So King Rehoboam made bronze shields to replace them and assigned these to the commanders of the guard on duty at the entrance to the royal palace. Whenever the king went to the LORD's temple, the guards bore the shields, and afterward they returned them to the guardroom. (I Kings 14:25–28)

To readers of these royal histories, the records seem depressing and curious. The writers make it obvious: bad things follow departure from God. For some reason, this wasn't apparent to the actors in the drama. We get a hint here that Rehoboam repented on some level and spent the rest of his life worshipping in the right place. The same wasn't true for his son, Abijah, who we're told "committed all the sins his father had done before him" (I Kings 15:3). It wasn't until Rehoboam's grandson, Asa, that things improved:

Asa did what was right in the eyes of the LORD, as his father David had done. He expelled the male shrine prostitutes from the land and got rid of all the idols his fathers had made. He even deposed his grandmother Maacah from her position as queen mother, because she had made a repulsive Asherah pole. Asa cut the pole down and burned it in the Kidron Valley. Although *he did not remove the high places*, Asa's heart was fully committed to the LORD all his life. (I Kings 15:11–14; emphasis added)

For some reason that we're not told, Asa chose the right thing; and he did it in a big way, expelling prostitutes not just from the temple but from the land. He even found courage for the socially dangerous move of deposing the queen mother. Asa was "fully committed to the LORD all his life"; yet, we run into this curious institution I've been noting. He didn't remove "the high places". He was almost a shining example of a good king but was unable (or unwilling) to perform the final act of purification. Why? We speculated on this when we started out, but let's try to go deeper.

The Problems of Taking on the Idols

We can state the problem simply. Eliminating all the high places would be hard. First, there were lots of them. We're told high places could be found "on every high hill and under every spreading tree". The numbers alone made this a daunting task. How many soldiers would be required? How long would it take just to visit every hill in the nation, much less attack? The soldiers would need food and provisions, making the expense enormous.

The expense might increase even more, depending on the devotion shown to individual deities. Some would go down easily; others might have followers willing to die for their god. What would it be like to get the casualty reports? Scores of the troops could perish at the hands of frenzied "true believers"; or, maybe an emotional appeal would suffice to stop reform. Tears and pleading might wear down anyone opposed to the nearby pagan temple.

Next, the problem can be complex. Note the first action of the good king was to remove idols from the temple of God itself. Often, idolaters aren't content to merely create a new god and keep it at home. They want others to follow. The principle of popularity is important, you know. You can't always do this with an unfamiliar god. Sometimes, you must make your god resemble familiar, popular gods. Perhaps you can borrow words used when worshippers of the true God approach Him. Using these and similar words in worship make your new creations more acceptable.

When there's enough power behind your god, the next step is to take over existing structures. It wasn't unusual during low times to see statues of other gods finding their way into the Jerusalem Temple itself; this results in a confused populace. Add further that some gods "aren't all that bad". "Our god doesn't call for child sacrifice," some might plead. "We just have a lovely temple prostitute. Where's she going to find employment? How is she going to support her family if we send here away?" The whole reform movement can be made to look mean-spirited. Who wants to look mean?

Because of the number, expense, and complexity of removing all the idols, you'd need a special leader. You'd need a man of great understanding. He would need to comprehend the threat the idols represented. He would need to understand that perseverance was worth the trouble. After the initial sweep, it would be tempting to look out from the palace veranda and think, "This looks pretty good. Maybe the rest of the problems will take care of themselves somehow." The fighting could end right there. The expense could be kept in check, allowing funding for "more important matters". No—the king would need to be a man of vision, willing to look beyond the palace gardens.

If he understood the threat, he'd need to possess courage. It wouldn't suffice to be convinced of the threat personally. There would be many in the palace uncertain that the cleanup was worth the effort. Fighting internal politics can be as difficult as fighting on the battlefield. Worse, local politics can become deadly. Maybe there'd be an assassin from the old school floating around? Having to check around every corner and wondering about every shadow can wear down otherwise brave souls.

As such, courage and understanding would have to combine into leadership. Ultimately, the leader and his people would have to ask an important question: Is the goal merely to knock down statues, or is the goal to make people "behave"? Students of the Scriptures know God isn't interested in a society of people who merely follow His laws on the surface, while quietly harboring a longing to follow other gods in their hearts. A godly leader would need a deep belief in the value of personal commitment to God, while striving constantly to win over the hearts of his subjects. He would need to reach everyone, from the powerful in his court to the lowest of workers in the field. Could any human do this all by himself?

This is why theologians, when discussing the history of God's working through the ages, speak of something called *revival*. Revival occurs when God's Spirit moves in people's hearts, leading them to seek Him. A godly king isn't enough; there must be revival among the populace for any changes to last.

Finally, what if all this had something to do with God's initial warning? What if the government of the Promised Land wasn't intended to be a monarchy? Maybe faith in the lives of a populace isn't best achieved through governmental structures. Perhaps it's God's desire to have another type of kingdom.

What would such a kingdom look like?

Chapter 15

The Kingdom of Heaven: Part I

The King of the Kingdom

We now fast-forward centuries. The cycles of rebellion have gone on for so long and have resulted in such depths of darkness, God allows the Hebrew people to be invaded and deported to the lands of their conquerors. The residents of the southern kingdom of Judah were led away as captives to the land of Babylon. There, they were forced to live as second-class citizens surrounded by idolatry. After seventy years of experiencing a land officially given to the other gods, the old generation was more than ready to repent and lead a new generation back to rebuild their homeland.

For a short time, the Hebrews lived in freedom, though their country possessed only memories of the power and respect of former days. Sadly, it didn't take long for the people to forget their God again. So, they were overrun by surrounding nations; first it was the Greeks. Israel broke away after some years of subjugation, but fell again in 63 BC to the onslaught of Rome. The time is still dated with the letters *BC*; that's because an individual will be born in the Hebrew nation whose life will be so influential that His birth marks the turning point in Western dating systems to this day. That individual's name was Jesus. He's known to the Jews as Jesus, son of Joseph. To the Muslims, he is Isa the great prophet. To Christians, he is Jesus Christ.

I mentioned previously the Scriptures written by Moses are agreed upon by three of the major world religions: Judaism, Christianity, and Islam. Up to this point, anyone from any of those groups could read this book, and although they might not agree on all points, they would at least have to acknowledge the ideas they saw were supported on some level by Scriptures recognized by their respective faiths.

In this chapter, I'll explain the perspective of the Christian faith. Let's start by looking at the requirements someone must have if he/she claims to speak for God. As we stated, there must be prophecy associated with this individual. For generations, the Hebrew people have looked forward to the coming of one called the *Messiah* or "Anointed One". There are a number of prophecies about this individual, which Christians believe were fulfilled in the life of Jesus. Following are a few.

Requirements for the King

On his deathbed, Jacob, the grandson of Abraham, prophesied about his children. Here's what he said about his son, Judah:

> The scepter will not depart from Judah,
> nor the ruler's staff from between his feet,
> until he comes to whom it belongs
> and the obedience of the nations is his. (Genesis 49:10)

Jacob prophesied that one day, all nations on earth would become obedient to a descendant of Judah. In the New Testament of the Christian Bible, four books are dedicated to the life of Jesus. Two of them, Matthew (chapter 1) and Luke (chapter 3), have genealogies tracing Jesus' lineage to Judah.
The prophet Isaiah further refines this lineage to King David:

> There will be no end to the increase of His government or
> of peace, on the throne of David and over his kingdom, to
> establish it and to uphold it with justice and righteousness
> from then on and forevermore. (Isaiah 9:7)

The genealogies mentioned in the gospels also include this Davidic link. It's important to note here that we've already eliminated lots of possibilities. The Messiah can only be someone directly descended from the Hebrew king, David. Later, the prophet Micah predicted the Messiah would be born in the city of Bethlehem:

> But as for you, Bethlehem Ephrata, too little to be among
> the clans of Judah, from you One will go forth for Me to be
> ruler in Israel. His goings forth are from long ago, from the
> days of eternity. (Micah 5:2)

This is where Jesus was born. It's particularly interesting because the parents of Jesus, Mary and Joseph, didn't call that place home at the time. They were forced to travel there during Mary's pregnancy because the Roman emperor of the day decreed that a census be taken in all the regions ruled by Rome. To make sure the count was accurate, everyone had to go to his/her ancestral place of origin. For Joseph, that was Bethlehem.

Once born, the Messiah would have miraculous work to do. Healing stands out among the many things mentioned: "And on that day the deaf shall hear words of a book, and out of their gloom and darkness the eyes of the blind shall see" (Isa. 29:18).

This may be one thing Jesus is best known for. As we mentioned, any prophet must be able to predict when something miraculous will happen. For Jesus, this happened countless times when He announced He could heal people stricken with disease. Their healing immediately followed.

The list goes on; and it goes places most people wouldn't make up. In particular, the prophecies state that the life of the Messiah wouldn't be the proverbial bed of roses:

> Who has believed our message
> and to whom has the arm of the LORD been revealed?
> He grew up before him like a tender shoot,
> and like a root out of dry ground.
> He had no beauty or majesty to attract us to him,
> nothing in his appearance that we should desire him.
> He was despised and rejected by men,
> a man of sorrows, and familiar with suffering.
> Like one from whom men hide their faces
> he was despised, and we esteemed him not. (Isa. 53:1–3)

The Messiah wouldn't be a movie star. He wouldn't be an impressive-looking man who caused women to swoon. In fact, He would be downright unpopular in many circles. He would know and understand suffering. It wasn't unusual for Jesus to be loved one minute and despised the next. He was eventually condemned to be executed based on false charges and nailed to a cross. One prophecy is particularly stunning here. The Psalmist David wrote of someone experiencing intense suffering:

> I am poured out like water,
> and all my bones are out of joint.
> My heart has turned to wax;
> it has melted away within me.
> My strength is dried up like a potsherd,
> and my tongue sticks to the roof of my mouth;

you lay me in the dust of death.
Dogs have surrounded me;
a band of evil men has encircled me,
they have pierced my hands and my feet.
I can count all my bones;
people stare and gloat over me.
They divide my garments among them
and cast lots for my clothing. (Psalm 22:14–18)

The sentences above describe what crucifixion would be like. The act of hanging for hours would pull bones out of joint. Between bleeding and exposure to the hot sun, blood in the body would thicken, causing strain on the heart. Dehydration would cause the mouth to become like dry cotton. Jesus was certainly surrounded by evil men on the day of His death. Perhaps strangest of all, the writers who recorded the death of Christ noted that He owned one good outfit that was taken from Him before execution. The Roman soldiers who attended the crucifixion cast lots to see who would own it after the prisoner's death (Matt. 27:35).

Here's the most important part: These prophecies were written centuries before the life of Jesus.

The Work of the King

Why all this suffering? The prophecies continue:

Surely he took up our infirmities
and carried our sorrows,
yet we considered him stricken by God,
smitten by him, and afflicted.
But he was pierced for our transgressions,
he was crushed for our iniquities;
the punishment that brought us peace was upon him,
and by his wounds we are healed.
We all, like sheep, have gone astray,
each of us has turned to his own way;
and the LORD has laid on him
the iniquity of us all. (Isa. 53:4–6)

We now return to the problem of sin. We discussed it at length earlier. Now our discussion calls for some expansion. Without expanding, we'd consider sin a serious problem, knowing only what we've already learned; but sin causes yet one more serious problem for humanity: "Your iniquities have separated you from your God" (Isa. 59:2).

Isaiah describes humans as *separated* from God. Previously, we've talked about the effects this has on our earthly existence. Now, we consider the *eternal* consequences of sin. It's one thing to live on earth separated from God. However, if we live our whole lives separated from God, what happens when we die? The answer to this question is one of the most frightening things taught in the Scriptures. If we live our lives separated from God, we enter eternity in the same state. Only now, *the separation lasts forever.*

In the Hebrew Scriptures, we see numerous statements concerning this. In one prophecy about the last days of humanity, the prophet Daniel describes the scene:

> There will be a time of distress such as has not happened from the beginning of nations until then. But at that time your people—everyone whose name is found written in the book—will be delivered. Multitudes who sleep in the dust of the earth will awake: some to everlasting life, others to shame and everlasting contempt. Those who are wise will shine like the brightness of the heavens, and those who lead many to righteousness, like the stars for ever and ever. (Daniel 12:1–3)

Daniel portrays incredible events; first, there will be a "time of distress" unlike any seen by humans. The cumulative effects of all humanity's sins will cause massive eruptions of evil and violence. After this, there will be a second event: the dead will awaken. This is called *Resurrection*. To those who follow these Scriptures, death isn't permanent. There's more to our existence than our physical parts, which are temporary. There are elements of our being that remain after our earthly bodies suffer destruction. Those parts have been assigned words like "soul" and "spirit". After death, these elements continue in a state resembling sleep. Then, an event occurs which is completely supernatural and fantastic. The eternal elements of our being are reunited with the earthly elements needed to reestablish conscious existence. We live again.

If the story stopped here, we could all look forward joyously to this thing called Resurrection. However, there is one more event; this is the most important of all. The Resurrection is followed by *judgment*. Some will leave the judgment in a happy state called "life"; others will leave the judgment in "shame and everlasting contempt". Here's the point where this all becomes very sobering. Whatever the state an individual is in when he/she leaves the judgment, Daniel describes it with the words *eternal* and *everlasting*.

What are the requirements for making it through this judgment on the "life" side of things? Daniel doesn't give a detailed description. He says some have their names written in a book. The way they got into the book was by being "wise" and by being among "those who lead many to righteousness".

Jesus expanded significantly on this teaching. Remember, His life was surrounded by the kinds of miraculous events identifying Him as a true prophet. Based on this, He has the authority to proclaim God's truth concerning any issue. The apostle Matthew records Jesus on the subject:

> Woe to the world because of the things that cause people to sin! Such things must come, but woe to the man through whom they come! If your hand or your foot causes you to sin, cut it off and throw it away. It is better for you to enter life maimed or crippled than to have two hands or two feet and be thrown into eternal fire. And if your eye causes you to sin, gouge it out and throw it away. It is better for you to enter life with one eye than to have two eyes and be thrown into the fire of hell. (Matthew 18:7–9)

This amplifies Daniel's teaching; Jesus picks up on the concept of "leading many to righteousness" by discussing its opposite, leading others into sin. Those who do so and those who follow them will be thrown into a place called hell.

The word we translate as "hell" is an ancient Greek word, *Gehenna*; It's associated with a valley near Jerusalem called Hinnom. In this valley, ancient, idolatrous kings sacrificed children to Molech. Later, the good king Josiah desecrated the valley by throwing in dead bodies, which were burned there. Use of the valley as a place to dispose of the dead persisted past that time, so the image of burning and death made for a clear and dramatic illustration of Jesus' teaching on this subject. Jesus used the phrase, "fire of hell". The idea involves a sense of equity. Evil people burned children as offerings to their gods. They will suffer the same fate, along with all those being punished for their sins. The gospel writer Mark records Jesus telling the same story to another crowd. Here, Jesus goes further; hell is a place "where the fire never goes out" (Mark 9:44). The suffering of those who go there is like this: "their worm does not die, and the fire is not quenched" (vs. 48). This would appear to indicate that the suffering of those consigned to hell never stops. Some who believe in hell would say the suffering there isn't eternal. People who go there are annihilated and cease to exist. Based on what we've read in Daniel and Mark, I would think the suffering is, in fact, eternal.

This is a very frightening thought: when we die, we aren't just buried in the ground. We don't float blithely into an "over soul", or automatically enter a happier place. We face judgment. Those who pass the judgment enter eternal happiness. Those who don't go to a horrifying place called hell. Avoiding hell, Jesus teaches, is worth anything. A note: He uses hyperbole to illustrate this. There are no records indicating that any of Jesus' apostles cut off their hands or plucked out their eyes. Jesus is merely employing standard literary tools to state that there is nothing on earth worth having if it results in an eternity of punishment.

Perhaps for some readers, though, this isn't so frightening. "I'm pretty good," they think. "I'm not so bad," think others. Well, let's consider the prophet Isaiah. He was a godly man, chosen to write one of the longest books in the Bible. One day, he had a vision of heaven, which he described with these words:

> I saw the Lord seated on a throne, high and exalted, and the train of his robe filled the temple. Above him were seraphs, each with six wings: With two wings they covered their faces, with two they covered their feet, and with two they were flying. And they were calling to one another:
>
> "Holy, holy, holy is the LORD Almighty; the whole earth is full of his glory."
>
> At the sound of their voices the doorposts and thresholds shook and the temple was filled with smoke. "Woe to me!" I cried. "I am ruined! For I am a man of unclean lips, and I live among a people of unclean lips, and my eyes have seen the King, the LORD Almighty." (Isaiah 6:1–5)

Isaiah was a righteous and good man; but when he stood before God, something about his self-perception changed. He could only proclaim, "Woe to me!" He said the angels cried out, "Holy, Holy, Holy." Holiness refers to a complete lack of evil or moral stain. More than that, it describes a quality similar to health. When someone is healthy, it means not only they lack signs of illness, but they also radiate life. In the same way, God's holiness means He is not only free from evil, but He shines with goodness. When compared to normal people, Isaiah appeared righteous. When compared to God, though, he appeared something much less.

What was God's answer to Isaiah's concern?

> Then one of the seraphs flew to me with a live coal in his hand, which he had taken with tongs from the altar. With it he touched my mouth and said, "See, this has touched your lips; your guilt is taken away and your sin atoned for." (vs. 6–7)

Even though Isaiah was a better man than most people, he needed to have "guilt taken away" and "sin atoned for". The word *atone* refers to appeasement of God's righteous anger and judgment toward sin. Isaiah was unable to do this himself; he needed a supernatural act of God.

Here's the hardest part for most people. First, everyone is stained with sin. We quoted Isaiah a few paragraphs back saying, "We all, like sheep, have gone astray, each of us has turned to his own way." Notice, Isaiah included *himself* here by using "we". He then includes everyone (we all). This places everyone in danger of judgment, because everyone is stained with sin. Second, *we cannot save ourselves from sin.* Isaiah couldn't, and neither can anyone else.

Imagine a point in space and time where we and God maintain a sort of equilibrium. We don't owe anything to God. God certainly doesn't owe anything to us. Consider, then, the things God has given to us. He made us, including our bodies. Without Him, we wouldn't exist. In a sense, we owe Him. He also made the air we breathe, the water we drink, and the food we eat. We owe Him for all that. As such, we start our lives owing God, but wait—God's generous. He gave all those things as a gift with no strings attached. So, we're back to that happy equilibrium where we don't owe God anything.

Now, let's say we commit a sin. Not a big one, mind you; just a teeny, tiny little sin. Guess what? We now owe God. We broke a law. So, we say, "I'll do something good to make up for the bad thing I just did." This makes sense at first, and a lot of people think this way. Here's the problem, though. What are you going to use to pay God back? He made your body. He made the air you breathe, the water you drink, and the food you eat. As such, you have nothing with which to pay God back. Committing one little sin makes you instantly bankrupt before God.

The average human being doesn't stop at one little sin. The theologian John Calvin is credited with saying that no one knows the one-hundredth part of the sin clinging to his/her soul. This is the problem of being self-standardizing. When we compare ourselves to no one, we look pretty good. Seeing as the world is filled with others stained with sin, we look pretty good in comparison.

However, if we could stand before the perfect and holy God as the prophet Isaiah did, we would look much dirtier than we might otherwise imagine.

Previously, when we discussed sin, one of the conclusions involved needing God's help. It's certainly true that sin causes us to need God's direction and God's help in many areas of life. Most important of all, we need God to take away our sin. There is no other way for our sin to be handled if we are to survive the great judgment. This is why the earlier quote from Isaiah includes the words, "We all, like sheep, have gone astray, each of us has turned to his own way; and *the LORD has laid on him the iniquity of us all*" (emphasis added).

This was the main work of Jesus Christ. He did many things during his visit to this world, but most important was to *take away the sins of the world* by allowing them to be *laid on Him.*

From the earliest days of humankind, God left us images of how our help would come. After Adam and Eve sinned, God took away their leafy garments. They supposed leaves were sufficient to cover their shame. God replaced those leaves with the skins of animals. In doing so, He implied that only through death could the stains of sin be covered. Centuries later, when the Hebrews lived as slaves in Egypt, God gave another image. He consummated the final plague, the death of the firstborn, with instructions that the Hebrews were to slaughter a lamb and place its blood on the doorposts of their homes. Only then would the judgment pass over them. Those families who didn't seek shelter under the sign of the blood suffered death. When the prophet John the Baptist saw Jesus, he said to his followers, "Look, the Lamb of God, who takes away the sin of the world" (John 1:29).

Space doesn't permit us to give all the details of Jesus' life. Fortunately, there are lots of good books out there—and don't forget the New Testament of the Bible. That's the best place to start. For now, here are the important details:

Unlike every other human, Jesus wasn't stained by sin. He was born miraculously to Mary, a virgin. This, along with God's power, allowed Him to live a sin-free live. Because of this, Jesus was the only human ever qualified to take the sins of others. After living a perfect life, Jesus was falsely accused of crimes and condemned to die by crucifixion. Jesus used this event to offer Himself as a sacrifice for the sins of the world. When He died, He died in the place of sinful people; it is as though you and I were nailed to the cross. Jesus took our places. God poured the judgment of all the world's sins on Jesus instead of us. Remember what we read, "the LORD has laid on him the iniquity of us all." This was all proven to be true by one of the greatest miracles of history: Jesus came back to life three days later. The empty cross was a sign to the world that all this took place with the authority of God.

Chapter 16

The Kingdom of Heaven, Part II

Who Was (Is) Jesus?

There is just one more thing that you must understand about Jesus to fully appreciate His work and His place in history. To do this, let's revisit the prophecy of Jesus given by Micah:

> But as for you, Bethlehem Ephrata, too little to be among the clans of Judah, from you One will go forth for Me to be ruler in Israel. His goings forth are from long ago, from the days of eternity. (Micah 5:2)

Someone is going to "go forth" from the little town of Bethlehem. He'll be a great ruler, but more than that, He is "from long ago". He's associated with "the days of eternity". Isaiah also wrote of Him:

> For to us a child is born, to us a son is given, and the government will be on his shoulders. And he will be called Wonderful Counselor, Mighty God, Everlasting Father, Prince of Peace. (Isaiah 9:6)

Isaiah speaks of a child who will be a great leader. In the same breath, he says the child will be called "Mighty God" and "Everlasting Father" (the last title can also be translated, "Father of Eternity"). The Hebrew prophets who predicted the coming of the one called Messiah stated He wasn't going to be a normal person like you and me. He wouldn't be like anyone else. *He would be God in human form, visiting the earth.* Christian theologians refer to this as the *incarnation*.

Earlier, when discussing the calling of Moses, we met a being referred to in the Scriptures as "the angel of the Lord". During that event, we spoke of

God creating a point of contact between Himself; an eternal being who exists outside His creation, and the temporal universe He created. This allowed Him to converse with Moses from the burning bush, a truly amazing event, but what if God desired something even more? What if He wanted not just a point of contact, but a point of *entry?*

Is it possible for God, who is infinite and separate from His creation, to actually enter into it? Even more, the creation is said to be broken by the sin of mankind. Can God, who is holy and free from evil, enter a sinful world?

There is one more question. The angel of the Lord was a manifestation of God seen on several occasions by the people of Israel. However, he came and left. The prophecies speak of God entering our universe by becoming a human child. Human children start as single egg cells in the wombs of their mothers. Could God, who is infinite and unimaginable in size, fit into the smallest of containers and then grow through the stages of childhood into a human adult?

Mary, the mother of Jesus, needed help understanding this, so she asked for it from the angel Gabriel when He announced God's plans to her. Here is his answer: "Nothing is impossible with God" (Luke 1:37).

Yes, God can do anything He wants. The Maker of the universe exercises total control over every part of it. If He wanted to turn the earth upside-down, He'd only need to speak it. The same is true with our sun, our solar system, or our galaxy. Nothing is too big. Nothing requires too much intelligence. Nothing requires too much ability. God can do anything He wants. The question isn't "Can He do it?" The question is "Why would He want to?"

Indeed, why would God want to do this? Answer: Because He's loving and generous beyond our wildest imagination. Sadly, many fail to see this. Many misunderstand. Many succumb to short-sighted interpretations of His actions. When God placed the tree in the Garden of Eden, He was offering Adam and Eve an opportunity to participate in the divine gift of choice based on godly virtues. Many look at this and say, "Well, isn't this a bit unfair? God put that tree in the Garden and watched while Adam and Eve fell into sin and shame. Later, God allowed Cain to choose how he would deal with his anger, even if it meant the life of Abel. Isn't that unfair for Abel? What kind of a god would let this happen?" All through the ages, people have made bad and, in many cases, evil choices. When they do, others suffer at the hands of the guilty. Humanity has seen wars and pestilence, slavery and oppression. Countless people have suffered horribly because of the bad choices of others. Many believe God passively watched from a distance.

Is this fair? Is this thing called *choice* worth all the pain?

To God, it is. He stubbornly continues to offer all people the opportunity to make choices, even when their choices hurt themselves and others. As I said earlier, He could sterilize the world. He could take away all the evil. However, *to have true choice, people must be able to choose badly. Otherwise, it's not choice.* Without choice, we're merely machines—robots who wander around doing things that look good but are preprogrammed into us.

So, rather than sterilize the world, rather than remove choice and all the pain it creates, God did something amazing: H*e chose to enter the world and live in it with us.* Because He did this, He experienced all the pain we feel and more. He was born a defenseless child entrusted to the care of a poor family. His father died before Jesus was an adult, so as the oldest child, Jesus knew about taking responsibility for a family. He provided for his family by working long hours as a carpenter before the days of power tools. He lived in a nation invaded by one of the harshest conquerors in history: Imperial Rome. After living a life marked only by service to God and others, he was falsely accused of terrible crimes and forced to suffer the cruelest of sentences: death by crucifixion.

Crucifixion was a torturous form of death. Pain was extended for hours and sometimes days. Hands and feet were nailed to the wood of the cross, with the pain amplified when the cross was hoisted from the ground into an upright position. Even worse, the excruciating pain was experienced publicly before a mocking crowd. Clothing, a valuable commodity in the days of Jesus, was confiscated. So, the victim likely hung naked in front of the jeering mob. The victims of crucifixion experienced every kind of pain possible, both physical and emotional.

All that pain was nothing compared to having the sins of the world poured upon Jesus. In one moment, he experienced the pain of every victim of every crime ever committed. He languished in every prison, He suffered in every labor camp, and He felt the blows of every beating. In one moment, He bore the responsibility of every brutal jailer, every sadistic tormentor, and every oppressor. The apostle Paul wrote, "God made him who had no sin to be sin" (II Cor. 5:21).

Have you ever seen something or heard of something that made you really angry? A bully beating someone much smaller? A thief stealing from an elderly person on the street? A war criminal taking the lives of thousands of people just to satisfy some bizarre sense of cruelty? Think of the angriest moment you've ever had. Then think of that anger multiplied by as many people as have ever lived on earth and as many people as ever will. This much anger and far more is what God, the righteous judge, felt in His heart when

He beheld the sin of the world. The flames of the sun don't equal the burning of God's righteous anger at so much sin.

God poured all of this anger out on Jesus Christ as He hung on the cross. Because of this, God can say that He understands our pain. He experienced every pain that a human being can feel and far more.

Imagine this: Go back to the time when God was thinking about the creation of the universe. What to put in it? Stars? Yes. Planets? Yes. A place called Earth? Yes. Plants and animals? Sure. How about some human beings? Yes, human *beings* who would not be just animals that wander around eating and existing, but beings who think and ponder. They would be beings who possess some of the qualities God Himself possesses, culminating in the ability to make true choices based on virtue and not mechanistic drives.

Then the thought comes: If these humans are to be given true choice, they will one day choose to disobey. Then what? In the infinite mind of God, He saw all the possibilities. He saw every choice, good and bad, that would ever be made. He foresaw all the evil, and He foresaw the wrath He would feel. Then what? He could wipe away choice and plan something else, something easier, but no. Instead, He decided to enter the world and walk through it with the humans He planned to create; *and He decided He would bear all the penalties for all their sins.*

He saw all this before He created the first molecules of the cosmos.

What could possibly make God want to do such a thing? The answer is *love*. He loved His creation even before He created it. He wanted to give humans not just existence, but something of the life He Himself experiences. He wanted them to have some of His heart. He wanted to walk with us, laugh with us, and watch with joy as we learn, grow, and become more like Him in character and heart each day.

Because God entered the body of a human being and experienced all this, He can truly understand our pain. There is no person who can say they suffered more than Jesus Christ. Because Jesus paid the penalty for our sins, we can be reunited with God and remain united with Him for all eternity.

In order for all of this to work, we must do something. Based on everything you've read about God in this book, do you want to guess what that is?

God wants us to make a choice. We must choose to accept His gift. Millennia ago, our parents Adam and Eve made a choice to turn away from God. They wanted to be their own god and live a life without obedience to their Creator. The result was all the pain and evil we've experienced in the world ever since. In the years that followed, humanity has turned to all kinds of sin and idolatry in an ongoing attempt to dethrone the legitimate king of the universe. Again, look at Isaiah's words: "We all, like sheep, have gone astray, each of us has turned to his own way." We have turned the wrong way; *God wants us to choose to turn back.*

Jesus and His followers used a word to describe this action: Repent. The verb *repent* comes from a Greek word that means "to have a change of mind". Before hearing any of this, we all thought our lives were pretty good. When we "turned to our own way", our way seemed fine. Our values seemed legitimate. Then, we hear of a God who revealed Himself to Moses and others in the book called the Bible, and we start to read. As we meet Him in the pages of this book, we, like Isaiah, begin to realize that next to Him, we are far lower than we thought. Then, we change our minds about our ways. We realize we need to seek God's values instead of our own. We need to do things His way, not ours.

This brings us to the foundation. Some hear this and don't feel they need to respond. That's because they don't *believe* what they're hearing; others do. The question of whether you believe or don't is crucial because this is what the Scriptures identify as the first step:

> For God so loved the world that he gave his one and only Son, that whoever *believes* in him shall not perish but have eternal life. For God did not send his Son into the world to condemn the world, but to save the world through him. Whoever *believes* in him is not condemned, but whoever does not *believe* stands condemned already because he has not *believed* in the name of God's one and only Son. This is the verdict: Light has come into the world, but men loved darkness instead of light because their deeds were evil. Everyone who does evil hates the light, and will not come into the light for fear that his deeds will be exposed. But whoever lives by the truth comes into the light, so that it may be seen plainly that what he has done has been done through God. (John 3:16–21, emphasis added)

A few years later, Paul stated it more succinctly: "*Believe* in the Lord Jesus, and you will be saved" (Acts 16:31).

The Scriptures refers to this as the "Good News". The more familiar term from old English is "Gospel". God offers to save us from the penalty of our sins as a loving gift; this is known as *salvation*.

Don't Make a Mistake

It is here that many people make crucial mistakes.

Mistake 1: They run. We're told in the passage above that many fear having their deeds exposed. That's very sad. God offers us a gift that is unimaginable. If you don't believe right away, isn't it at least worth staying around a bit so you can have a look?

> Taste and see that the LORD is good;
> blessed is the man who takes refuge in him. (Psalm 34:8)

Mistake 2: For some reason, this "believe" stuff sounds too simple to be true. Since most people have some sort of business relationship with their idols (I do something for you; you do something for me), they assume God works the same way. So, they try to purchase salvation. Salvation, under this approach, means a person must do some number of good deeds throughout their lives. At some point, the good outweighs the bad. At this point, you've got your ticket into heaven.

One of the starkest examples of this that I've seen in recent history came from one of the world's richest men, Warren Buffet. In June of 2006, he announced he was contributing 1.5 billion dollars to the Bill and Melissa Gates foundation. Included in a statement he made about his reasoning were these words: "There is more than one way to get to heaven, but this is a great way" (USATODAY.com—Warren Buffett). Now, mind you, this gift is certainly generous, and the money will accomplish a lot of good. However, it would appear Mr. Buffet is under the impression that his donation has secured a seat in glory. If this is the case (and I would certainly be happy if I'm misinterpreting his reasoning), he's going to be in for a tragic surprise when he meets God someday. I'm afraid the message to Mr. Buffet and every other member of the human race is this: No one purchases heaven—not with a billion dollars and not with a billion-billion dollars. Only the sacrifice of Jesus Christ on the cross is sufficient payment for our sins. The apostle Paul later drove this home: "For it is by grace you have been saved, through faith—and this not from yourselves, it is the gift of God—not by works" (Ephesians. 2:8–9).

When you think about it, the idea that you can pay God for salvation is totally inconsistent with everything we've learned so far. When God created Adam and Eve, He placed them in a garden paradise on a perfect planet. Did He then say, "OK, A&E, now I want you to do about a thousand years of work to pay for all of this"? No. He gave paradise to them *for free*. That's what a loving parent does; He gives good gifts to His children.

More than this, the thought that salvation can be bought totally misses the size of the gift God has given to us through Jesus Christ. Jesus died a horrible death to bring us this gift. To understand this better, imagine that you're trapped in a burning building. You're high enough that you can't jump; but wait—you're in luck. The city has a fire truck with a mechanical ladder high enough to reach your floor. Taxpayers paid a lot of money for it. A firefighter who spent a lot of time learning his skills is hoisted up to you. He's risking his life for you—at any time the building could collapse, killing you both. You watch nervously as the ladder extends to your window. Then, the fireman arrives. To be saved from certain death, all you need to do is believe the fireman wants to save you and believe the ladder can carry you both. All you must do is trust the fireman and step out of the window into his arms. Imagine, though, when the fireman gets within reach, you put your hand into your pocket and pull out a one-dollar bill. You say, "I'm sure you want me to pay. This should cover it, right?" Not only would this be stupid, it would be deeply insulting to the fireman who's risking his life to save yours.

No, you can't purchase salvation. If the richest man on earth offered his whole fortune in payment, it would be as foolish as offering the brave firefighter a dollar.

An Invitation

You've been doing a lot of reading to this point. The message is simple to summarize: you and I have "turned to our own way". Adam and Eve turned away from God. Cain turned away from God. The whole population of the earth before the flood turned away from God. What is the message to us? *Turn back to God*. Turn back to God, who was revealed in the Scriptures by Moses and the other great prophets. He wants you to make a decision. As He always does, He offers you a choice. What will you do with this opportunity?

Is there anything stopping you from making that decision right now? If you're ready, you just need to do some talking with God (also known as praying). When you talk with God, include at least the following:

- Acknowledge that you have turned away from God in your life. This is called confession.
- Ask God to forgive you, based on the work of Jesus Christ dying on the cross.

- Tell God that you want to turn back (repent). Ask for His help. He'll gladly give it.

If you do this, we are told in Scriptures: "to all who received him, to those who believed in his name, he gave the right to become children of God" (John 1:12).

If you've talked to God in the spirit we just discussed, and if you truly believed, you are now a child of God. This means that someday, you will pass the judgment and see God in heaven for all eternity.

However, you'll likely remain on earth for a while until that day. How does that work? What does it look like? We'll consider that in the next chapter.

Chapter 17

The Kingdom Explained, Part I

New People, New Values—a Kingdom of the Heart and Mind

The apostle Paul wrote a letter giving advice to his friends in Rome. In it, he said:

> Therefore, I urge you, brothers, in view of God's mercy, to offer your bodies as living sacrifices, holy and pleasing to God—this is your spiritual act of worship. Do not conform any longer to the pattern of this world, but be transformed by the renewing of your mind. Then you will be able to test and approve what God's will is—his good, pleasing and perfect will. (Romans 12:1–2)

Prior to meeting God, we think of our lives as the sum of our experiences and possessions. We have memories of places we've been; that includes our homes, our travels, and our education. We also have a collection of possessions. For some, the collection is small: a few coins in the pocket. For others the collection is huge, including multiple grand homes and massive bank accounts. However, no matter where we've been and what we have, we imagine ourselves as sitting in the center of it all. We are in control. It's as though we have a little kingdom, and we are sitting on the throne.

Paul tells us the first requirement for those wishing to be part of the kingdom of heaven is to recognize who the King is. God is the King; we are the subjects. *The first step, then, is to emotionally and mentally move off the throne of our lives and offer that throne to God.*

Once we've done this, we begin the process of being renewed. This starts as a supernatural act of God in our hearts. Jesus once told a leading teacher of His day, "I tell you the truth, no one can see the kingdom of God unless he is born again" (John 3:3). Jesus went on to explain that He was talking about a spiritual rebirth. He was very clear in saying that the business of understanding spiritual truth requires spiritual help.

This spiritual action by God is the foundation for change, but the building blocks involve our most important possession—*our minds*. This is where many make a tragic mistake. They think becoming godly means shutting down our minds and passively opening up to God. When I first learned this principle, my friends compared this to the act of leaving your coat with a coat-check person upon entering a high-class restaurant. In other words, many people think following God means "checking your brain at the door." This couldn't be further from the truth. *The Bible teaches that our brains and our conscious use of them are vital parts of our walk with God.* This is because our minds are the tools we use to choose our values. Because choice is important to God, our minds are important, too.

Most of our values come from our experiences. Things happen to us. We spend time with parents, family, friends, and a host of other people. Those people influence us. We make decisions about what's important based on all these experiences. Paul called this the "pattern of this world" (Rom. 12:2). This is normal, but because we live in a broken world, the patterns we see are often different from God's patterns and values. Sometimes our influences include people who desire to follow God, making some of our values right; but sometimes the influences are wrong. How can we tell the difference?

I've spent significant time in this book demonstrating that God reveals Himself and His values through the writings of the Bible. As we read the Bible, we meet God in its pages. As we meet Him, we learn His values. Here's the important part: because we've placed God on the throne of our lives, *we begin to let His values displace our values.* We change from being self-standardizing to God-standardizing. We measure our values and the values we see around us against God and His values. This process involves thinking, pondering, and reflecting.

It even involves asking questions. Sometimes the questions are simple. Sometimes, though, the questions are hard. Have you ever played the psychological game: "What's wrong with this picture?" Someone shows you a picture, and you select things that don't make sense. Sometimes God allows us to be placed in hard situations—they don't make sense at first. We find ourselves asking, "What's wrong with this picture?"

You'd be surprised at how many times godly people ask tough questions of God. In the Psalms, one phrase that regularly occurs is, "How long?"

> My soul is in anguish. How long, O LORD, how long?
> (Psalm 6:3)

Asking how long God is going to be before He helps someone in need doesn't appear to be a manifestation of deep faith. It implies someone is feeling left out and forgotten. Sometimes, God places His people in situations where they might feel this way. It's part of His plan, and He understands that it's hard. In these situations, God doesn't castigate people for asking honest questions. Honest questions work on the assumption that God is in control and that He cares about us, even if it doesn't seem apparent at the moment. The individual who wrote the prayer above later added, "The LORD has heard my cry for mercy; the LORD accepts my prayer" (v. 9).

On the other hand, sometimes questions are thinly veiled excuses for rebellion against God. Cain's didn't ask his famous question, "Am I my brother's keeper?" because he wanted to learn more about God. People who ask "Cain questions" tend to receive something other than satisfactory answers. People who ask good questions often receive good answers, even if the answers don't come immediately.

So, following God starts with spiritual renewal and involves our minds, as this renewal spreads in our lives.

One more note before moving on: Another sad mistake made by many is to assume the Scriptures are intended to be a "score card" for faith. Each day, people who follow this line of thinking keep a mental checklist of things they feel are in compliance with the principles of the Bible. Consider the Ten Commandments. If we don't kill anyone, we get a point. If we don't commit adultery, we get another point. Now, let's say that we lie at some point. That must cause a sort of demerit. Perhaps the two points we got by not murdering or committing adultery counterbalance the demerit we got from our "small indiscretion". This isn't the way of faith presented in the Scriptures. We are warned in the Scriptures that if anything, understanding the writings tends to remind us of how far we need to go, rather than causing pride in our accomplishments. We read the Scriptures to meet God, not to purchase His favor.

A Continuous Kingdom

Was all of this new? Was Christianity meant to be a new religion separate from the Jewish world in which Jesus was born? Jesus Himself answers, "No."

> Do not think that I have come to abolish the Law or the Prophets; I have not come to abolish them but to fulfill them. I tell you the truth, until heaven and earth disappear, not the smallest letter, not the least stroke of a pen, will by any means disappear from the Law until everything is

accomplished. Anyone who breaks one of the least of these commandments and teaches others to do the same will be called least in the kingdom of heaven, but whoever practices and teaches these commands will be called great in the kingdom of heaven. (Matthew 5:17–19)

As a young person who didn't know much about his own religious heritage, much less that of others, I believed Christianity and Judaism were separate religions. When I started reading the Bible for myself, I was surprised to discover Jesus was Jewish. Not only was Jesus Jewish, but He loved the Jewish people. He taught that He was sent to them first and foremost, before He was sent to other people groups. Everything Jesus did was based on principles given to the Jewish people over centuries, but now, something important was about to happen: the Jewish religion was ready to *blossom*. For centuries, God focused on a piece of real estate. Now, the message of the Good News would explode out to all the nations on earth. For a long time, the faith of the Jewish people was like a caterpillar locked in its cocoon. Now, it was ready to emerge, like a beautiful butterfly ready to soar over distant meadows throughout the world.

Because of this blossoming, some aspects of the faith would undergo a surface change. Prior to the time of Christ, the Jewish people were given numerous symbols to demonstrate their separation from the evil and false gods of the world. One example was their food. The Jewish people were sternly commanded to avoid foods that weren't "kosher" (clean). Now, however, they were going to be messengers teaching that the evil of people's hearts could be washed away through the work of Christ on the cross. As such, the followers of Christ could eat all the foods eaten by the nations around them. They were to have "kosher hearts" rather than "kosher stomachs". They were to go out into the world and live the life previously symbolized by kosher food. They were to live lives where their righteous deeds spoke even more loudly than the symbols that were so revered by the followers of Moses.

On the other hand, Jesus often amplified things that were written centuries before, but which had been misunderstood:

You have heard that it was said, "Eye for eye, and tooth for tooth." But I tell you, Do not resist an evil person. If someone strikes you on the right cheek, turn to him the other also. And if someone wants to sue you and take your tunic, let him have your cloak as well. If someone forces you to go one mile, go with him two miles. (Matthew 5:38–41)

Someone once asked me, "So, if you believe the Bible, does that mean you think someone should have his hand cut off for stealing a piece of bread?" My response was, "No, because the Bible doesn't teach that someone should have their hand cut off for stealing a piece of bread!" When Moses gave the Law to the Hebrew people, among its provisions was a responsibility on the part of society to punish crime. This punishment should include consideration of the pain caused to victims. At the core of the Law is respect for the value of human life and the right of all people to live their lives free from fear of their fellow man. As such, it's appropriate for properly convened courts to prosecute crime. "Eye for eye" and "tooth for tooth" are symbolic statements indicating that penalties for crime should be assigned in a manner reflecting damage done to a criminal's target. This goes for excessive punishment as well as deficient. Bodily mutilation over minor offenses is exactly the kind of thing the Law is intended to prevent.

Further, in every society, individuals are tempted to exact revenge for perceived offenses without going through courts. Such isn't the approach of godly people. Even if the legal system is unable to properly punish the guilty, individuals aren't to take revenge. In these cases, God says, "It is mine to avenge; I will repay" (Deut. 32:35). No society can live in peace when it's filled with vigilantes and lynch mobs.

This principle was followed by King David centuries before the time of Christ. Before becoming king, David led a group of soldiers who provided protection for individuals living along the borders of his country. There, the residents lived in fear of marauders and plunderers from neighboring nations. In one case, David and his followers protected a man named Nabal for an entire season. At the end of the season, David sent messengers to this man requesting payment. Nabal expressed no sense of responsibility and sent the messengers away. When David heard this, he intended to attack the man for his stingy ways. Fortunately, Nabal's wife was wiser than her husband and arranged payment for David and his men. David responded with these words: "May you be blessed for your good judgment and for keeping me from bloodshed this day and from avenging myself with my own hands" (1 Sam. 25:33). David regretted his rash thinking and saw this woman's actions as a merciful provision from God. David was protected as well as his intended victim. Later, Nabal suffered a heart attack and died, demonstrating God's judgment.

So, when Jesus teaches that His followers aren't to take revenge when offended, He's reminding everyone of eternal principles given by Moses centuries earlier. Better to be abused than to respond in kind. In the modern world, whole nations are wracked by violence, as people feud over hurts from centuries past. In some cases, no one even remembers who started the fight. What would these societies look like if everyone stopped taking revenge?

Here's another important point: I often hear people say things like "In the Old Testament, God's full of wrath and punishment. The New Testament teaches a different god; a god of love and forgiveness." To this, I can only recommend people read the Bible themselves. Look at the first chapter of Genesis. God created a world and offered it to humans, with the invitation they rule with Him. Where's the anger there? Even after Adam and Eve fell, God didn't punish them with lightning bolts. In the next generation, Cain killed his brother, yet God protected him from the vengeance that should have followed. Only after centuries of disobedience and corruption did God bring the flood. God has always shown generosity to humans. Although there are exceptions, He has most often shown mercy when people disobey, usually reserving judgment for the worst of long-term offenders. Older translations of the Bible use phrases like "long-suffering" to describe God's reaction to the world's evil. When Jesus spoke of mercy and forgiveness, He only clarified and expanded what people already knew.

A Kingdom with Things You Wouldn't Think Of

We mentioned earlier that following God involves using your mind. As important as this is, it's also important to understand there are limits to our minds. There are some things about God we'll never fully understand. For example, how did God figure out the way to become human? We'll never know. That's why some people reject the idea outright. It doesn't make sense to them. Since this idea doesn't fit into their views of God, they assume it simply can't be.

If that's hard, Christians discovered something about God that humans would never predict; this involves the complexity of God. Prior to the time of Christ, theologians concentrated on the unity of God. The Hebrew people were told, "Hear, O Israel: The LORD our God, the LORD is one" (Deut. 6:4). This was stated, among other things, to distinguish God from the pantheons of other gods existing in the mythologies of nations surrounding Israel. From this comes the idea of monotheism (one God) as opposed to polytheism (many gods).

Christians certainly believe in one true God, not a pantheon. As they studied the Hebrew Scriptures, though, they came upon some curious statements. For example, when Moses wrote of God creating human beings in the first chapter of Genesis, he didn't quote God as saying, "I'll make man in my image." Rather, God says this: "Let *us* make man in *our* image, in *our* likeness" (Gen. 1:26; emphasis mine). Some think God already made the angels, and He was including them in His discussion. There's one problem with this, however; human beings aren't made in the image of angels but in the image of God. Moses quotes God in the next verse, "So God created man in *his own image*, in the image of *God* he created him" (vs. 27).

As the early Christians studied further, they ran across interesting descriptions of God. Early in the creation story, Moses wrote, "Now the earth was formless and empty, darkness was over the surface of the deep, and the *Spirit of God* was hovering over the waters" (Gen. 1:2). Later they ran into a being we discussed earlier, "the angel of the Lord". This being wasn't like other angels; he spoke the words of God authoritatively, as though God Himself was speaking. The early followers of Christ expanded on this idea of one who speaks the words of God. The apostle John starts his biography of Jesus with these words:

> In the beginning was the Word, and the Word was with God,
> and the Word *was* God (emphasis mine). He was with God
> in the beginning. Through him all things were made; without
> him nothing was made that has been made. (John 1:1–3)

Only a few sentences later, John gives clear meaning to these words: "The Word became flesh and made his dwelling among us. We have seen his glory, the glory of the One and Only, who came from the Father, full of grace and truth" (vs. 14).

After considerable study and reflection, Christians accepted the idea of the Trinity. Prior to this, God was considered as one being. After considering the writings of Moses, and later expansions by those who walked with Christ, it became apparent God was complex but unified. Three beings were identified: Father, Son, and the Holy Spirit. They were all equal and all God; yet, they're discussed as one. This is not "one + one + one = three," but rather "one + one + one = one." The second member of the Trinity, known as the Son, "became flesh" and died for the sins of the world.

Time won't allow further discussion of this important topic. We'll highlight just a few things. First, many of our Jewish and Islamic friends would say something like this: "Moses taught that God is one. Christians made up this idea about three." In fact, Christians believe it was Moses who taught the complexity of God from the opening sentences of the Bible. Jesus and His followers helped us to understand the existing concept.

Second, Christians believe in Father, Son, and Holy Spirit as Beings who co-existed together from eternity. Some think Christians believe in "Father, Mother, and Son". This is totally inaccurate.

The reason I mention these things is that idolatry involves making up ideas about the spiritual realm. These ideas are incorporated into "other gods". When people make things up, they tend to draw from their earthly experiences. Hence, the mythologies of many ancient peoples involve ideas like one important god who got married and had little gods. Or, perhaps one of the gods liked some human females and decided to have sex with them. This resulted in everything from god-like humans to monstrous creatures. The interesting thing about the Trinity is that no one would make up something like that. Father, mother, and children makes sense from an earthly perspective. One god making other little gods makes sense, too; but Father, Son, and Holy Spirit all co-existing together from eternity past? Three beings existing in such perfect unity that they're discussed as one? No, that doesn't fit any earthly pattern.

When we meet God and learn about Him, we must be ready to learn uncomfortable things that are outside the earthly patterns surrounding us from our births. We must be ready for a kingdom full of things we wouldn't imagine—things so fantastic no one could make them up.

A Public Kingdom

Some suggest the spread of Christianity was meant to be a sort of "good infection". As believers traveled into the world, they would share the message of Jesus with others, hoping the others would believe and become followers of Jesus. For this to work, though, the message would have to be shared publicly. In our modern world, we place a lot of stress on "private faith". You can believe anything you want if you don't bother others with it. Jesus would have nothing of this:

> You are the salt of the earth. But if the salt loses its saltiness, how can it be made salty again? It is no longer good for anything, except to be thrown out and trampled by men.

> "You are the light of the world. A city on a hill cannot be hidden. Neither do people light a lamp and put it under a bowl. Instead they put it on its stand, and it gives light to everyone in the house. In the same way, let your light shine

before men, that they may see your good deeds and praise
your Father in heaven. (Matthew 5:13–15)

As we've looked through the Scriptures together, we've seen a message
repeated many times: There is one true God. He revealed Himself to Abraham
and his descendants. He spoke face to face with Moses and revealed Himself
to the children of Israel with great power. He wants us to turn away from
the other gods and turn to Him. He wants us to turn from our sin and accept
His salvation. He wants us to replace our self-standardizing values with His
values. If we don't do this, we're in terrible danger of being separated from
God for all eternity. God sent Jesus Christ into the world to offer Himself
as a sacrifice for our sins, so we could be saved. Finally, all we have to do
to enjoy eternity with God in Heaven is come back to Him, believing in the
gift of Jesus Christ.

Why would anybody who believes this want to keep it to him/herself?
When you're excited about something, you can't help but share it with
everyone around you. I've had friends over the years who've shared the
benefits of exercise, vitamins, and meditation. They've share the benefits of
quitting smoking, reading a certain author, watching a movie, or going to their
medical practitioner (be they traditional or something exotic).

We always share things that excite us with our friends. We always share
things we believe make our lives better. Of course we would share the message of the Good News of Jesus Christ.

So again, why would anybody who believes this want to keep it secret?

Chapter 18

The Kingdom Explained, Part II

Persecution—A Kingdom with Cost

Sometimes it's tempting to keep this message to ourselves because it gets us into trouble.

Remember the story of Cain and Abel? It only took four people on the earth to produce a situation where one person was willing to kill another. Why did Cain want to kill Abel? Was it because Abel was mean to Cain or because Abel hit Cain first? No. Cain killed Abel because Abel wanted to follow God and Cain didn't. This made Cain feel angry and ashamed. Cain realized he couldn't physically strike God, so he dealt with his anger and shame by striking Abel. Some people aren't interested in having their values challenged, I'm afraid.

Cain's tragic pattern has been replicated countless times over the millennia following the first humans. Sometimes it's expressed as mere inconvenience: it's the person who rolls his/her eyes when a believer behaves in ways obviously communicating a desire to follow God. Sometimes it's uglier than the murder of Abel.

When evil kings arose in Israel, the prophets of God often had to hide. Notorious among the ancient royalty was Jezebel, wife of King Ahab. She rejected God and followed the local deity Baal. Her persecutions included attempts to slaughter the prophets of God living at the time. (1 Kings 18:3-4)

Centuries later, early Christians underwent horrible persecutions under Roman rule. Some were thrown to the lions as a public spectacle. Others were impaled on stakes, coated with oil, and set on fire to provide light for garden parties.

Even today, people who declare faith in Christ face persecution. In some places, they might be arrested and sent to work camps. In other parts of the world, believers are left to fend for themselves when they're robbed and beaten by angry mobs, while government officials look the other way. In the

Western world of Europe and the Americas, the populations enjoy religious freedom. Many are unaware their freedom and relative safety aren't the norm for many. Some say this religious freedom won't last forever.

A Kingdom where Mercy Balances Judgment

When Jesus died on the cross, He wasn't alone. On the day of the execution, two others were on the docket; both were thieves. Likely, they were violent robbers and/or repeat offenders. All three men were nailed to separate crosses on the same hillside at the same time. One of the men was so bitter he hurled insults at Jesus. The other, though, realized who Jesus was and said something remarkable:

> "We are punished justly, for we are getting what our deeds deserve. But this man has done nothing wrong." Then he said, "Jesus, remember me when you come into your kingdom" (Luke 23:41–42).

How did Jesus respond to a violent criminal who waited until only moments before his own death to ask Jesus for mercy?

> Jesus answered him, "I tell you the truth, today you will be with me in paradise" (v. 43).

Jesus responded by granting salvation. An entire life of rebellion against God, culminating in violent crimes punishable by death, was forgiven because of one moment of belief and true repentance. Note, however, although faith allowed this man to see heaven, it didn't remove the earthly consequences of his crimes. He still died on his cross.

So, Jesus showed mercy and generosity to anyone who came to Him expressing belief. What did He do with people who behaved otherwise?

> As the time approached for him to be taken up to heaven, Jesus resolutely set out for Jerusalem. And he sent messengers on ahead, who went into a Samaritan village to get things ready for him; but the people there did not welcome him, because he was heading for Jerusalem. When the disciples James and John saw this, they asked, "Lord, do you want us to call fire down from heaven to destroy them?" But

> Jesus turned and rebuked them, and they went to another vil-
> lage. (Luke 9:51–56)

In the days of Jesus, Israel was divided into territories managed by the Roman Empire. Jesus spent significant time in the region of Galilee to the north, but often traveled to Judea, the southern region. Between those two territories lay Samaria. Samaria was a place where people of Jewish heritage had intermarried with people from surrounding nations. As such, the people there were considered half-breeds by people in Judea; this resulted in animosity between the people of these regions. Jews who wanted to travel to Jerusalem through Samaria were often met with hostility from the locals. Jesus, despite being a well-known teacher, was no exception as far as the residents of one village were concerned.

So, what should Jesus do? He knew who He was: God visiting the earth. He was met with hostility by an insignificant group of know-nothings. In a sense, His disciples had it right. Such people deserve harsh treatment, but this isn't how God does things. He didn't call fire from heaven for Adam and Eve. He didn't do it for Cain. Extreme judgments such as the Flood and fire from heaven are rare, and reserved for extreme cases. No. Jesus merely said, "That's too bad," and moved on to the next village. Furthermore, He rebuked those who suggested He do otherwise.

The followers of Christ who've taken the time to understand Him in the Scriptures follow His lead. *We don't kill all the people who disagree with us.* We don't beat them into submission or force them to convert with swords held to their throats. We're told something different:

> You have heard that it was said, 'Love your neighbor and
> hate your enemy.' But I tell you: Love your enemies and
> pray for those who persecute you, that you may be sons of
> your Father in heaven. He causes his sun to rise on the evil
> and the good, and sends rain on the righteous and the unrigh-
> teous. (Matthew 5:43–45)

If I'm commanded to love even my enemies, how much more should I extend God's love to people with whom I peaceably disagree? I have friends and relatives that I value highly who don't agree with a word I've written in this book. The love of Christ allows me to value them despite our differences.

Sadly, there are cultures and religions who've fallen to the temptation of eliminating all who disagree. Sadder yet, some of those who followed this practice thought they were following Christ. How could this happen?

An Imperfect Kingdom

On several occasions, Jesus described His kingdom using parables. On one occasion, He shared this mysterious story:

> Jesus told them another parable: "The kingdom of heaven is like a man who sowed good seed in his field. But while everyone was sleeping, his enemy came and sowed weeds among the wheat, and went away. When the wheat sprouted and formed heads, then the weeds also appeared. The owner's servants came to him and said, 'Sir, didn't you sow good seed in your field? Where then did the weeds come from?' 'An enemy did this,' he replied. The servants asked him, 'Do you want us to go and pull them up?' 'No,' he answered, 'because while you are pulling the weeds, you may root up the wheat with them. Let both grow together until the harvest. At that time I will tell the harvesters: First collect the weeds and tie them in bundles to be burned; then gather the wheat and bring it into my barn.'" (Matthew 13:24–30)

Theologians get into discussions (sometimes heated) about how to interpret the parables. Some think you should break them down into specific details, but others (I would say most) feel the parables were intended to give a "big-picture" view of something. In this case, the big picture is clear: The earthly kingdom of Jesus will be imperfect in some ways. In particular, people will sneak in who don't belong there. They'll create problems, but one thing is apparent: lightning bolts won't fall from heaven to obliterate them.

Why doesn't God remove them? Again, we're viewing the big picture here. God knows who they are, and He's able to remove them; but He won't. He has His reasons for that. He had reasons for making the Garden of Eden with no fences and for allowing the serpent in. God often has ideas about how things should run that don't make sense to us at first. That's because He's God, and He knows what He's doing.

Personally, I'm glad about this. You see, I have a vested interest here. If God wanted His earthly kingdom to be perfect, the first thing He would have to do is get rid of *me*. I'm very imperfect. I have a lot of problems. I sin sometimes, maybe more than I know. In a perfect kingdom, I'd be shown the door, and quickly. I might be shown something much worse. God tolerates imperfect people in His kingdom *because that's all there are.*

The business about not knowing the difference between weeds and good plants isn't for God. Obviously, He knows the difference; it's for us. We don't always know the difference. Later, Jesus gave some specific instructions for handling extreme cases, but for most people, we try encouragement rather than judgment. Skeptics of Christianity might be surprised to find there's no "Book of Witch Hunts" in the Bible. We aren't instructed to run around rooting out heretics, using techniques like torture and forced confessions. Those are for tragically misguided fanatics, not students of the Master, Jesus Christ.

All this will cause a public relations problem for people in the Kingdom. Jesus tells another parable:

> The kingdom of heaven is like a mustard seed, which a man took and planted in his field. Though it is the smallest of all your seeds, yet when it grows, it is the largest of garden plants and becomes a tree, so that the birds of the air come and perch in its branches. (Matthew 13:31–32)

What a nice picture. The kingdom starts out small and grows so big, all kinds of pretty songbirds fly in to make music. There's only one problem with this interpretation: if Jesus was talking exclusively to modern city people, it would be legitimate to think of birds like peacocks, parrots, and canaries. In ancient times, though, most societies had a much larger agricultural component than modern metropolitan audiences might imagine. To farmers, birds were annoying. They ate your seeds. They left smelly droppings all over. That included droppings all over you if you were in the wrong place at the wrong time, and there weren't any laundry machines back then. To confirm this, Jesus later told a parable where He compared the Kingdom to a farmer scattering seeds. Some seeds were eaten by birds. Jesus gave a specific interpretation of this parable to His close followers: He associated seeds with the gospel and birds with the devil (Matt. 13:1–23).

Based on this, the parable of the mustard seed seems to indicate the Kingdom will, in fact, become very large. Unfortunately, it will attract people who desire its power and resources over its holiness.

It's a funny thing; when I see a beautiful tree, I'm drawn to different parts of it. I may look first at the leaves. Next my eyes may wander to the trunk. I might continue to the limbs, which divide into graceful branches. Being a human being, though, I'm drawn to motion. So, if there's a bird flitting from branch to branch, that stands out. If I stand too long under the bird, I may regret it, even though we've since invented the laundry technology our ancestors lacked.

That's how it is with the history of the church. There have been countless, untold stories of people whose lives were changed by an encounter with Jesus Christ and who later fed the starving and sheltered the homeless. They built hospitals, orphanages, and schools of all sizes. Some were scientists, some were statesmen, and some were artists.

Then, there were those who wanted for some perverse reason to bear the title "Christian", who lacked interest in reading about the kindness and mercy of God in the Scriptures. Those people clouded the great works of the Christian church. I've often had conversations like this:

> Me: Let me tell you about Jesus.
> Skeptic: Spanish Inquisition.
> Me: Well, yes that was tragic. How about Mother Theresa? Look at all the people she's helped.
> Skeptic: Spanish Inquisition.
> Me: Well, how about great scientists like Isaac Newton who was a dedicated Christian? There are a number of others like him . . .
> Skeptic: Spanish Inquisition.
> Me: I guess you don't want to hear about the Salvation Army and all the people they've helped or William Wilberforce who led the English people to abolish slavery or anything else?
> Skeptic: Spanish Inquisition.
> (and so on)

As disheartening as these conversations are, they raise an important question. It's one thing to say God doesn't immediately destroy evil people, but why do evil people sometimes get so powerful?

A Kingdom in the World but Not of the World

One of Jesus' best-known miracles was the feeding of five thousand:

> When Jesus looked up and saw a great crowd coming toward him, he said to Philip, "Where shall we buy bread for these people to eat?" He asked this only to test him, for he already had in mind what he was going to do. Philip answered him, "Eight months' wages would not buy enough bread for each one to have a bite!" Another of his disciples, Andrew, Simon Peter's brother, spoke up, "Here is a boy

179

> with five small barley loaves and two small fish, but how far will they go among so many?" Jesus said, "Have the people sit down." There was plenty of grass in that place, and the men sat down, about five thousand of them. Jesus then took the loaves, gave thanks, and distributed to those who were seated as much as they wanted. He did the same with the fish. When they had all had enough to eat, he said to his disciples, "Gather the pieces that are left over. Let nothing be wasted." So they gathered them and filled twelve baskets with the pieces of the five barley loaves left over by those who had eaten. (John 6:5–13)

In the modern Western world, few people understand the life of those in poor agrarian cultures. Finding food wasn't always easy. Many worked an entire day to make barely enough to get by for that day. This may have been the first time many in the crowd experienced the sensation of being full. Here before them stood someone who could feed them for a lifetime. How did they react?

> After the people saw the miraculous sign that Jesus did, they began to say, "Surely this is the Prophet who is to come into the world." Jesus, knowing that they intended to come and make him king by force, withdrew again to a mountain by himself. (vs. 14–15)

This miracle caused everyone in the crowd to recognize Jesus as the Messiah. They intended to lift Jesus up on their shoulders and make Him king. Considering Jesus was prophesied to be "the one born to be King of the Jews" by wise men thirty years earlier, it would make sense for Jesus to grab a crown and accept the invitation.

That's not what He did. Jesus quietly left, leaving only an air of mystery behind Him. The exuberant crowd was left wondering why it got so quiet. Why in the world would Jesus do that?

The answer came later when He was arrested. He was interviewed by local leaders, including the Roman governor, Pontius Pilate. Pilate asked Jesus if He was a king. After some back and forth, Jesus replied, "My kingdom is not of this world" (John 18:36).

This culminated a long series of statements and actions that no doubt confused those who wanted Jesus to start an earthly kingdom. Jesus instructed His followers to pay taxes to Rome, a nation that invaded Israel. On one occasion, Jesus said, "If someone forces you to go one mile, go with him two miles" (Matt. 5:41). He was possibly referring to a practice put in place by the Romans: any Roman soldier who got tired carrying a load could command a resident of a vanquished nation to carry the load one mile. Some would protest; others would grudgingly travel the minimum required by law. Jesus told people to "go the extra mile."

This philosophy was explained more fully by the apostle Paul:

> Everyone must submit himself to the governing authorities, for there is no authority except that which God has established. The authorities that exist have been established by God. Consequently, he who rebels against the authority is rebelling against what God has instituted, and those who do so will bring judgment on themselves. For rulers hold no terror for those who do right, but for those who do wrong. Do you want to be free from fear of the one in authority? Then do what is right and he will commend you. For he is God's servant to do you good. But if you do wrong, be afraid, for he does not bear the sword for nothing. He is God's servant, an agent of wrath to bring punishment on the wrongdoer. Therefore, it is necessary to submit to the authorities, not only because of possible punishment but also because of conscience. This is also why you pay taxes, for the authorities are God's servants, who give their full time to governing. Give everyone what you owe him: If you owe taxes, pay taxes; if revenue, then revenue; if respect, then respect; if honor, then honor. (Romans 13:1–7)

If this surprises you, consider this: Paul was writing to his friends in Rome, the seat of Caesar. The Jewish people watched the Romans roll through their nation as ferocious conquerors. Furthermore, Paul spent time as a prisoner of Rome; yet, he instructed his friends to "submit . . . to the governing authorities" (v. 13). This all conforms completely with Jesus' teachings.

What does this mean for believers as they relate to government? It means we see our governments as enactments of God's will for the world. We follow the rules. We obey the laws. We pay the taxes. We drive at the posted speed limit (or at least we try; that one can be hard).

Perhaps even more important, we pray for our leaders. While giving advice to his protégé Timothy, Paul stated:

> I urge, then, first of all, that requests, prayers, intercession and thanksgiving be made for everyone—for kings and all those in authority, that we may live peaceful and quiet lives in all godliness and holiness. This is good, and pleases God our Savior, who wants all men to be saved and to come to a knowledge of the truth. (I Timothy 2:1–4)

If Paul's earlier instructions about rulers of the day seemed unusual, at the time Paul wrote this, Christians were experiencing direct persecution under Emperor Nero.

This raises an important question: Obedience might make sense when you get along with a ruler, but what if you disagree with your government? Believers have several options.

1. We can appeal to our leaders. As salt and light in our world, we seek the ear of our leaders as much as anyone else. In the modern world, this means speaking, writing, and using media any way we can. In democracies, this includes voting.

2. If the government turns against us, we can run. This was the response of Joseph and Mary when they learned King Herod decreed the slaughter of all children in their region to kill Jesus.

3. Finally, when there's no place to hide, we experience persecution. From the first days of the church onward through the modern age, believers have suffered mockery, imprisonment, seizure of possessions, torture, and death in the name of Jesus. Through all this, they continue to influence their world in whatever way they can, even if it means paying the ultimate price.

In all the above, there's one thing we don't do: *We aren't revolutionaries.* It's the job of the government to raise a police force to keep local peace and an army to defend against invaders. We shouldn't be a cause of concern for either. In some cases, believers may even choose to serve in these forces when they're properly constituted by government. When we disagree with our governments, we may gather in the park to pray, but we don't riot. We lift our voices, not our fists.

Jesus was given numerous opportunities to start a revolution, but He didn't take any. Instead, He allowed Himself to be arrested, tried, and sentenced to death. When Jesus was arrested, the apostle Peter pulled out a sword and lopped off the ear of someone in the arresting party. Rather than encourage this action, Jesus rebuked Peter. Jesus then supernaturally healed the man injured by His overzealous follower. (Luke 22:49-51, John 18:10-11)

It seems Jesus' goal wasn't to create an earthly, political kingdom. What was His goal? To create a kingdom with residents who are *in this world, yet not of it*. His will be a kingdom whose consummation will occur sometime in the future.

What should we do in the meantime?

> So when they met together, they asked him, "Lord, are you at this time going to restore the kingdom to Israel?" He said to them: "It is not for you to know the times or dates the Father has set by his own authority. But you will receive power when the Holy Spirit comes on you; and you will be my witnesses in Jerusalem, and in all Judea and Samaria, and to the ends of the earth." After he said this, he was taken up before their very eyes, and a cloud hid him from their sight. They were looking intently up into the sky as he was going, when suddenly two men dressed in white stood beside them. "Men of Galilee," they said, "why do you stand here looking into the sky? This same Jesus, who has been taken from you into heaven, will come back in the same way you have seen him go into heaven." (Acts 1:6–11)

Jesus tells us we're to be His witnesses. We're to tell people about God. We're to spread the good news of the Gospel.

Centuries ago, Jesus gave us a picture of how He'd prefer His Kingdom to come. On one occasion, Jesus entered Jerusalem riding a donkey. Here's how the scene is described:

> When they brought the colt to Jesus and threw their cloaks over it, he sat on it. Many people spread their cloaks on the road, while others spread branches they had cut in the fields. Those who went ahead and those who followed shouted, "Hosanna!"
> "Blessed is he who comes in the name of the Lord!"
> "Blessed is the coming kingdom of our father David!"
> "Hosanna in the highest!" (Mark 11:7–10)

Jesus entered Jerusalem on unexpected transportation. A great conqueror should ride into town on a beautiful stallion, or he could ride an ornate chariot, followed by his army. Instead, Jesus rode on a donkey, a beast of burden. This was a humble King, not a conqueror. The crowds who came to that great parade came because they loved Jesus. They loved Him so much; they gladly threw their cloaks on the ground in front of Him to soften His ride. If someone chose to stay home that day, it was his/her loss. None were dragged from there residences and forced to bow before the king at the point of a spear.

When Jesus left, His followers were told that one day He'd return. We're told He'll come back in physical form; His return won't be symbolic or spiritual. On that day, we'll see the Jesus a rebellious world should expect. That Jesus will be a conqueror who will drive out the evil infestations of this world. His ride will be flames of fire, and He'll bring the previously missing armies. As part of our message, we're to warn the world of that day.

Until that day, we share the message of a peaceful kingdom whose residents choose submission to the great King. We live under the rule of earthly governments, but ultimately our home is someplace else.

Chapter 19

Bridges to the Kingdom in the Modern Age

Jesus lived a long time ago. Science fiction fans might add "in a galaxy far, far away". I didn't throw that in just to be colorful—to modern people, it might seem there couldn't be anything further from their daily lives than ancient books filled with records of ancient people and ancient religions. We've been reading about people like Moses and the Hebrew kings who followed him; they all lived thousands of years ago in a little corner of the world far from readers in any of today's major population centers. Even the life of Jesus is now so far past, we've entered a third millennium after His birth.

To many, Christianity isn't ancient. Residents of the Western world are accustomed to the sight of church buildings somewhere in their communities. Some are grand cathedrals built from stone; others are new and boast modern facilities like food courts. How did a movement including names like Noah, Abraham, Moses, and Jesus, make it into the modern age? How did the great battle for the hearts of mankind, started so long ago, spill over into today?

Faithful Historians

The next time you play a trivia game, make sure you know the name of the most-printed book of all time. It's the Bible. Estimates put its numbers in the billions; that's a lot of books. In itself, this figure doesn't prove anything, but it's a testament to the number of people who find meaning in the records of the great Hebrew prophets and the Christian writers of the early church. The earliest of the Bible books are attributed to Moses, who lived over a thousand years before Christ. The last book of the Christian Bible, The Revelation of John the Apostle, was probably written late in the first century AD. The Bible is a collection of writings by different authors whose lives spanned centuries; it's all believed to be inspired by God.

Don't all religious books claim to be inspired by God? Actually, not all do. However, it's true lots of books claim to be revealed by divine beings. Why do we think the Bible is inspired?

First, its writers make that claim. Here's something Paul said to his young friend Timothy:

> But as for you, continue in what you have learned and have become convinced of, because you know those from whom you learned it, and how from infancy you have known the holy Scriptures, which are able to make you wise for salvation through faith in Christ Jesus. All Scripture is God-breathed and is useful for teaching, rebuking, correcting and training in righteousness, so that the man of God may be thoroughly equipped for every good work. (II Timothy 3:14–17)

There isn't much that's more bound to an individual than breath. Paul says the Scriptures are "breathed out" by God. More than that, they're "useful"; they're meant to be studied and employed for personal growth.

Second, it would be fair to expect a divinely inspired book to have unique qualities, making it stand out from other books. The raw numbers we mentioned a few paragraphs ago attest to the uncommon impact of the Bible.

Another standout quality of the Bible is its accuracy, when compared to other ancient texts. It's surprising to learn how few original copies we have of many ancient books. Also surprising is the fact that often the few copies we have of ancient books don't agree with each other much. The only thing more surprising than these facts is the amount of authority historians gives to such books. Currently, we have only forty-nine early copies of the writings of Aristotle. He wrote these words more than three hundred years BC, yet our earliest copies appear over a thousand years later (AD 1100). That leaves a lot of time for copying errors. Compare this with the New Testament of the Bible—we have over twenty thousand early copies, with some passages appearing as early as a few decades after the original books were written. These texts all look pretty much the same. They're not perfect, but there's a high degree of agreement. We have so many copies, and these copies agree with each other so much, we can be certain the original text was accurately preserved.

Even more amazing are the writings of the Hebrew Scriptures. Many have heard the name "Dead Sea Scrolls", but few know what they are. The Dead Sea Scrolls were a collection of parchments found in caves near the Dead Sea (hence the name). They were stored in jars in a very dry area, so the parchments were well preserved. The jars contained copies of the Hebrew Scriptures (among other things) dating more than a hundred years BC. What's most important about these documents is what occurs when they're compared with copies of the Hebrew Scriptures that appear centuries later. The amount of agreement is uncanny.

This is because the Hebrews had great respect for the writings. They were copied with the utmost care, using tedious techniques meant to ensure accuracy. Because of this, the Hebrew Scriptures have an even higher level of accuracy than the writings of the New Testament. An amazing feat!

Why is this so important?

Because the writings are the bridge to the future; let me repeat a statement I made earlier in this book:

> *Humans have no ability to completely sense ultimate reality*
> *on their own. They never did, not even in their perfect state*
> *in the Garden of Eden.*

Think about it: If humans had a natural ability to sense ultimate truth in the cosmos, wouldn't we all agree more? The reason humans disagree so much is there are billions of us, and not one can communicate with the cosmos on their own.

That's why we need the writings. It's in the words of scripture that we meet God. It's there our minds actively engage revealed truth from Him. Without scripture, we get only a vague picture of reality. We can peer into the heavens and know they must have been created by something much greater than us, but specific knowledge of God can only be obtained when we read the words that He "breathed out".

More importantly, as I've pointed out numerous times, not all roads lead to God. Jesus once warned His followers:

> Enter through the narrow gate. For wide is the gate and broad
> is the road that leads to destruction, and many enter through
> it. But small is the gate and narrow the road that leads to life,
> and only a few find it. (Matthew 7:13–14)

Sadly, it's easy to go in the wrong direction. Even more sad; there are many who are all too willing to lead you there. Jesus went on to say: "Watch out for false prophets. They come to you in sheep's clothing, but inwardly they are ferocious wolves" (vs. 15).

Early church leaders started running into these people right away. Paul once wrote to his friends:

> But even if we or an angel from heaven should preach a gospel other than the one we preached to you, let him be eternally condemned! As we have already said, so now I say again: If anybody is preaching to you a gospel other than what you accepted, let him be eternally condemned! (Galatians 1:8–9)

False prophets started popping up shortly after Christ's death, and they've continued through the history of the Church. Leaders like Paul had to confront them. One of the things early church leaders recognized was the tendency of these individuals to produce writings that competed with known, dependable sources. What to do?

To understand this dilemma, consider the following illustration: Imagine you're the child of an important historical figure. Let's make it a president of the United States. Shortly before his death, the president writes you a letter. In it, he tells you how proud of you he is. He also talks about his reasoning behind some important decisions. You would, of course, cherish this letter. (To keep things simple, let's assume you liked your father and agreed with his politics.) Later, as you come to the end of your life, you give the letter to one of your children, encouraging them to take good care of it. They also regard the letter with high esteem. In fact, they have it framed and hang it prominently in their home. Likewise, when it's time, they pass the letter on to one of their children.

Here's where a problem comes in; we're now looking at the third generation of ownership. A visitor wanders into the home and sees the framed letter. "Is this really a letter from a president?" they ask. The current holder beams and proudly asserts it is. The guest goes on, "How do you know it's real? It's old. Maybe it's a fabrication? Someone could have tricked your parents." You, the original recipient of your father's letter, know that it's real. Your children have good reason to believe it's real, because someone they trust (you) has attested to its authenticity. As the generations pass, though, the question of validity becomes more pronounced. How would you deal with that question?

In modern times, this is why we have presidential libraries. People who have documents from a president often donate them to the president's library early while there's good evidence to demonstrate the legitimacy of the document. If a document appears years later, outside of these collections, the documents can be tested for things like similarity of handwriting from authenticated documents.

Early church leaders addressed this problem through a series of councils where they carefully researched existing documents to ascertain their validity. By the third century AD, they recognized the current twenty-seven books of the Christian New Testament, along with the Hebrew Scriptures that Christians refer to as the Old Testament.

Some skeptics doubt this. They suggest the Bible is merely a document made up by people who disregarded the *real* books about the life of Jesus for scurrilous reasons. Modern books, such as *The Da Vinci Code* by author Dan Brown, follow this path. Writing such books is a good way to make a lot of money. In a short time, Dan Brown went from a nobody to a famous man with a mansion in one of the most expensive areas of New York. Unfortunately, this book faces significant challenges with facts and history. People looking for an excuse to disregard the real life of Christ can find satisfaction in works produced by Brown and others like him. More serious people can enter the words, "Da Vinci Code Hoax" into any Internet search engine and find numerous critiques. I think Paul L. Maier, professor of ancient history said it well:

> This is a very deeply flawed literary product that should not be taken seriously. In fact, were this book an automobile or appliance, the manufacturer would doubtless be forced to issue a full recall. (Hanegraaff 2004, 87)

To illustrate further, in 2008, authorities in New York arrested a man named Bernie Madoff. Madoff was a respected financier who ran a Ponzi scheme. He managed to trick some intelligent people into giving him money for an investment, whose details he kept secret. Investors were promised returns that weren't outlandish, but which were sizable and said to be very secure; but the investors had to be "players in the big league". No small-timers were allowed. Madoff milked billions of dollars out of wealthy individuals and, in some cases, charitable organizations. Otherwise intelligent and business-savvy people were tricked into losing millions of dollars.

How did Madoff accomplish this? Investigators scratched their heads. Apparently, this should have been obvious to anyone, much less experienced investors. Suffice it to say, there are people who can sell anything. These people lack the stuff called "common decency". Some of Madoff's victims were people who worked hard for a long time. They entrusted their life savings to him. As I said, other victims were charitable organizations; groups responsible for helping people with all kinds of problems.

Sadly, people like Bernie Madoff pop up often in religious circles. They have arguments, which appear convincing. They say they've got facts; however, they have no conscience. Jesus warned of them, using descriptive terms like "wolves". That's why early church leaders worked so hard to establish a set of standards to recognize scripture.

You might be convinced, or, you may not. My recommendation is to read these writings for yourself. As a Christian, I would recommend starting with one of the books known as the Gospels, or histories of Christ's life. They're found at the beginning of the New Testament: Matthew, Mark, Luke, or John. After that, you might want to jump back to the beginning and read Genesis. When you're done with those books, read the rest of the Bible. Perhaps you could read a few pages of Hebrew Scripture in the morning and a few pages of New Testament in the evening. At any rate, whatever you do, read the books for yourself. The original manuscripts of the Bible were written in ancient languages, so you'll need a modern translation. I've been using the New International Version (NIV) for this book. You might also try the New American Standard Bible (NASB), the New King James Version (NKJV), or the English Standard Version (ESV). I don't recommend starting with the original King James Version (KJV), as some of its language is old and difficult to understand. However, if it's all you have, go ahead.

Behind the Mask

At this juncture, we need to consider one of the Ten Commandments:

> You shall not make for yourself an image in the form of anything in heaven above or on the earth beneath or in the waters below. You shall not bow down to them or worship them. (Exodus 20:4–5)

This commandment warns against images. Some have asked though, "What if someone drew a picture that could make worshippers understand God better?" In other words, we understand we shouldn't make an image of a cat and bow down to it. Since Christians claim Jesus to be divine, is it appropriate to draw or paint pictures of Him? Churches all over the world are filled with such images. Most represent Jesus as a man with long hair and a beard, wearing a robe and making noble gestures. Religious educational materials are filled with pictures like this, such as Jesus holding little children and baby lambs. Could anything be wrong with this?

We can't solve the problem here, but artists who want to enhance religious experience are warned: be very careful, because we get our knowledge of God from the Scriptures. The Scriptures in their original form conspicuously lack illustrations. There are no "God-breathed" images of Jesus in the Bible (or Moses, or anyone else for that matter). Perhaps that says something.

Here's the reason for this: Such images can be limiting. Jesus was certainly viewed at times as a kind man. On at least one occasion, He encouraged children to come to Him, so He could bless them. At another time, though, He grabbed a whip and drove merchants from the Temple of Jerusalem because they inhibited worship. Jesus died on a cross, so many artists have portrayed Jesus going through this experience. As important as this event was, it's thought by many to be superseded by the Resurrection. For those people, the empty cross is more important than the occupied one.

A bigger problem is the fact that an image has a horrible weakness. *It can be easily transformed into a mask.* Masks can be worn by anyone. Sadly, there are many places in the world where Christ's image has been associated with malicious activities.

For example, the Scriptures portray Jesus as a Jew who had a deep love for the Jewish people. He is described on one occasion as weeping over the city of Jerusalem. Later, Anti-Semites used His name as an excuse to persecute Jews. Though I may strongly disagree with my Jewish friends about the person of Jesus Christ and His proper place in history, no true Christian would seek harm for the nation that gave us the Scriptures and the Savior of the world.

The Scriptures portray Moses as a man who fled Egypt after a failed attempt to free his people, using force. He returned only after being personally instructed by God to rely on divine power, not a sword. The Scriptures portray Jesus as a man who avoided taking Jerusalem by force, even though He was offered the opportunity on several occasions. In modern times, though, Moses and Jesus are portrayed by some radical groups as militants in combat gear, encouraging people to start a revolution.

The Scriptures portray Jesus as a leader who invited people to follow Him, chiding people who suggested immediate punishment for those who refused the invitation. In later centuries, leaders arose who initiated witch hunts and inquisitions in Jesus' name, seeking to force whole populations to follow with fear of imprisonment, torture, or death.

Jesus invited people to follow Him. In doing so, He presented Himself as a continuation; in fact, a fulfillment of God's revelation to humans. He used the Hebrew Scriptures for proof; yet, there are some today who speak of rescuing Christianity from those who interpret the Scriptures literally. In doing so, I'm afraid all they're doing is rescuing Christianity from *Jesus*. As a part of the fulfillment of promises made to Abraham, Jesus stands in a long line of prophets encouraging humanity to turn away from idols to the true God. Some would portray Jesus as a passive soul, who accepts every behavior under the sun in the name of love. Those who do this totally miss the clear images in scripture of a Jesus who will return as the coming King. When He returns, He'll lead the final judgment of mankind; a judgment culminating in Jesus overseeing the assignment of rebellious souls to a dark eternity in hell.

Without the Scriptures, Jesus and other great people of biblical history become whatever anyone wants. They become empty masks with the face of Jesus and the prophets painted on them, with holes where the eyes should be. Those holes allow imposters to look out upon their followers as they mislead for reasons ranging from delusional to insidious.

New Times, New Idols

Jesus warned of new kinds of idols waiting to tempt humanity. The number of entities competing for attention with the God of Scripture is alarming. In the days of Moses, people who wanted something other than God tended to find it in a statue. The exterior might look like a cat, bird, bull, or just about anything else wandering the planet; but the beings thought to be represented by the idols acted like people. In times following Jesus' life, some of this would change.

Today, there are still lots of places where people worship beings with the faces of animals. However, in the time of Christ, some gods become more refined. The Egyptian gods were replaced over time by Greek and Roman deities. These new gods all looked very human. Visitors to Roman temples saw statues of Jupiter, the master of the gods, pictured as a bearded man holding lightning bolts. Down the road, people could visit the temple of Venus, goddess of love. She enjoyed portrayals as a beautiful, shapely woman. Other visits might include Mars, god of war: a muscular, armored man. Some could go to Neptune, the broad-shouldered god of the seas. If you wanted good times, you could drop in on jovial Bacchus, god of wine and merriment. As the god who brought alcohol to the party, you can imagine Bacchus was popular. All these gods were pictured as ideal human beings.

We spent time previously explaining that idols draw followers by claiming to provide things for those who approach them the right way. It's really the *stuff* offered by false gods that make them popular. The Roman gods, though growing in sophistication, gave all the same stuff as their more primitive predecessors. They, too, provided prosperity, protection, pleasure, popularity, and power.

Jesus predicted the gods of the world would change over time. He pointed people to the stuff the gods would promise:

> No one can serve two masters. Either he will hate the one and love the other, or he will be devoted to the one and despise the other. You cannot serve both God and Money. (Matthew 6:24)

This was a new way of looking at things: *Money could be a god.* We mentioned it earlier in the book, but here's more on the topic. Money could demand service just as any of the more animate gods. How could money be a god? Here's how: money provides the things the images promise. Money can buy a home with walls. It can buy weapons and maybe some hands to yield them. As such, it provides protection; and let's not forget the myriad of ways money can be used to provide pleasure and popularity. If you live for money, it becomes your god. This is why Jesus warned:

> Do not store up for yourselves treasures on earth, where moth and rust destroy, and where thieves break in and steal. But store up for yourselves treasures in heaven, where moth and rust do not destroy, and where thieves do not break in and steal. For where your treasure is, there your heart will be also. (vs. 19–21)

Unlike the treasures we seek that fade over time, Jesus points us to something longer lasting. Here, He asks the key question: where is your heart? That's because your heart shows what's valuable to you. This is significant because the next question someone will ask is, "But isn't money important? Don't you need money to pay the rent and buy food, and so on?" The answer is yes; of course, you need money to get by; but Jesus warns us we must ultimately watch our motives.

How do we know our motives? Jesus continues:

> Therefore I tell you, do not worry about your life, what you will eat or drink; or about your body, what you will wear. Is not life more important than food, and the body more important than clothes? Look at the birds of the air; they do

not sow or reap or store away in barns, and yet your heavenly Father feeds them. Are you not much more valuable than they? Who of you by worrying can add a single hour to his life? And why do you worry about clothes? See how the lilies of the field grow. They do not labor or spin. Yet I tell you that not even Solomon in all his splendor was dressed like one of these. If that is how God clothes the grass of the field, which is here today and tomorrow is thrown into the fire, will he not much more clothe you, O you of little faith? So do not worry, saying, 'What shall we eat?' or 'What shall we drink?' or 'What shall we wear?' For the pagans run after all these things, and your heavenly Father knows that you need them. But seek first his kingdom and his righteousness, and all these things will be given to you as well. (vs. 25–33)

According to Jesus, our motives are identified by feelings and actions. *When we want something, how do we go about getting it? If we don't get it, how do we feel?*

Worry is one big indicator. Looking at the number of self-help books available today on worry, you'd be tempted to think modern people invented this bothersome emotion. However, worry has been around for a long time.

Economics were different in Jesus' day. Most people were happy if they had enough food to eat and a set of clothes. If that meager amount was in danger, they worried. So, Jesus started there. Imagine you're sitting on a hillside in ancient Israel. Jesus directed His audience to the birds that flew overhead, and which hopped around close by while He spoke. Birds made a great illustration of this principle. There never seemed to be any shortage of them. One source puts the total number of birds in the world somewhere between two hundred and four hundred billion. (Drum 2017) I can't help but picture a man lying on a chaise lounge with a pair of binoculars counting the little critters, but I'm sure the researchers employed much more sophisticated methods. No matter how you count them, that's a lot of birds. Who feeds them? Jesus told His audience, "God does."

There's something profound here. Theologians like to debate the relationship between God's provision and our energies. We won't solve that one here, but Jesus gives us a strong hint. The birds don't sit around waiting for a magic hand to drop food in their mouths. They expend constant energy searching for food. Somehow, there's enough food for billions of them if they're willing to look for it.

How about clothing? Jesus says God clothes the grass of the field with flowers. It's a beautiful and poetic image. Jesus tells us we're more important than birds or grass—if God takes care of them, He's certainly willing and able to provide for us.

Who worries? People labeled by Jesus as "pagans". The modern English word here sounds a little mean, but it's an appropriate translation of the original language. Jesus doesn't mention Rome, but it was the dominant power in the world then. Jesus may have been referencing those who knelt before Jupiter and all the Roman pantheon. Sometimes, these people ran to their false gods when they wanted things. Relying on false gods only leads to worry.

The problem is, the gods were imperfect. Take Vulcan, the blacksmith god. He lived deep in the earth and fired up things down there. If he made a mistake and added too much fuel to the furnace, a volcano could erupt. How about Jupiter? As we mentioned, he was often pictured with lightning bolts in his hand. Get him mad (and who really knows why he gets mad?), and you get a thunderstorm. The worst of it came when the gods got mad at each other. The conflicts they created resulted in all kinds of havoc being poured out on the earth. Storms, volcanoes, floods, pestilence, and earthquakes could fly from the gods at any moment. How could you even schedule a picnic with gods like these? Any reasonable person would worry.

Jesus says the true God isn't like this. He lovingly cares for and protects His children.

The skeptics are getting antsy. "Do you really expect us to believe in this day and age that God is going to feed and clothe people?" The answer: Yes. There's a saying attributed to G.K Chesterton: "Christianity has not been tried and found wanting; it has been found difficult and not tried." Jesus told people who put God first in their lives not to worry. God knows what you need. This is the God whose constant message to His people is that He cares for them. He's able and willing to provide. He's committed to keeping our little planet spinning at just the right place in the solar system, so there's plenty of sunshine for millions of acres of grass and flowers. Billions of birds can live off the seeds and insects growing in those plants. They've done so since God created the planet.

So again, the question: "But don't people need food, clothing, and money to live?" Again, the answer: Sure. The bigger question is, what do you do when you don't get what you think you need? Jesus tells us we should "seek first His kingdom and His righteousness." In saying this, Jesus gives us a pattern.

The Pattern of Choice

You want something. Maybe you want it badly. Perhaps you believe you need it to survive. The problem is that you're not getting it, at least not when you expect it or in the way you expect it. That's where the moment arrives. You have a choice. You can choose to believe God is able and willing to provide what you need. As a result, you choose to act in ways someone would act if they're seeking God's Kingdom first and foremost. You choose to avoid activities and attitudes that displease God. You can partake of the divine plan offered to Adam and Eve in the Garden of Eden. You can make choices based on godly virtues like humility, wisdom, faith, and love. Doing so may or may not give you what you want. If you get it, you receive it with thanks. If you don't get it, you choose to rest in the knowledge that God is all-knowing, all-powerful, and infinitely loving. Either way, if you make the right choice the right way, you enjoy the blessing of becoming more like God in the way God intends for you.

Alternately, you can choose something else. You can choose to worry and maybe become angry. You can choose to entertain doubt in God's word, God's power, and God's character. At some point, you can choose to disobey. You might even run after other gods, hoping they'll give you what you want. Those gods can have a religion attached to them, or they can be something more abstract.

This is the core challenge for everyone.

I just stated the principle in general. To get more specific, we'll need to identify the gods of the modern age. Who are they? What are they? Where did they come from? What do their followers look like? When we meet them, will we be able to identify the behaviors and attitudes of their followers, so we can turn away? We'll discuss all this in the next chapter.

Chapter 20

Some Modern "Gods" and How They Came to Power

Lots of "Gods"

How do you start a chapter about gods of the modern age? It's difficult, because the Western world prides itself in its lack of deities. Visitors to places like New York City see towers of steel, glass, and concrete. Many are so high; it's hard to see sunlight. Occasionally, in between the shining towers, you find an old church or synagogue. Years ago, these were the tallest buildings in sight. Today, they're dwarfed by their architectural, younger brethren. It's hard to find gods in the "concrete jungle".

Perhaps you can find them more quickly on the Internet? I called up a popular search engine and typed the word *god*. I was greeted with sixty-three million hits. Before continuing, I was reminded by my search engine that I live in the modern age: it informed me I might have typed "gods *and goddesses*". I can take a hint. After giving an apology to the virtual machine for my chauvinist attitude, I read on. There was a lot to read. One site boasted, "Thousands of NAMES OF GODS, GODDESSES, DEMIGODS, MONSTERS, SPIRITS . . ." (Lowchens). It really had thousands. For the casual viewer, it offered a summary section before diving into the pantheons of the world:

* Norse Gods and Goddesses
* Roman Gods and Goddesses
* Greek Gods and Goddesses
* Celtic Gods and Goddesses
* Japanese Gods and Goddesses
* Hawaiian Gods and Goddesses
* Polynesian Gods

* Irish Gods and Goddesses
* Welsh Gods and Goddesses
* Gods and Goddesses of War
* Gods and Goddesses of Love and Sexuality
* Slavic Gods and Goddesses
* Chinese Gods
* Gods of Thunder

My, my. That's a lot of gods, and this was just the summary. No one takes those gods seriously today, right? You might be surprised. However, since most Westerners don't have a shrine to the Celtic goddess Danu in their homes (or any other Celtic gods/goddesses), we'll just leave these gods as a historical footnote for now. The gods we're interested in are abstract. This makes them more troubling because they're harder to see.

What are today's gods? To find them, let's look at their roots in Western history.

The Political Bridge to the Modern Age: The Roman Empire

During the early years of the Church, Christians suffered from an unsteady relationship with the ruling power of the Mediterranean region, where the Jewish and Christian faiths were born. The Roman Empire, proud of its civilization and religion, attempted to advance these in conquered territories. However, the Empire was also very practical (at least during much of its rule). The Romans realized they couldn't force everyone to follow Roman religion. Some religions were recognized as acceptable. These were the "approved" religions. The temples of Egypt, for example, weren't wiped out when the Romans took over; the Egyptians could worship the gods they worshipped previously. The Jewish religion was also permitted to continue. People of different religions could travel freely in the Roman Empire if they didn't cause trouble and if their religion was recognized.

Enter the Christians. Many thought they created a new religion. Hence, early Christians were considered troublemakers. They defended themselves by pointing out they were an outgrowth of Judaism. As such, they were a sect of an established and recognized religion. In fact, the book of Acts records several discussions between the apostle Paul and Roman leaders in which the Romans had difficulty seeing any significant difference between the Jewish religion and this new group (Acts 25:16–21; 26). Still, the Christians caused rumbles.

These rumbles reached the level of political earthquake when some of the Caesars left their tolerant ways and started thinking they were gods. Gods must be worshipped. Christians and Jews believed in resisting false gods. If they were small in numbers and quiet, hiding might have worked, but Christians have a funny notion: They believe they should tell others about their faith. Because of this, their numbers were increasing. This resulted in several periods of persecution. Some were bloody. One of the most notorious occurred under Nero who blamed Christians for the great fire of Rome in AD 64. Despite this terrible persecution, Christianity continued to grow.

A few centuries later in 313, the Emperor Constantine signed the Edict of Milan, legalizing Christianity. Think about this—for over two hundred years, anyone declaring faith in Christ might suffer fines, confiscation of property, imprisonment, torture, and death. Suddenly, Christians could stop hiding. In fact, the edict included the return of confiscated property. To top it all off, Constantine acted in ways one would hope for the first Christian-influenced emperor. When he legalized Christianity, he didn't ban other religions. Everyone was free to choose. Religious toleration ruled the day.

As wonderful as all this was, many Christians today look back with mixed feelings. It was marvelous for believers to be finally free. On the other hand, something troubling began to happen. Christianity wasn't only legal; it eventually became the *government-endorsed* religion. "Wait a minute, isn't that good thing from a Christian perspective?" some ask. The answer: yes and no. Yes, because the Christians exerted a positive influence on their culture. Rome benefitted from the adoption of a cultural ethic that valued human life. Previously, Roman citizens practiced things like infant exposure. This was a way to dispose of unwanted children. If babies or young children were considered undesirable, they could be left in the woods to die of exposure or to be torn apart by wild animals. Such barbaric practices decreased when Christian culture dominated.

On the other hand, when a partnership between faith and government becomes too close, it creates problems. One of the biggest problems is the large number of people who don't care about their beliefs, but care a lot about popularity and political power. Previously, popularity and power were associated with the Roman gods. Presenting a few offerings to the local deity gained favor with the political elite, whether you believed in the deities or not. Now, the newly legalized Christians could hold political office. Those seeking favor would want to please the new leaders. Sitting in church and smiling once a week is a small price to pay when it makes you look good to the emperor.

Thus started a centuries-long struggle that Jesus predicted in the parable of the mustard seed. There were times when true Christians used their positions of freedom and, in some cases, political power for great societal benefit. Great works of charity relieved the needy. Wonderful works of art were painted on canvas and chiseled into stone, as beautiful cathedrals rose to dominate the skylines of medieval cities.

Sadly, there were also times when people who didn't understand Jesus took over. They donned a mask with His likeness, while instigating massive persecutions and oppressive practices not even hinted at in the Scriptures. At those times, the poor suffered most while rulers, and in some cases even corrupt church leaders, enjoyed riches obtained through virtual enslavement of the masses.

Perhaps the biggest problems of those times came when some church leaders saw a complete fusion between leadership positions in the church and the governments of their day. It's one thing to disagree about theology when the disagreement involves two individuals. It's a wholly different matter when church and state combine. When this occurs, disagreements become a matter of political loyalty and even criminality. Religious leaders of those days became the antithesis of biblical faith. I can't say this too much: God offers people the divine opportunity to choose, whether they choose well or poorly. True faith is never the product of coercion.

Science and Atheism

I read something once in the book of Psalms that confused me: "The fool says in his heart, 'There is no God'" (Psalm 14:1).

What's confusing about this? It may be strongly worded, but at first glance it's not confusing. The words, "there is no God" are words from what today is called an atheist. The psalm writer labeled such words foolishness. What confused me was the time of writing. It's attributed to King David, which means it was written over a thousand years before Christ. Here's why this seemed unusual: *prior to reading this, I thought atheism was invented in the modern age.*

I was taught the following: ancient people worshipped deities of all forms. When modern science arrived, there was no longer need for those outmoded ways of viewing the world. Science, I was taught, provided a better understanding of how things worked. Some even believed science disproved the existence of God. Atheism, as such, was the product of modern thought.

This verse indicated something different: there have always been people who thought God didn't exist. They believed this long before anyone invented computers or microscopes. There's something profound here. These individuals came to believe there was no God *when there was no scientific reason for believing so.* They didn't arrive at their belief because they hooked electrodes to a beaker of fluid and measured the flow of electricity between electrodes. They didn't develop their philosophy after they built a rocket, flew into space, and looked down from orbit. They came to their belief for another reason.

How did this happen? In the letter to the Romans, Paul explains:

> What may be known about God is plain to them, because God has made it plain to them. For since the creation of the world God's invisible qualities—his eternal power and divine nature—have been clearly seen, being understood from what has been made, so that men are without excuse. For although they knew God, they neither glorified him as God nor gave thanks to him, but their thinking became futile and their foolish hearts were darkened. Although they claimed to be wise, they became fools. (Romans 1:19–22)

Although we cannot perfectly discern ultimate reality, we can get some general notions by looking around. It's difficult to gaze into a starry night and avoid the sense that something is responsible for what we see. If the skies cloud over, we can look somewhere closer: we can marvel at birds in flight or enjoy the beauty of flowers. In each case, we see something amazing. Wherever we look, we see evidence of a grand design.

For some, the process isn't so easy. Why? To put it bluntly, some people hate God. These people inherited the mind of Cain. They have no desire to seek God. They have no desire to obey Him. For these people, life is one long act of avoiding God. The longer they do this, the more they become vulnerable to what Paul called "clouding of their vision" and "darkening of their hearts".

I witnessed something resembling this process once. While visiting friends, I met a young child named Mikey. Mikey was having a bad day. When dinnertime arrived, Mikey's mother called to him. Mikey didn't want to come. His mother repeated her call, but Mikey's mind was made up. He stayed in place, playing with his toys. Mikey's mother became annoyed, so she walked closer, repeating the call to dinner. Mikey put his hands over his ears, closed his eyes, and sang a song. His mother walked over, reached down, and gently lifted one of Mikey's eyelids with her thumb, allowing eye contact. "I'm still here," she quietly said. Mikey got a puzzled look on his face. The look seemed to say, "How can this be? I thought I made you disappear!" Mikey wound up coming to the table and eating dinner. Once he started eating, he enjoyed it.

Child psychologists call this principle *object permanence*. Children need to learn objects exist, whether you can see them or not. Closing your eyes doesn't make them go away. Placing objects behind an opaque object like a wall doesn't make them go away, either. Learning this is an important step in a child's development. If a child fails to learn this principle, it's a detriment in life. As much as it's fun playing "Peek-a-boo" with a child, most parents hope for the game to end as the child grows older.

Adult people also have an important principle to learn; I call it *God permanence*. God is there whether we want to see Him or not. Because we're limited, we may not be able to discern Him perfectly, but we should realize He exists. Sadly, many adults never learn this principle. If children fail to learn object permanence, they're labeled "developmentally disabled". If adults fail to learn God permanence, they're labeled "atheists".

Apparently, there have always been atheists. In past ages they were considered odd, and from the standpoint of scripture, foolish. In modern times though, atheists have managed to change their status. Today, they consider themselves as the model of sophistication. They've convinced many their self-adulation is merited. In the marketing world, this activity is called "rebranding". How did the atheists do it?

They did it largely through the *misuse of science*.

Science, when properly applied, is wonderful. Many are surprised that someone who believes in the Bible can feel this way, but that's a misperception. We can all agree on the benefits of good science. I like being able to take a pill when I'm sick, knowing I'll feel better. I'm happy to get into vehicles that deliver me to far-away destinations much faster than walking. Let's not waste space talking about how much biblical believers value good science as much as everyone else.

Now, I'm using the phrases "science properly applied" and "good science". The clear implication: There's "bad science" and "science improperly applied". What's the difference?

Definitions of science vary, but here are four important elements: knowledge, systemization, observation, and experimentation. We want to learn about the universe (knowledge) because it's interesting and because it's useful. So, we look around (observe). We group our observations into useful categories (systematize). It's not long before we run into mysterious things that can't be explained with simple observation. When this happens, we set up situations allowing us to control various things that affect what we're observing. We attempt to predict how something will behave when exposed to things in this controlled environment (experiment). Once we establish predictable and repeatable behavior, we believe we've discovered a law. We can then move on to other mysterious things, building on what we learned. The main point is we start with what we can observe and advance in a disciplined way to things we can't. Using this approach, humanity has learned amazing things.

However, there are problems with this system. To illustrate, let's imagine you and I live in a different age. We'll go back to the Middle Ages, a time before modern approaches to science. There, we'll become university students. At that time, if you asked a professor the question, "Where do living things come from", you'd get the following answer: "Living things come from two places. First, they come from other animals. Male dogs and female dogs produce puppies. Second, living things come from 'spontaneous generation'. This means inanimate objects can become living things. A leaf floating on a lake eventually becomes a frog."

At this point the professor smiles and awaits acclamation from his students. Unfortunately, I've always been a troublemaker. "Excuse me, professor," I respond, "but doesn't it say in the Bible that animals come after 'kinds'? I mean, God created the first two frogs male and female, and from there we get little frogs, right? Doesn't it take living, parental animals to make child animals? I don't think the Bible teaches 'spontaneous generation.'"

The professor gets a look on his face that says, "Oh no—we've got one of those strict ones again." "Look," he'd say, "go out to the lake. Look around. You'll see a lot of leaves. Come back a few months later, and you see frogs. I'm afraid the evidence is undeniable." Not being convinced, I try again. "But there's a lot of time between those two observations, and there's a lot we don't control. Perhaps there are other factors we should consider?" Again, the professor glances around the class with a knowing look. "You have the beginnings of a scientific mind; if only we can wean you away from your religious predispositions. As it turns out, we can control such observations. Let's take a piece of meat and put it under a cover. If we come back in a week, there are maggots crawling around the meat. Where did they come from? The only logical explanation is spontaneous generation."

Well, now I'm stuck. The professor certainly makes some good points, and he's presented evidence obtained from a "controlled experiment" to support those points. I'm having trouble leaving behind the Scriptures which I thought provided a sufficient explanation of this phenomenon, even if I don't have "science" to back up my beliefs. The whole room seems to nod in agreement with professor, who represents the establishment. I'm alone. Still, I end up saying, "I'm sorry professor, but with all due respect, I must maintain my belief in the Scriptures. Someday there will be an explanation for this apparent conflict." The professor appears a bit upset but keeps his composure. He finally says, "I just don't know how you 'believers' can so stubbornly hold to your beliefs in the face of *so much compelling evidence!*"

"Compelling evidence." Ah, yes. We hear that a lot. As it turns out, the "compelling evidence" allowing spontaneous generation to be taught for centuries was flawed. Frogs don't come from leaves; they come from other frogs. Concerning meat and maggots: Maggots come from eggs so small they're difficult to see with the human eye. Those eggs can be deposited on meat before a cover is placed on it. If your cover isn't tight, flies and other insects can easily crawl in and deposit eggs, even if there were none to start. It took a series of experiments, starting with Francesco Redi in the 1600s through Louis Pasteur in the 1800s, to put the theory of spontaneous generation to rest.

To modern students, the idea that anyone ever believed in spontaneous generation is silly, but was it silly at the time? Weren't scientific minds making observations? They saw lots of leaves and later lots of frogs. In some cases, investigators made attempts to control the environments of their observations; this included activities like placing meat under a cover. What was the problem? There were two. First, *scientists failed to understand the limits of their instrumentation.* In this case, "instrumentation" was bare senses and simple implements, such as a cover placed over a dish. With these limitations, observers missed a lot. Second was *the problem of preconceptions.* Once a theory is established, it's difficult to displace.

The first problem was helped as scientists developed better instruments. This allowed them to make more detailed observations. Some tools available for research today were the stuff of science fiction a generation ago. The findings obtained with these devices are amazing. Having said that, there are still times when scientists would do well to understand that even the most advanced instruments don't show everything. Even the best equipment is useless if users are unwilling to allow for evidence that challenges their preconceived notions.

Here's where the second problem becomes manifest. Everyone grows up in a world full of mysteries. We all find ways to understand as best we can. If you, as a child, let go of your lollipop, it has a nasty way of traveling down to the ground where it gets dirty. Always. Every time. So, at first you just accept it and learn to hold on to your lollipop until you've licked the last bit of sugary goodness out of it. Later in school, you learn about something called the "Laws of Gravity". This fits with what you already know, so there's no problem. Sometimes, though, we develop explanations for mysterious things that seem right when they're suggested, but which get challenged later. We tend to lean on whatever worked for us in the past instead of giving way to new ideas. Sometimes this is good and sometimes not so much. The things that make sense to us most form our preconceptions. This brings us to a vitally important point: *all human beings have preconceptions about how things work.*

To me, this is the key to good science versus bad science. Actually, it's not just good science and bad science; it's a good way to run your life versus a bad way to run your life. *The key is to be able to identify and admit to your preconceptions.* If you can't do this, it doesn't matter what information you possess. Your preconceptions always win. *Facts and reason are no matches for an unidentified preconception.*

One of the biggest forces behind preconceptions is *authority.* When things don't make sense, what do you rely upon to make decisions about how to proceed? I've tried to make the case that since the Garden of Eden; most humans are self-standardizing. That means we make choices based on our own experience and what feels good. Different people have very different ideas of what makes them feel good. I've also made the case that God desires for us to have Him as our authority. His design for us is that we function differently than the other created things on the earth.

So, let me be the first to admit—what I'm stating is a personal preconception. When I see evidence that this is the right way to go about things (and there is lots of it), it makes me feel good. I will also be the first to admit there are times when I see things that don't fit into this scheme. I either need to explain those things or accept the problem of an information/preconception mismatch.

Right now, an atheist in the audience has jumped to his feet and yelled, "Amen!" He'll probably sit down and suffer some embarrassment when he realizes he doesn't believe in religious things and shouldn't be using religious words. His more controlled friends are elbowing each other and saying, "It's about time one of those Christians admitted his preconceptions!" Well, not so fast. The problem is, atheists have some preconceptions, too. They don't like the idea of God. Their worldview says everything is a result of random processes. When they see things appearing to support this belief (admittedly, those things exist), they're happy. The problem occurs when they see things not matching their preconceptions. It's not so much that they become unhappy; it seems they just *can't see* evidence contradicting their positions. In fact, most atheists don't believe they have preconceptions. In their minds, they're a superior breed of human being who just "gets it". Their way of thinking is simply right. Period. Over the years, they've managed to convince a lot of people that their way of thinking has merit. As such, many atheists sit in tenured seats of the world's most prestigious universities.

So, how did this group of people move from being considered foolish centuries ago to being considered intellectual leaders of today's world? As I previously mentioned, Jesus introduced the idea that gods can be abstract. With this in mind, I'd like to introduce an abstract god right now. It's one of the most important gods of the modern age.

I call it the *"god of smart"*.

Where Does the ""God of Smart" Come From?

Everyone desires to prove they're worthwhile — perhaps even important. One way to do this is proving to others you're intelligent. The words "you're *smart*" have amazing power over people. Conversely, there's great power in the word *stupid*. No one wants to look like a dummy. In any society, the smartest people become scientists, healers, and teachers, or so it's thought. Anyway, if you can demonstrate you're smart, you're important. Next in line to being smart is being able to hang around with smart people. If you can be seen in the spotlight with smart people, the implication is you're smart, too.

Now, challenging the smart people is costly. If you're proven wrong, you're labeled a dummy. Again, no one wants to be a dummy. As such, challenging the smart people is usually avoided.

In the time of the early church and later into the Middle Ages, the recognized owners of "smart" were the Greek and Roman philosophers. We still read the ancient philosophers because much of their teaching makes sense even day.

Then, of course, there are theories like spontaneous generation. The ancient philosophers, the smart ones, taught it (Brack 1998, p. 1). Therefore, in the old days it had to be correct. Then came the Bible. Reading the first few pages of Genesis provides the correct view of how living things appear. Parent organisms produce child organisms "according to their kind" (Gen. 1:11–12, 21). What do you do when you believe the Bible is inspired by God, but its teachings appear to conflict with established opinions of the day?

Enter a man named Augustine (AD 354–430). He was a remarkable thinker and a great leader of the early church. He faced this challenge. Here's his solution: Augustine chose to work on the assumption that the establishment was to be deferred to in matters of scientific knowledge. As he searched the Scriptures, he noticed the statement in Genesis, "Let the water teem with living creatures" (Gen. 1:20). From this, he suggested that although God created creatures to procreate from parent creatures of their kind, he may also have allowed for spontaneous generation in the oceans. This appeared very scholarly and allowed Augustine to appear smart to the philosophers of his day; this turned out to be a tragic error.

There comes a point where believers practice abundant humility. They listen thoughtfully to the teachings of leading thinkers. If they hear something appearing to conflict with their understanding of Scriptures, they return to the Scriptures and consider carefully whether they're interpreting the relevant passages correctly. After doing this, though, believers may conclude the Scriptures state a given truth clearly and undeniably, even though it may conflict with teachings of the day. At that point, they must have the courage to say, "I know my views don't agree with current consensus, but I still believe them. Perhaps someday we'll see new evidence proving the Scriptures correct. In the meantime, here I stand." Having admitted their preconceptions, believers must be willing to accept the fact that the owners of smart may look down on them.

Had Augustine done this, he would have eventually been credited with proving the superiority of scripture over the ancient philosophers. Spontaneous generation, as taught by the philosophers of Greece and Rome, is now a small (and might I add laughable) footnote in the history of science. Instead, people who read Augustine caused Western thought to be impeded for centuries.

Believers and nonbelievers alike have suffered for this, but believers still hurt today. If you've ever sat through a lecture by a modern scientist or philosopher, you may have heard something like this: "People in Europe got stuck with a religion based on the Bible. Bible, Bible, Bible. The Bible taught nonsensical things like spontaneous generation. Because blind believers followed the Bible, Europe was mired in the Dark Ages. Then came 'Science'. Science freed people from superstitious thought, and we've moved happily forward ever since." The clear implication is, smart people don't read the Bible. Doing so may cause a return to the Dark Ages; but as you've just read, it wasn't belief in the Bible that held Western civilization back. The problem occurred when the early church allowed itself to believe that the establishment of its age had all the answers concerning science. When that assumption became fused with theological thought, the result was centuries of stifled thinking.

This fusion led to the greatest embarrassment the church has ever seen: the inquisition of Galileo Galilei in 1615. Before getting into this, let's dispel a few myths. There are surprising amounts of people saying things like, "The Bible teaches the earth is flat. That's why the church attacked Galileo." Sorry, no. Early church leaders such as Clement and Origen (second century AD) accepted a round earth. Also, Columbus had already discovered America in 1492.

The question at the time of Galileo over a century later wasn't the shape of the earth, but its relationship to the sun and the other planets. Galileo proclaimed the heliocentric views of Copernicus. Leaders of the established Western church espoused the geocentric view. Because of this conflict, Galileo was tried for heresy, found guilty, and sentenced to house arrest for the remainder of his life.

Often missed in discussions about this sorry chapter of church history are the religious views of Galileo. He believed and studied the Scriptures. He didn't find in the Scriptures any contradiction with the heliocentric view; neither do modern biblical scholars. The problem was not that Galileo was an early pioneer of atheism. The problem was Galileo's interpretation of scripture. It disagreed with the church establishment. Acknowledging that the views of a layperson could be superior to church leadership wasn't to be allowed at the time. Scripture wasn't the problem; it was pomposity. So, church leaders of the day convicted a brilliant and devout man of heresy and gave Christianity a black eye from which it has never recovered. Later believers came to understand that even though humans are highly valued, they aren't the center of the universe. God is.

Prior to this, the beliefs of Christianity weren't subject to large-scale challenge in the Western world. With this horrible mistake, a crack was created in the dike, which eventually led to a flood of challenges to scriptural faith.

Why So Much about Atheists?

Isn't this a book about idolatry? How does atheism relate? We're discussing this for two reasons. First, atheism is a form of idolatry. When Adam and Eve reached for the forbidden fruit, they thought they could become like God. Atheists imagine the same thing. They want to be their own god. They want total authority over their lives, and they can't have it while God exists. So, they imagine Him away. That's not how things work, and atheists will receive a very unpleasant surprise someday when they enter eternity. What's important for now are the methods modern atheists employ to support their imaginations.

That brings us to the second reason for this discussion. When Adam and Eve realized things had gone wrong, they attempted to make God go away. In their case, they hid among the trees of the Garden. Their efforts were as effective as little children who hide from their parents under the bed, but don't realize they left their legs sticking out. Still, there was something about hiding behind a tree that made Adam and Eve imagine God was out of the picture. Here's the point: in essence, *atheists use science and other modern disciplines to build virtual trees.*

This makes atheists useful to idolaters. Something funny happens when atheists convince people the true God doesn't exist. Some people respond by becoming atheists. A lot more people shun the atheists and move on to other gods, whether established ones or gods of their own making. Atheists become pawns of the other gods, doing their dirty work for them.

Note: this includes agnostics. Although different in theory, agnosticism is the practical equivalent of atheism. Both leave the adherent with no ruling authority in life. Hence, both allow people to imagine they're their own gods.

Let's see how atheists and all their friends went about creating a new forest of virtual trees, and how to break through.

Chapter 21

Answering Challenges Posed by the Modern "Gods"

Archeology

After the mistreatment of Galileo, the children of disbelief grew bolder. Some scholars announced in the eighteenth century the Bible couldn't be believed. Why? The Bible spoke of ancient peoples who didn't appear to exist. One such group was the Hittites. No one could find evidence of this ancient people. The English had England; the Finnish has Finland. Where was Hittiteland? If you're going to talk about a group of people, shouldn't there be some record of the people's existence? With this "compelling evidence", the skeptics nodded confidently to each other. The Bible was merely a book of myths and mythological people. Many listened to the skeptics, and some lost faith.

Enter the archeologists. Archeologists love to find hidden things. Some of them wandered out to the Middle East and began to excavate. Guess what they found? Hittites! Not living ones, but the civilization they left centuries ago. It was buried beneath the sands of antiquity; and not only did they find the Hittites, but numerous other people mentioned in the Bible: Canaanites, Moabites, Ammonites, and other lost people groups all appeared when ancient sands were removed by the skilled hands of archeologists. Archeology is an example of a science that, rather than disprove the Bible, has done the opposite. Thanks to archeologists, we know the Bible is filled with references to people truly existing in history. This alone doesn't prove faith, but it does a good job dispelling one pile of "compelling evidence".

Spiritual Vacuums

Let me introduce an important concept here; I call it the "*spiritual vacuum period*". A spiritual vacuum period is the time that occurs between two events: the first event is the act of someone declaring they have "compelling evidence" that the Scriptures aren't to be believed. The second event occurs when an authoritative source declares the first statement to be invalid, backing up their new ideas with "compelling evidence" of their own. The time between the original statement about missing Hittites and the time archeologists found them was such a vacuum period. Significant mischief was perpetrated by unbelievers on believers during this time, with some believers losing faith. Other believers were made to look foolish in university settings. They had to live with persecution.

I've seen numerous vacuum periods. I've been shocked at how much "common knowledge", purportedly supported by "compelling evidence", is complete nonsense. Understanding this principle is very helpful when dealing with the god of smart.

The General Sciences

From Galileo to today, the general sciences have been led by believers and nonbelievers alike. For example, Isaac Newton believed solidly in Christianity. His faith didn't conflict with the laws of gravity.

By analyzing what they see, scientists discover all kinds of useful information. Often, they hand this information to engineers and inventors. The job of engineers and inventors is to take the discoveries of scientists and use that information to create useful things. Everyone likes useful things.

Problems come when things aren't immediately useful. In some cases, we understand a phenomenon and assign a scientific principle. However, the phenomenon is too rare to apply the principle economically. That's not a problem because rare and hard have a way of becoming abundant and easy with ongoing study. In 1947, John Bardeen and Walter Brattain invented the transistor. They likely would be awestruck if they could look only a few generations into the future. Transistors have become so small, millions can be placed on a standard computer chip the size of a fingertip.

A bigger problem comes with *theories*. Theories come when scientists have observed phenomena enough to believe they can predict the future concerning the subject of their observations. What they believe will occur just hasn't happened yet.

A good example of this occurred in the early twentieth century when a young Albert Einstein introduced his theory of relativity. One peg in his theory involved a prediction that light could be bent by gravity. To observe this, you'd need a massive object—like our sun. You would then need to find a powerful source of light emanating from behind, and just to the side of, the sun—like one of the distant stars visible near the sun's edge. If you could measure the position of the light from the star and demonstrate that our sun's gravity made the star appear to be in a different position than it was known to be, you could prove the theory. This was an awfully hard proposition. It involved looking up to the sun at a time when the sun's light didn't obscure the stars, and this only happens during a total eclipse. The proper type of eclipse would only occur a handful of times during Einstein's life. Because his theories were so compelling, there were dedicated scientists willing to haul specially built equipment to remote places at just the right time to test Einstein's ideas. They eventually found light from distant stars bending as it passed close to the surface of our sun. Einstein's theories were proven.

How does all this relate to faith? Here's the problem: The Bible isn't a book of science, per se. It's a book of history. The problem with history is it's all in the past. If someone states a theory of something that's happening now, or will happen in the future, the theory can be proven or disproven once the appropriate events are observed. What happens with theories about the past? Many times, people are curious about things that happened long ago. Since no one alive today was around then, the curious must gather evidence about what *might* have occurred. After enough evidence is gathered, they can develop theories. The problem with historical theories is *they can never be proven*. Once the events happen, they're done. You can have all kinds of discussions about what might have been. You may be able to find evidence. If you're lucky, you may gather enough evidence to win others to your theory. That makes a theory "generally accepted". However, until someone develops a time machine allowing us to visit the past, historical theories will always remain theories.

Here's the challenge: what happens when someone develops a theory of what happened in the past that conflicts with the historical records presented in the Bible, a book claiming to be inspired by God? Enter a man named Charles Darwin.

The Question of Origins

Charles Darwin was born into a wealthy English family in 1809. He attended university at a time when thinkers felt free to ask questions about ultimate reality. Although a free thinker, Darwin wasn't strongly influenced by the extreme views challenging fundamental beliefs in Christianity surrounding him—at least not at first. At one point, he prepared for ministry with the Anglican church. His interest in science won out, though, and Darwin eventually left England for an adventure aboard a ship called the *Beagle*.

During his voyage, Darwin collected a number of specimens from South America, the most famous coming from the Galapagos Islands.

The following two paragraphs are familiar to anyone who's read a high school biology book, but we need to quickly review the topic to establish a line of thought.

Among Darwin's findings were some creatures Darwin thought to be insignificant, such as some finches. Later, he came to believe these birds were significant. They appeared similar but had distinct beaks. Darwin theorized the birds were all descendants of a common ancestor. Each group of birds developed unique beaks, as they became separated over time and found different foods. Darwin theorized that the parent bird itself came from an earlier type of bird. Here's the important part: if you went back far enough in the lineage of the bird, you'd find an animal that wasn't a bird. If you went far enough, eventually all life could be traced to a single organism. Darwin theorized this process took place slowly, covering millions of years. The process became known by one word: *evolution*.

Also prominent in Darwin's theory was the dynamic of this process. Changes occurred through "natural selection". Let's say we observe a group of animals. Some are born with lots of fur, some with little. The assignment of fur is random. Also random is the animal's environment. At one point, it gets colder. The animals with abundant fur stay warm and live longer than their less-furry brethren. Longer-lived animals can mate more often, producing increases in animals with heavy fur. Over many generations, changes become great enough that a new species appears, a process called *speciation*.

That was a whirlwind overview of Darwin's work. Let's summarize the major points as they relate to the topic of this book:

- Darwin stated life was the product of long processes, with current species evolving from previous species. Current species are better adapted to their environments than their predecessors. Complex organisms evolve from simpler organisms. In opposition to this is the record of scripture. The Scriptures teach life is the product of a Creator. He created "kinds" of living things. It takes one from a kind to make another of the same kind. Kinds can experience significant variation but don't become other kinds.
- Second, evolution requires abundant time—millions of years. At first reading, the opening chapters of Genesis state the creation took place in a short period of time: seven days.
- Third, all species come about through an unguided, natural process. There is no room in this plan for an intelligent being guiding the

213

process (Eliot 1909, 94–95). The Scriptures clearly state an intelligent being implemented life with a planned architecture.

- Finally, the dynamics of the process involve one goal: survival. Only organisms left alive after environmental changes can breed and create more organisms. As such, the phrase "higher life" is irrelevant. There are only winners and losers, survivors and extinctions. The Scriptures teach that God has a purpose for all life, and that humans were created as the highest form of life on our planet. His goals for us are much more complex than mere survival.

Scientists say there are mountains of compelling evidence (there's that phrase again) to support the Darwin's theory. Let's address some of the conflicts.

Conflicts with the Theory of Origins

Time: The Scriptures state the heavens, the earth, and all living things were created in a time span of seven days. After that, there's a recorded series of events tending to indicate a "young earth". There are three ways people have attempted to resolve this apparent conflict.

- The Bible is wrong. Find another religion or become an atheist.
- The Bible is right and is to be interpreted literally. Current scientific understanding is wrong. People in this camp refer to themselves as "creationists" and propose a "young earth" theory of origins. They have their share of PhDs, and they've compiled evidence to support their views. I suggest that you type "creation science" into a search engine and read for a bit before you write off these people.
- The Bible is right, but it should be interpreted at some points symbolically. There are either no conflicts or limited conflicts with current scientific understanding. Some people in this camp hold to a partially symbolic view. They note the Hebrew word for "day" (*yom*), often used for a literal twenty-four-hour day, also occurs in the Scriptures to describe periods of time over twenty-four hours. Hence, long time spans are no conflict. Others believe the Scriptures involve greater use of images. Augustine, for example, believed God created everything at once and then developed the one-week concept as a symbolic way to describe His activities. To understand, let's say you found a genie in a bottle and were given one wish. You choose the perfect spouse. Would you want to receive an infant, requiring you to wait

until it to become an adult? Or would you want a person in the prime of life? If you've got a genie, why wait? Some suggest God lives outside of time as we know it and created a mature earth in His own time. We look at that maturity as "age". If you or I were to make it, it would take billions of years. God isn't you or me. He's working with infinite resources and power.

- The final group suggests the concept of "intelligent design". Proponents of this view believe there are things in the universe indicating an intelligent force behind its existence. Adherents believe they can assemble scientific evidence to support this theory without a required point of intersection between the Bible or any other religious book. Many followers of this theory would identify as Christian or Jewish, but technically, you can be an agnostic and hold this view.

Speciation: belief in speciation is the result of big problems in the ways scientists work.

Darwin collected more than finches on his famous voyage. He collected numerous specimens from the living and fossil worlds. Since then, scientists have collected warehouses full of fossils and zoos full of living creatures. They've arranged the fossils and animals into the schemes that we've all seen on charts in biology textbooks. These arrangements, it is felt, prove evolution.

To illustrate why this is a problem, consider this story. On the way home from work, a man decided to visit a toy store to find a surprise for his young son. He chose a puzzle. The puzzle displayed a picture of a baby monkey. His son accepted the treat and happily assembled all the pieces—not too many, as this was an age-appropriate gift. Proud of his accomplishment, he called out to his family. Unfortunately, his father had stepped out for a moment. The only person to arrive was an older boy from next door. He took one look at the monkey and began to laugh. "What are you, some kind of baby?" he mocked. "You should be playing with things like this." The older boy held up a toy rocket. He made a rocket-like sound ("swoosh," "zoom," you can make one up) and ran from the room, holding the toy like it was flying. The father came in just in time to witness the tail end of this conversation. His heart-broken little boy looked up at him and said, "I don't want any more baby monkeys. I want a rocket!" This story could have ended with another trip to the toy store. Unfortunately, the budget being what it was, this father had to be clever. He said, "Let's see if we can put together the parts of the puzzle *differently*." He then took some pieces and shaped them into a rocket body. He took pieces that previously composed the monkey's ears and made them into tail fins. The links between the pieces didn't fit like they used to, but no matter. The end product was a rocket. The little boy was happy again.

Those of us who disagree with the theory of evolution understand there are warehouses full of fossils and zoos full of animals collected by scientists. We can see it's possible to place pictures of these specimens on charts and declare they form a chain leading back to an original, single cell. However, we disagree with the arrangement of the pieces. Here's the problem: it feels like we're back in the days of spontaneous generation. From the scientist's perspective, if you want to create something to support the status quo, you can assemble pieces as you wish. You can ignore holes in the big picture and forget pieces that don't fit. From the student's perspective, if your goal is acceptance from the owners of "smart", you'll accept these conclusions without question.

If you're more open-minded, you'd be shocked at the ways pieces can be arranged into alternate theories. I've heard numerous presentations from people with PhDs, suggesting the fossils we have don't support evolution at all.

A tougher question: if there are alternate ways to arrange the puzzle pieces, why doesn't the average person know about them? Because scientists who align themselves with the status quo often refuse to acknowledge the legitimacy of competing theories. Competing theories are generally not included in classroom lectures. Few are given a choice in the matter. Scientists who disagree with evolutionary theory have charged for a long time that their voices are silenced. This atmosphere has created a massive problem of numbers. If you want to get a scientific degree from a good school, you had better not give any hint that you're open minded when it comes to theories that compete with evolution. Compliance means scholarships, fellowships, foundation funding, tenure, and respect. Questioning evolution results in losing of all the above. Members of the status quo will lift their noses slightly and declare, "If you can come up with evidence, we'll listen to your theories!" That's nice, but when funding is pulled from anyone challenging the core of modern philosophical belief, you don't get many takers. Hence, the scientific establishment is left with the upper hand. The average student doesn't even know evolution is a theory, much less one with significant problems. It's taught as fact. Because of the hold on all the resources, followers of the god of smart collect an ever-growing pile of data, which is the only material allowed when considering the concept of origins. Thus, challengers are faced with an ever-growing mountain of "compelling evidence".

It's not just a problem in the scientific realm. Challenging scientific theory is impractical for other disciplines. This leaves students with little else to do but follow evolutionary theory without question; and this is a big problem because universities are the entryway to power in our world. Challenging the status quo isn't just an intellectual problem. It's a way to ensure you're hampered in every area of life. Those in the public eye who challenge evolution are met with armies of journalists and media personalities all too happy to destroy heretics. It's much easier to worship at the feet of the god of smart if you wish to be successful in life.

Unguided processes and the goal of life: It's here that we hit not only bad science, but the worst science. Challengers of evolutionary theory fall into two groups. First, many believe evolution conflicts with the Scriptures. Scripture present a Creator who made everything and who sustains everything. More than this, God created the universe for a purpose. Based on everything you've read so far, this group shouldn't be surprising. The second group, however, surprises many. They challenge evolution based on science. This is because *the idea of unguided (otherwise known as random) processes conflicts with the most fundamental scientific laws.* Let me explain.

Once again, the following involves rudimentary science principles most learn in high school, but we need a quick review to establish the line of thought.

In the 1800s, physicists discovered the laws of thermodynamics. The one most important to our discussion is the second one, which involves *entropy.* In its simplest statement, things have a way of becoming equal. An easy illustration is an ice cube and a glass of water. If you place an ice cube in a glass of water, the ice cube starts to receive energy in the form of heat from the surrounding water. This causes the cube to melt. The water in the glass will cool, as it's passing its heat to the cube. This process will continue until the water from the ice cube has reached a state where its temperature is equal to the water in the glass. When this happens, we have *equilibrium.* At this point, there's no more cube because the solid water has become liquid. Because of this law, we can turn a room-temperature glass of water into something cool and refreshing on a hot day.

Entropy also involves *randomness.* Let's grab that glass of water and go a little further. It's good that it's cold, but we want it to be sweet. So, we drop in some sugar. The sugar comes out of its container in the form of crystals, molecules that have been locked into orderly patterns. Once the crystals hit the water, the formerly stable and orderly molecules begin to disperse among the molecules of the surrounding water. This process will continue until all the sugar molecules have been evenly dispersed into the water. One of the implications of the second law of thermodynamics is that things in nature tend to move from orderly states into less organized states. *Order tends to be displaced by randomness.*

Here's the conflict: Evolution states all of life came from a single cell. That cell came from randomly appearing chemicals that came together under random conditions. *So, life came about as a result of random molecules becoming orderly.* From there, with no help, the cell became something more complex. Cells cooperated with other cells to move from single-celled organisms to simple, multi-cell organisms. From there, they grew to a fantastically complex array of organisms. This array formed an ecosystem that has kept life on this planet in balance for billions of years. This pattern breaks one of the most fundamental rules of physics. In nature, things go from complex to simple, not the other way around. The most obvious way for things to go the other way, from simple to complex, is for an *organizing force to make them go that way.*

Hence, it is perfectly scientific to state the universe requires an organizing force if it is to achieve and maintain high levels of complexity. If you state otherwise, you're the one who's unscientific; yet, the core of evolutionary theory says randomness grew into orderliness over billions of years *with no help.*

Surprisingly, many scientists understand what I just stated. What are scientists supposed to do when they have major holes in their theories? Well, if you have a theory about how something works, but there are some things appearing to conflict, you're allowed to stick with your theory. You can do so if you acknowledge the fact that there are things about your theory still needing to be reconciled.

Is this what evolutionists do? No. Evolution is taught as proven fact from the highest levels of academia down to elementary school. Why is this?

Let's revisit the medieval university we discussed earlier. You remember—the one where I challenged spontaneous generation, the accepted teaching of the day. When I challenged, I had to say something like, "I know my views don't match the currently accepted school of thought. This is because I have a preconception about how the world works. I have faith that someday, evidence will be found to support my beliefs." In doing so, I've been honest. I stated the conflict, and I was frank about the fact that the conflict occurs on my part because of my religious preconceptions. That's what people with religious preconceptions do. Compare this to the statement of most evolutionists today. They insist their ideas about origins are undeniable facts. Challengers of evolution consider this practice to be intellectually dishonest.

In actuality, things are slightly different in privileged scientific circles. If you're in "Biology 101", and you're concerned about the things I've written, you're allowed to raise a question that will produce a slightly different statement. Please, for your own sake, when you ask this question, don't say something like "I read a book that said evolution breaks fundamental laws of science like the second law of thermodynamics, and that seems like a pretty good argument to me." That will cause you to be scarred for your entire academic career. Instead, pose the question like this: "I have a superstitious relative who insists on challenging evolution. He mentioned something about the laws of thermodynamics. I know he's an idiot, but I'm new at this, and I didn't have a reply. Can you help me straighten him out?" If you do this, you'll get a much more sympathetic reply. You'll hear something like this from your professor: "We don't have an explanation for that yet, but we have *faith* the evidence will come in the future."

Wait a minute. Faith? I thought faith was only for religious people. Here is why I'm calling this bad science. The idea that evolution is the only answer for origins, and that it can only occur through unguided, natural processes looks more like religious dogma than a statement of scientific observation. In fact, the followers of evolution act more like religious zealots than they care to admit. Most evolutionists have a preconceived notion about how things should look. They don't realize they have it; and because they don't realize they have it, they don't state it.

It would be tempting to spend time describing the "mountains of compelling evidence" I've seen, which contradicts the evidence of evolutionists. Further details on that need to be left to the people with PhDs in science who challenge evolutionary theory. There are lots of them, and they're a very brave group of people. For now, we must be content leaving further discussion to the experts and move on to the ways evolutionary theory has influenced other disciplines.

Chapter 22

Surprising Areas of Thought Influenced by the Modern "Gods"

I f we looked at the history of the Hebrew people, we'd expect to find true faith in the great Hebrew temple of Jerusalem. If idols existed, they would be found "out there" in the countryside. Surprisingly, in the saddest episodes of the Bible, idols sometimes found their way into the great temple itself (II Chron. 33:4). Centuries haven't changed the way the idols work. Today, their influence can be found in surprising places.

Theology

Theologians attempt to systematize our understanding of God. The topic falls out of scientific circles because no one can put God in a test tube. You can't experiment on God. So, theologians gather data based on what people have observed about ultimate reality over time. For Jewish and Christian theologians, this at one time meant attempting to understand their respective writings in the Bible. For Jews, it meant understanding the Hebrew language in which the Scriptures were mostly recorded, and also reviewing the work of great rabbis over centuries of Jewish thought. For Christians, it meant understanding Hebrew and Greek (the language of the New Testament), along with review of teachers throughout the days of the Church. Christians have always acknowledged rabbinical teaching, but in recent years numerous Christian thinkers have put special emphasis on understanding Hebrew thought. Jesus was Jewish. Understanding Jewish perspectives on the Scriptures mean gaining a better understanding of His world.

Here we run into a problem. Let's say you've been taught the Scriptures are the main source of information about God. Later, you're told scripture has been proven inaccurate by the "mountains of compelling evidence" generated by science. You have several choices. If you choose to say, "Well, I know that my views do not match current consensus, but . . ." you must be ready for the consequences of your choice. You're going to look stupid. The god of smart who's worshipped by all around you will frown, and so will his followers. You'll no longer be invited to the best parties, and your career options will be limited. If you don't like this, you can become an agnostic or even an atheist. This will get you a ticket to the best parties, but not all parties. You'll lose some friends on this road, too. You'll feel better intellectually, but seeing old friends waving on the way to church may leave you doubting your decision.

There's a third choice. It's called *liberal theology*.

In 1883, Julius Wellhausen, a noted theologian, published a work in Germany called "Prolegomena (critical introduction) to the History of Israel." In this work, Wellhausen stated his belief that the Pentateuch (the first five books of the Hebrew Bible) were not written by Moses, as traditionally believed. Instead, it was supposedly a collection of works by four sources, all of whom lived long after Moses. The sources were combined by an editor; they could be identified, it was said, by different writing styles. The "documentary hypothesis" took off quickly and was widely accepted in scholarly circles. Other theories like it were added by later theologians.

Scholars at the time failed to notice two problems; one was pointed out years later by Christian writer C. S. Lewis. He wrote a number of works using different literary styles. In some cases, he wrote children's literature. In other cases, he wrote adult science fiction. As a professor of a major university, he also wrote scholarly papers. He authored all of them, even though the styles may have differed. Here's the interesting point: Lewis noted that when critics attempted to guess at his motivations, they were universally wrong (Lewis 1967, 159–160). If you can't correctly identify the sources and motivations of modern authors who live in your day, the idea that you can guess at sources in an ancient document is fundamentally flawed.

More important, though, was the underlying reasoning of the documentary hypothesis. Wellhausen believed writing hadn't been invented in Moses' time (Harrison 1969, 201). Hence, Moses couldn't write anything down. If he couldn't write anything down, anything concerning Moses would be handed down through oral tradition over centuries until writing was available. The only things which could then be recorded, would be highly exaggerated and romanticized stories about this figure. If this is true, Moses is nothing more than a "tall tale", much like the early American legend of Paul Bunyan. This is a very disturbing thought for people of faith.

Once again though, those pesky archaeologists come knocking at the door. As it turns out, archaeologists discovered writing which existed long before Moses (Harrison 1969). The Egyptians, the Babylonians, and the Phoenicians all had writing systems. Having been raised in Pharaoh's court, Moses certainly had access to Egyptian hieroglyphics. He may have been required to understand other writing systems as well, to properly discern affairs of state. Thus, Moses was certainly capable of recording his thoughts. As with modern writers, he may have had assistants who helped him to compile his work. This would explain unusual things like the statements describing Moses' death at the end of Deuteronomy.

Sadly, these observations were unavailable, missed, or simply ignored at the time the liberal theologians entered the academic scene. The statements of Wellhausen started one of the most damaging spiritual vacuum periods of the modern age.

A few paragraphs back, I asked the question of what to do if you're a believer and you're confronted by the "compelling evidence" of science. Now it gets harder. What do you do if you're a theologian or a religious worker and you're faced with "compelling evidence" in your own discipline? What do you do when you've spent your life in religious service, and you come to believe that the foundational writings of your faith are nothing more than fairy tales?

Once again, you have several choices. You can choose to remember theories are sometimes overturned under the weight of new evidence. You can once again declare, "Well, I know that my views do not coincide with the current consensus, but . . ." Again, you'll look stupid. Or, you can do what Wellhausen did. He realized the implications of his "discovery". As an intellectually consistent man, he resigned his position as a trainer of Christian ministers and took a position as professor of ancient languages in a different school.

In our modern age, people who wish to enjoy the respect of modern readers attempt to avoid being judgmental. Being so is considered bad, even mean. I'm afraid, though, I will have to indulge in some judgmentalism. You'll note I used the words "intellectually consistent" for Julius Wellhausen. I say this because he did the right thing. He realized there was no point in teaching Christian or Jewish theology when you believe the writings forming the basis of these belief systems are nothing more than a collection of myths. Sadly, there were many others of his day who did otherwise.

You have to understand the position of ministers and religious workers in Europe and America back then. These people had professions, which commanded respect from society at large. Not all positions paid well, but at least they provided a salary and a place to live. Of course, some positions at larger churches provided more generous compensation. In Germany, for example, the Lutheran church was state-sponsored, funded with tax dollars. This wasn't just a good income, but a steady one. Add to this the fact that most in ministry were people who invested heavily in an education preparing them for one thing: the pulpit of a church. In many cases, they could do little else. There were no used cars in those days, much less used-car salesmen. You could dig ditches for a much lower salary and live in a little rented room somewhere, but this is hard when you've grown accustomed to an orderly office and a clean parsonage. The upper classes who drove by in fancy carriages had a way of looking down on common laborers, but a minister? You almost always got a smile and a nod if you wore a clergyman's uniform.

What a dilemma—to have such a good life and to know it will all disappear if you admit you've lost your faith in traditional views of scripture; but wait, there's an answer. There's a way to go on enjoying your lifestyle: *convince yourself it's perfectly reasonable to teach religion based on fairy tales.* With this, the movement called "liberal theology" was born. Liberal theology takes many forms today, but there are always four basic components: (1) the Bible is not the infallible expression of God; (2) it's possible to generate faith from ancient myths and tall tales; (3) there is some good reason to provide a salary for religious workers who believe numbers 1 and 2; and (4) it's possible to call this new religion "Christian".

Of course, your work isn't done by merely convincing yourself. You need to keep the current flock together if you're going to fund all this. To be honest and upfront, you'd need to hold a meeting and state the following: "I've come to doubt the traditions on which this church was built, so I suggest we follow a new path where we discard the Bible as the foundation of our faith." However, this is risky; you might be fired. Maybe it's better to start small. You assume people who come to your church are attached to phrases and images associated with the church. So, you keep the phrases. You just *change the meanings.* You also keep the images. You just *change the associations behind the images.*

First, the Bible is no longer the perfect expression of God's will for us. The Bible is a collection of fairy tales. Wait! Did I say "fairy tales"? That will never do. How about "faith stories" or some such? Centuries ago, people were sitting around campfires in the Middle East thinking warm thoughts about God. While thinking warm thoughts, they adapted their fairy tales (I'm sorry, I keep saying that—let's try "morality tales") to include their warm thoughts of God. This made them moral. So, the core of religion is to think warm thoughts about God and to be moral. You think I'm kidding? I attended a church years ago where the pastor declared with a smile on his face that sophisticated people in the modern age don't take the story of Noah's flood literally. Instead, they take it as encouragement to be kind to animals.

After making this statement, the minister stopped for a moment and beamed, appearing quite proud of his revelation.

Now, if the Bible isn't an authoritative representation of God's will, then we certainly have to do something with words like *sin*. In the Bible, sin is what happens when we disobey God's laws and fall short of His perfect character. Without the Scriptures, we can't know either of these things. So, to the liberal theologian, sin becomes bad behavior as determined by whatever people feel at the moment.

In fact, if you think about it, can we know anything for certain? If the Scriptures were the product of people sitting around a campfire thinking warm thoughts, who's to say their warm thoughts are better than anyone else's warm thoughts? This means all religions are equal. All roads lead to God. Maybe God is a creator. Maybe he's (she's? it's?) just a force. Maybe he expresses himself in the forms of many gods. Maybe he appears in different ways to different people, depending on his mood at the time. He's Jesus to one person and a large bird to another. I had a friend who worked at the denominational headquarters of a group guided by liberal theology. She was a believer. She had to leave when the heads of this one-time Christian denomination installed a totem pole and suggested all employees should have meditations and prayers in the presence of this statue.

Since the enlightened know all religious thoughts are equal, the biggest sin is to suggest otherwise. Sin is now defined as being *intolerant* or *judgmental*. Who are we to judge another's lifestyle or religious preferences? We just need to get together and think warm thoughts; and please, let's not talk about hell. Let's not even go there. How about if we just forget that one for now?

Finally, if there's no sin, then you must figure out what to do with the cross of Christ. Scripture teaches Christ was the God-Man who offered Himself as a sacrifice on the cross. We deserved to die because of our sins. We deserved the anger of God; but Christ allowed the wrath of God and the penalty of our sins to be placed on Him while on the cross. These are all offensive ideas to the modern theological elite; but the cross is the main symbol of Christianity and has been for centuries. So, you keep it, but you change its *meaning*. Liberal theologians say something like "Sacrifice sounds good, so let's keep that. Dying for a cause sounds very noble, so we'll keep that, too. So, Christ died *as an example*. Of what, no one is sure. But the thought generates lots of warm feelings, so it will do the trick nicely."

Once we've updated the church dictionary, we can consider church images. The liberal theologian starts again, "Surely Jesus had a lot of warm thoughts about God, just like us. So, we can keep the stained-glass windows with pictures of Jesus looking thoughtfully skyward. And oh yes, all the pictures of Jesus holding little children and baby lambs; those are great. Let's keep them around"; and so on. If you have the privilege of designing a new church building, you can limit images to those which generate warm feelings. If you want, you can throw in a few traditional images, such as a man with long hair staring at you with a blank expression while holding his hand in the "blessing" position.

Somewhere in this orgy of warm thoughts, though, we must ask the question "Why?" At some point, someone has to come to the realization that without the Scriptures, we really can't know anything about Jesus with certainty. There are vague references to Him in other historical literature of the day, but they don't tell us much other than He existed.

Of course, you can start a quest for the "historical Jesus". This is popular in major news magazines around Easter because it generates sales. To do that, you must give equal weight to anything that anyone ever wrote about the man called Jesus.

Think of this in the modern age: Imagine some sort of holocaust hit the world and wiped out almost everything. Centuries later, archeologists start digging in the ruins and find a sensationalistic tabloid magazine. Can you imagine one of them saying, "Wow, apparently there were creatures called 'aliens' in those days. Here's a picture of one of them talking to someone called 'the president' of a place called 'The United States'. This has to be true, because someone took the time to write it!"

There were lots of people who wrote about Jesus in the days of the early church. Some were sincere but misguided. Others were con artists. Those writings are as useful as modern tabloid articles. As such, they were rejected as worthless by church leaders who were much closer to the original sources than we are almost two thousand years later. The books church leaders identified as proper components of the Bible stood up under scrutiny of experts living at the time.

So again, why? The term *Christian* literally means, "Little Christ". It refers to someone who wants to be like Jesus. Why try to be like someone when you aren't really sure who he/she was? Jesus might have been a carpenter, or He might have been a baker. He might have been kind to women like Mary Magdalene, or He might have been an abusive man who beat women. He might have liked little children, or He might have been a crotchety old man who only kissed a few babies to make Himself look good when the press was around. Without the Scriptures, we don't know.

Why use Jesus as an example when you don't know what the example was for? If a fireman hears a crying baby and runs into a burning building, saving the infant but later dying from his injuries, that would be a great example of sacrifice. However, what if the fireman knows everyone is out of the building? He yells, "I want to be an example" and runs in. A few minutes later the building collapses on him, and he dies an agonizing death. What kind of example is that? If Jesus died on a cross and no one (much less Him) knew why, that would be a very poor example.

In this world, you can believe anything you want. You can believe aliens brought religion to the world (Däniken 1999). You can believe major religious figures were really mushrooms. Yes, really, there's a book with that thesis (Allegro 2009). You can make up whatever you want and call it a religion, but why would you want your religion to be called "Christian" when you can't be sure who Christ was?

The answer is because when the originators of liberal theology began their craft, there weren't a lot of jobs for people who wanted to throw out historic Christianity and invent a new religion. Ministers, parsons, religion professors, and so on lived with salaries paid by institutions endowed with lots of money. Years before, people who believed in the revealed God of the Scriptures wanted others to hear about Him. They worked hard and sacrificed large percentages of their earnings to build beautiful buildings and leave big trust funds with the intention that those resources would be used by faithful people to spread the good news of Jesus Christ. Sadly, those resources were taken over in later years by people who wanted nothing to do with the God of the Bible, but who wanted to live comfortable lives. One by one, churches and whole denominations were stolen from the people who created them.

The individuals who stole churches did good jobs of hiding themselves until there were enough of them to take over denominations. Later, those who believed in the Scriptures were forced to fight or leave. Many of those who chose to leave were told their church buildings were owned by the denominations, so an exit meant starting with nothing. For many, leaving meant losing salaries and even hard-earned pensions; but with great courage, leave they did. They started new denominations and new churches, many of which still thrive today and correctly bear the title "Christian". We're thankful for the sacrifice of those good people.

Let me be fair here (if fairness is called for). There are many religious workers today who've spent their lives listening to liberal theology. This stuff has been around for a long time. For them, there's no blatant dishonesty as there was with early originators of this attack on true spirituality. Today, you can attend famous divinity schools and graduate to churches and other institutions who *want* their ministers to reject the Bible. For today's liberal religious workers, the question is whether they're *intellectually honest*. One more time, why call your organization "Christian" when you don't think it's possible to know anything about Christ with certainty?

When you know nothing about God for certain, you're left with only one thing to do. Make up a god. You can start afresh, locking yourself away on a mountaintop and opening your mind to the universe. Or, you can create a mosaic of images collected from all over the world and from all ages. In the end, you have nothing more than an image born of your warm feelings. In olden days, people carved idols and worshipped them. In modern days, people take pictures of all the idols ever created and combine them. In many cases, the idolaters then place their images inside a covering statue; one with long hair, a beard, and a long gown. When they're done, they call the name of their newly created god "Jesus".

So today, we face a harsh reality. I wonder what Abraham would think? His whole meaning for life was leaving the false gods of his youth. What would he think of organizations created to carry on his legacy, but who, in some cases, look no different than the religions he left behind?

All of this leaves the followers of these new (and sometime warmed-over old) religions with a terrible problem.

Guilt and Shame

Humans have an inconvenient ability: they're capable of feeling guilt and shame. The first, guilt, exists on two levels. On one level, it's an emotion. We experience a negative feeling when we believe we've done something wrong. Accompanying this feeling is a sense that we deserve punishment. Guilt is different than regret, the feeling that we made an unprofitable decision, but we don't feel any penalty need come from it. On a more concrete level, there's legal guilt. That's a state where we're judged to be responsible for a crime by an established authority, which has the power to assign penalties for wrongdoing.

Shame, on the other hand, exists purely as an emotion. Shame is the feeling something is wrong with us, making us deserve rejection from others. Shame asks, "How can you show your face here after what you've done?"

Again, humans have no ability to perfectly sense ultimate reality. So, in our state of disconnect with God, we sometimes feel guilty about things we needn't feel guilty about. On the other hand, there's such a thing as legitimate guilt. For example, the Ten Commandments tell us "You shall not commit adultery." If someone has been unfaithful to his/her spouse, hearing this commandment often arouses guilty feelings. This is because God has created in us an ability to respond to Him when He communicates with us.

Though imperfect, the feelings we experience at times like this indicate a real problem. We're guilty of breaking one of God's laws, and we deserve to be punished. The feeling we experience is "hard wired" into us and represents spiritual reality. What should we do in these situations?

The Scriptures tell us we should diligently study God's revealed words, so we can know what pleases and displeases Him. We need to know His laws well. We must understand the times in history when people did things that made Him angry. When we understand this, we'll understand whether the guilt we feel represents a spiritual reality (we've broken one of God's laws) or false guilt (we haven't done anything wrong by God's standards). For those times when we're guilty of breaking God's laws—and the Scriptures teach, "All have fallen short of the glory of God" (Rom. 3:23)—we're instructed to approach God and ask Him to forgive us. One of the main reasons Jesus Christ came to earth and died on the cross was to pay the real penalty our sins have incurred. If we sincerely ask forgiveness, God eagerly grants it. From there, we're told something amazing: "Therefore, there is now no condemnation for those who are in Christ Jesus" (Rom. 8:1).

"No condemnation." There's no penalty. God won't be angry with us ever again if we've sincerely asked for forgiveness through Jesus Christ. Give yourself a minute to consider this. Let it soak in. If you didn't respond the last time we invited you to consider forgiveness in Jesus Christ, maybe this is the time.

Sometimes our consciences have berated us for so long, we don't know how to handle forgiveness. Getting our consciences to catch up with this new spiritual reality can be challenging. However, with encouragement and prayer, people who understand this principle enjoy a powerful, freeing dynamic in their lives.

Again, though, there's a problem for people who don't wish to follow God. Guilt can be troubling. What to do?

One of the goals of liberal theology is to disqualify the idea that there is anything such as real guilt from God. Some try to solve the problem of guilt by suggesting humans do, in fact, have an ability to sense ultimate reality. If we all "perceive" together, we'll eventually come up with a correct sense of right and wrong. Anyone who wants to attempt to perceive ultimate truth can get in line and give it a try. His/her observations will be as good as anyone else's. One of the problems here is the tendency for the perceiver to miss anything wrong in his/her own life. "Right" tends to be whatever they're good at doing. "Wrong" tends to be what others do.

Unfortunately, you haven't solved the problem of guilt. It hasn't gone anywhere.

Legalism

One popular solution for guilt is something called *legalism*. Legalism is the belief that it's possible to earn God's favor by performing good deeds and avoiding bad deeds. Good deeds earn points; bad deeds earn demerits. For the legalist, life is a long, hard process of getting as many points as you can while avoiding demerits. They believe that one day when they stand before God, a scale will appear. Good deeds will go on one side and bad deeds on the other. Hopefully, the good will outweigh the bad. The biggest problem here is one we explained at length earlier. This is not how God works; God cannot be paid back. He certainly cannot be paid off. He gives the gift of Jesus Christ for free. Attempting to earn salvation insults God.

Even if God did work this way, how do you determine the weight of right and wrong? Most people think adultery is a bad idea, but, how bad? Can you make up for it by volunteering in a hospital? If so, how long do you need to volunteer? One hour? An afternoon? A day? A week? You'd never know. For people who believe in legalism, life is like the little wheel in the rat's cage. You run and run forever, never knowing when you've achieved your goal. Again, even if God worked this way, imagine you've spent your whole life performing one good deed after another. You arrive at the gates of Heaven, and the scale comes out. Your good deeds go on one side and bad on the other. You watch with great anticipation as the piles grow. Finally, the last deed falls into place. Guess what? After all that, you find out you're one point short. Sorry! You go off into judgment.

This is why people who follow a legalistic philosophy tend at the core to be afraid. Their standing with God is precarious.

So again, guilt hasn't gone away. What now? Perhaps we can get some help.

Psychology

With the elimination of an objective reason for guilt, what do you do if you still feel guilty? Answer: You can assume guilt is always an unrealistic feeling. Perhaps it's a kind of sickness. Enter psychology.

Before going on, I want to mention that psychology is a complex and sophisticated field. Over the last few centuries, psychologists have discovered helpful insights into the mind. Psychologists and other mental-health workers have helped multitudes. However, I want to focus on one aspect of psychology which is a cause for concern.

When I walked into my first college psychology class, I thought we were going to talk about Sigmund Freud and people lying on benches complaining about their parents. Instead, our class was shown pictures of nerves and eyeballs. If you understand the history of psychology, this makes sense.

Psychology grew out of neurology. Nerves are the way we interact with the world. We have special nerves all over our bodies that receive input from our surroundings. The brain itself is a massive collection of nerve cells managing information in the form of biological electrical circuitry.

To those who believe in a Creator, the nervous system is yet one more reason to revere the One who made us. The body for believers is a holy vessel, which allows a human soul to interact with the world. Our brains are wonderful things where heavenly and earthly realities meet. For someone who doesn't believe in a Creator, though, the body is something else. It's a *machine*, a complex one, but still a machine; nothing more, nothing less. As a product of random processes, there's no soul; nothing remains after the machine stops functioning. When you start with a materialistic base, problems in the mind are no different than problems in the body. Problems only occur because of injury or illness. Guilt, then, is merely a symptom of a sickness needing to be cured.

The most famous psychologist is Sigmund Freud. Freud was a product of his time. As far as religion goes, he had no time for traditional biblical faith. He loved evolutionary theory and applied it to problems of the human mind. Being no different than other animals, Freud stipulated, humans were driven to reproduce. Therefore, humans are motivated by a seething cauldron of sexual energy, which he called the "id." Now, if all humans listened to the id alone, chaos would follow. It's hard to keep a species going with chaos. So, Freud reasoned that humans evolved a controlling force called the "super-ego". The ego, or self, lived in between these two forces. The super-ego is where the rules of one's society live and hence, belief in God with its accompanying sense of guilt. Since there's no God in Freud's world, guilt is an illusion. When it becomes bothersome, it can be dispelled with increased self-awareness. This self-awareness is reached with the help of an expert guide, like Freud.

Returning to my previous caveat, because of the sheer volume of data collected by psychologists, there are many useful things to be gleaned from psychology. Fortunately, there are many people sympathetic with biblical faith who've joined the study of the human mind. They've also discovered helpful insights. However, believers approach the science of psychology with care because it's dominated by atheism. Centers of study are guarded by those whose beliefs make them adverse to a biblical view of the mind. Believers are once again confronted with "mountains of compelling evidence" appearing to contradict their beliefs. Faith is reduced to merely wishful thinking. Guilt is just a form of illness curable with the proper combination of medications and therapy.

Here's the biggest problem of all: guilt has a way of returning, no matter how hard we work to explain it away. It may change form. It may get suppressed, but there is only one way to completely and permanently cure guilt. Real guilt must be forgiven by the real God. Until the reality of God's love and forgiveness is grasped by our minds, and experienced in our hearts, guilt will always persist, plaguing individuals and entire societies.

Moving On

In this chapter, we've met some of the gods of the modern world. In the next few, we'll look more at the ways they've influenced modern culture.

Chapter 23

The Modern "Gods" and Sexuality

Who Will Be King?

In the last chapter, we looked at a series of events spanning centuries. We've been introduced to abstract gods like the god of smart, and we've seen how events unfolded to create a world atmosphere that's adverse to those interested in the God of Scripture.

This was foreseen millennia ago:

> Why do the nations conspire
> and the peoples plot in vain?
> The kings of the earth take their stand
> and the rulers gather together
> against the LORD
> and against his Anointed One.
> "Let us break their chains," they say,
> "and throw off their fetters." (Psalm 2:1–3)

Some of the world's residents aren't interested in following the world's rightful king. The Tower of Babel has returned, albeit in symbolic form. A rebellion is planned. The great battle continues. We've seen how foundations for the battles of this age have been laid. Let's move on to see the world those who rebel against God want to create; and let's look at the gods that will be worshipped in that world.

The "God of Smart" revisited

Not too long ago, "smart" was unpopular. "Pretty" or "handsome" were good ways to be popular. Lots of people want to look like fashion models. "Strong" was always good—athletes have long been admired by the crowds.

Strong and beautiful meet in Hollywood every week, as action heroes save the world in just a few hours. But smart? For a long time, smart was the way to lose your favorite girl to the muscle-bound guy on the beach. Smart boys and girls wore thick glasses and stayed home studying, while the good-looking and strong had fun at parties.

This all changed with the computer age. Suddenly, we realized smart people were inventing gadgets that earned them lots of money. The guy with the thick glasses now had an attractive woman on each arm and drove an expensive car (assuming he didn't have a driver). Soldiers who previously relied on strength now had computerized gizmos built by the guy with the thick glasses. With those devices, one highly skilled soldier can take on an army of hapless combatants equipped with only old-fashioned firearms.

The smart people are revolutionizing every aspect of our lives. Who would try to run an office without a computer? I grew up in a world where you always carried some coins, so you could make calls from something called a "payphone". With modern communication, payphones are ancient history.

The smart people are giving doctors tools capable of healing sicknesses that used to wipe out whole populations. They're helping farmers produce ever-increasing harvests. They're improving our lives every day. "Smart" has gained social value—and rightly so.

Unfortunately, the smart people also took some bad turns—not all of them, but enough to create problems for people of faith. Our universities have become filled with smart people who believe they've supplanted God. They certainly believe they've disproven the Scriptures of the Jewish and Christian faiths. How about those five "Ps"? Prosperity? The markets of the Western world are now filled with affordable food and clothing. In a large supermarket close to me, there's an entire aisle allocated to pet food. We have so much food; even our pets need weight-loss regimens. Protection? We have massive ships to patrol our oceans and supersonic warplanes to watch our skies. We have bombs so powerful they can destroy entire cities. Pleasure? We know how to distill the best ingredients out of just about everything. We experience the best flavors and the most complex sights and sounds. Of course, our psychologists and physiologists have analyzed sexuality. They've written enough material to keep us happy in the bedroom for years. When our body parts start to give out, there are happy little pills in bright colors to keep us going strong. I don't think I can even begin to address all the ways people pursue power.

In order to keep God at proper distance though, you need the fourth "P": popularity. If you can control access to this, you've got what it takes (or so it would seem) to pull off a peaceful coup in the Kingdom of God. One atheist writer states this clearly. He looks forward to a world where religion is eventually eliminated. His method? Something he refers to as *religious intolerance*. Thankfully, he's very quick to point out that he's not looking for a kind of intolerance that places people in prisons when they dissent. Rather, he advocates something he calls *conversational intolerance*.

> When people make outlandish claims, without evidence, we stop listening to them—except on matters of faith. I am arguing that we can no longer afford to give faith a pass in this way. Bad beliefs should be criticized wherever they appear in our discourse—in physics, in medicine, and on matters of ethics and spirituality as well. (May; Interview with Sam Harris)

On the surface, this seems reasonable enough. Shouldn't we all reject *out-landish* claims, whatever the topic? In practice though, I find that statements about faith get labeled outlandish more quickly than statements about science. In scientific discussions, it's normal to discuss evolutionary theory without mentioning that it conflicts with the laws of thermodynamics. Suggesting the same laws support the idea of a great organizing force in the universe is branded outlandish.

Practically speaking, the idea of creating conversational intolerance means that when the smart people talk, they shouldn't be challenged. If speakers are smart, and someone challenges them, what does that make the challenger? Obviously, it makes him/her a dummy.

With "smart" unbelievers solidly in control of centers of higher learning, those in power now work overtime to spread the gospel of a godless world. Those content with lower degrees and those pursuing nonscientific programs have no alternative but compliance. What kind of business major would challenge the instructor in an elective science class? The most talented accountant doesn't dare confront the masters-level student who teaches introductory classes, much less the revered professor who has obtained a PhD. Possession of a degree from a good school is often a ticket to the halls of power in society. So, most students choose to give complete submission rather than risk their keys to successful lives. Because of this, the elite echelons of society are now almost fully populated with those who have complied with their professors—those who knelt to worship in the temples of secularism that are now our major universities.

Sexuality

This is the "send the children from the room" section. Many people remember a time somewhere around puberty when a parent sits down with a youngster, and they have "the sex talk". It may sound strange, but after parents are done having this talk with their children, they might consider moving on to talk with their religious leaders, too. In this section, we'll find out why.

As we discussed earlier, Freud's view of human motivation involved a total reduction of human drives into the cauldron of sexual energy called the id. Humans started as lower animals no different than their cousins the primates. Higher functions such as ego and super-ego evolved later. According to Freud, much of the modern subconscious involved sexual thoughts that got repressed and mixed around, only to surface later in odd dreams or questionable, compulsive behavior.

With this as the foundation, psychologists began to describe people as "sexual beings". If this is true, what should humans do? Well, among other things, they should be involved in sexual relations, of course.

This idea advanced further when Abraham Maslow conceived the famous "Hierarchy of Needs". Humans have needs, which can be arranged in levels of progressive order, according to Maslow. First and foremost are physiological needs. Air, water, and food are required to keep our bodies properly fueled. Sleep, warmth, and the ability to eliminate byproducts of the fueling process are also necessary. Few would disagree. It's interesting, though, that Maslow suggested the possibility that sex belonged at the base of the pyramid. He stated, "Sex may be studied as a purely physiological need (Maslow 2013, 10). Maslow's discussion of the priority of sex is complex, leading some to draw his pyramid with sex in the base. Others leave it out. Sex can be merely reproductive, or sex can be associated with other, more complex emotional needs. The point is, sex is part of the list of needs. Unless the needs of each level are met, it is surmised, higher levels cannot be reached. What happens when major components of this hierarchy are missing? The result, Maslow suggests, is illness on some level, whether physical or mental. At first glance, this appears reasonable. Many are enamored with this theory of human motivation. Unfortunately, the theory has two problems.

The first problem is the assumption of a "need". I'd like to suggest you only have needs when you have a goal. Let's say I'm sitting in an automobile. I want to drive somewhere. In order to do so, I need fuel. So, my goal is a location. I have a need for fuel if I'm going to reach the goal of a certain location. Let's say, though, the car is a luxury car. All I want to do is sit in it and look impressive to attractive women wandering by. I don't need fuel for that. You can argue that the car is much more impressive if it's able to move, so reaching higher levels of prestige gets us back to putting something in the fuel tank.

The point is, needs are only relevant in relation to goals. If we carefully examine our goals in life, we may find things classified as needs that aren't such. We may desire them. We may long for them, but need them? No.

This leads the second point: It's the reason I challenge the inclusion of sex as a need.

Let's take the illustration further. Assume the car is a convertible, and you lower the roof. You look up and see a missile with a nuclear warhead hurtling straight toward you. It's going to hit you in ten seconds. Suddenly, fuel is irrelevant. In fact, air, water, food, sleep, and yes, sex, all disappear as needs. You're about to enter eternity. Your goals change completely.

"Isn't that a little extreme?" some might ask. Yes, it is. However, our world is in a more extreme position than most realize. If that illustration is unacceptable, how about something more common? The car has stopped at an intersection when a vehicle in the oncoming lane loses control. Unfortunately, our world can be a dangerous place. Eternity has a funny way of being thrust into our lives when we least expect it.

We stand each day at the feet of a Creator God who offers us fantastic gifts. If we don't accept, we enter a tragic eternity. What we *need* is the ability to relate to God, to please Him, and to have faith in Him. That's the only way to be prepared for the eternity we may enter at any moment.

More than this, God offers to help us in this life. If we seek Him, the apostle Paul says, "My God will meet all your needs according to his glorious riches in Christ Jesus" (Philippians. 4:19).

Even if you disagree with my theory of what people really need, history books are full of people who had all but the most basic needs taken from them. We know about them because they triumphed through strength in the depth of their spirits. They survived gulags and concentration camps. They watched their civilizations destroyed in wars. Their spirits helped them survive and even thrive.

On the other hand, many of us know people who whimper at the faintest suggestion they'll have to live without luxuries.

Granted, we need food, air, and water to survive any length of time. However, when your goal is to please God, other things higher on Maslow's pyramid become what I'll call "nice to haves". If you don't have God, your goal becomes surviving and obtaining comfort in this life. If you add to this empty life the pronouncements of the smart people that you have "needs", then getting those needs met becomes your goal.

This attitude becomes particularly significant when dealing with human sexuality.

To summarize scripture on this topic: We aren't sexual beings. We're spiritual beings for whom sexuality is a significant and powerful component. The first two humans were created male and female. They were "naked and unashamed" (Gen. 2:25). This relates symbolically to all levels of emotion, but it also concerns sexuality. God created Adam and Eve with the ability to relate sexually. They were not to be embarrassed about this wonderful gift from their Creator.

Sexuality is intended exclusively to be enjoyed between two adult human beings, one male and one female. It's intended to be part of a bonding relationship in which participating individuals make a covenant to love and serve each other for life. This covenantal relationship is, of course, better known as marriage. In the earliest mention of human creation, Moses wrote: "For this reason a man will leave his father and mother and be united to his wife, and they will become one flesh" (Gen. 2:24). When a man and a woman marry, they're "united" and become "one flesh". These are powerful phrases. The Hebrew word for *one* is the same word used to say that God is one. In this context, it denotes mystical unity—a powerful and permanent bond between two people.

When everything's working well, this often results in procreation. The covenantal bond includes caring for children produced by this union in a family. Some feel sexual relations are so special, they should only be employed when the intention is to have children. Others would say sex can be enjoyed by married people, even if they aren't intending for children to result. Sadly, there isn't room in this book to address that issue. Suffice it to say that sincere people disagree.

Sex is, of course, extremely enjoyable; it's *meant* to be. In fact, it's more than enjoyable. Sex is designed to make people want to come back for more. We often speak of a "sex drive", which compels people to seek sexual relationships. In the marriage relationship, this is a good thing.

In a broken world, sex becomes something different. Instead of being a force that drives people together in love, it becomes a force that compels people to seek self-gratification. Men and women approach each other only because they have urges. They're experiencing an itch they want scratched. If something more comes about afterward, that's great. If it doesn't, just move on to the next experience. Why should it be different? Don't our best psychological minds tell us sex is a need? When something is a need, you'd be foolish to avoid having it met somehow, wouldn't you? How can you become a "fulfilled person" when your needs aren't being met? Come to think of it, what kind of a person would try to prevent you from having your needs met? It seems only bad people would do something like that.

As such, the mention of Judeo-Christian morality is worse than old fashioned. People who suggest it's possible to be happy when "your needs aren't being met" and who discourage immediate gratification are thought to be weird. To people who assume the "sex as a need" line of thinking, that's all there is to it.

During all this, reality sneaks in. For some reason, the idea of lifelong love between a man and a woman continues to infest our children's storybook tales. The prince meets the princess, and they all live happily ever after. Our modern songs continue to be filled with lyrics of people promising true love and lifelong commitment to each other. The smart people call us out of our "idealistic fantasies" and back into a world where sex is a need that must be met in order to be happy. How do we work out all this?

In our open-minded world, everyone is free to do whatever works for them. One person goes to the bar every weekend and picks up a new lover with each visit, or at least that's the goal. Another looks for longer relationships but feels obligated to take the respective partner on a "test drive" to make sure the outcome of a commitment would endure. Living together becomes a normal status for couples.

Here's a big problem: what do you do when you can't find a partner? People are strange sometimes. They'll state at the party that we're sexual beings—and it's perfectly legitimate for people to have their needs met. When a man with such a "need" approaches a woman to have his need met, well, those uncaring females have a funny way of denying the request. "Sorry, you're not my type," they say to surprised males who thought having needs met was noble. How uncivilized of those women!

In some cases, individuals can be found who'll help for a price. At one time, prostitution was a profession looked on with disdain by the Western world; it was seen by some as a wholly unacceptable practice. Others viewed it as a necessary evil and sought to limit its practice to small areas of cities with names like "red-light district" and such. Today, there's discussion about making the practice legal. Some regions have done so; others are working on it. Even where prostitution is legalized, though, it's expensive.

Because of this, we've learned to produce sexual experiences based on *fantasy*. Early in this book, we compared the creative urges of animals with the creative practices of humans. Animals create by instinct. Their creative abilities are "hard wired", so most species of birds build nests that look similar. Humans, on the other hand, have a more complex range of creative abilities. One of the things making this possible is our ability to imagine. We can see what things will look like in our minds before we begin making them. This is one of the amazing abilities God placed in our brains, which allow us to share in His divine nature. He loves to create things; we love to create things. He plans His creative works in advance. So do we.

This quality of imagination is very powerful and can grow into fantasy. Our imaginations can produce experiences so vivid, they seem almost real. Sadly, in our broken bodies, these experiences can get out of control. We all hope for "sweet dreams" when we sleep, but sometimes our dreams go bad and become nightmares. We wake up in a cold sweat because the people chasing us or attacking us in the dream seem real. For people with mental illness, this experience spills over into real life. People with certain kinds of mental illness hear voices when nothing is there.

When fantasy intersects sexuality, the experience can seem very real. In the absence of a partner, one can simply imagine a sexual encounter. Merely by the force of such imagination, the bodily mechanisms that would otherwise result in intercourse can be aroused. When the mind reaches its limits, hands become involved, leading to self-stimulation, or masturbation.

Imagining can be hard work; it can also be repetitive and eventually boring. Enter pornography.

Finding attractive women who'll take off their clothes for any man is difficult. Such women are rare. If you can find one, they're usually expensive. However, finding women willing to remove clothing for an artist or a photographer is easier. They're still not the majority. Apparently, though, it's much easier to get a woman to strip in a controlled area when no physical contact is involved than otherwise. The resulting pictures can be shown to any man, but the emotional connection has been severed, making it easier on all who participate, whether producers or viewers. Years ago, this was limited to paintings. However, modern photography and printing have allowed this practice to blossom into an industry. The Internet has allowed this industry to become almost omnipresent.

The practice looks like this: A man wants sex but is told "no" by prospective partners. So, he just obtains pictures of beautiful women who have undressed for the camera and enters a fantasy. He becomes aroused and eventually masturbates. His "need" has been met, or so it seems. How about the attractive woman in the picture and her publisher? If she was providing real sex for money, she'd be called a prostitute and her facilitator a pimp. Now she's a "glamour model" or sometimes an "aspiring actress". The publisher becomes a savvy businessman. It's all perfectly legitimate now. By the way, when the "glamour models" discuss their work on television, they generally leave out the part about men masturbating after viewing the pictures. That doesn't fit the "glamour" template very well.

Again, all this has problems. The biggest problem: We weren't designed for most of the ways sex is experienced in the modern world. We were designed for marriage between a man and a woman; anything else is a cheap substitute. As much as sex can be a wonderful thing, in our broken world, it can be challenging even between committed people. It takes a radical commitment to God and to each other to enjoy God's gift of sex the way God intended. Anything less leaves people wanting. This causes more problems. Let's take a look at them.

As I said, sex leaves you wanting more. In marriage, that's good because you can come back later; but outside of marriage, the drive can get out of control. For some, it's the emptiness following a failed hunting expedition at the bar. For others, the sensations created by commitment-less sex grow into cravings. At some point, the normal substitutes can't keep up. The magazine purchase becomes the magazine subscription. The attractive feature model gets boring after a while and needs replacement. So, you get the new "girl of the month" with each issue.

The models in the magazine? They're perfect. However, they're rarely perfect in real life. To reach perfection, blemishes are carefully removed by photographers with computer programs. Body parts must be reshaped. Breasts must be enlarged. After a while, it becomes hard for many men to be motivated by the normal women surrounding them.

This is particularly sad for women, who become objects. Even those well above average in appearance get tired of looking perfect every minute of every day. If marriage occurs, there's the quiet suspicion women have about that pile of magazines in the closet. "Accepting" and "enlightened" women shrug off the feelings of unfair competition and assume their men are just acting normally. After a while though, it begins to sink in. The girl of the month doesn't age. She doesn't put on weight. She doesn't have "that time of the month". She's never upset. Month after month, year after year, there is a never-ending line of attractive women willing to take off their clothes for the camera. Month after month, real women watch as their men drift farther and farther away. Aging is challenging enough in marriage without this competition; but with it, women become devastated by the virtual wandering of their husbands. Who knows how many marriages have been destroyed by the "Girl of the Month"?

The problems get worse. Sometimes the quiet trips to the closet magazine stash grow into ever-increasing longings for more and more variety. Perhaps a little more "creative sex" can solve the issues? Maybe a little violence?

Whatever you "need", you need more of it. At some point, you have a full-fledged addiction.

What makes counterfeit sex addictive? On a larger level, what makes anything addictive? Sex, maybe more than any of our other drives, is complex. When it's working right, sex accompanies all kinds of legitimate human wants—it's not just pleasurable. Sex can come with companionship. Sex can come with love. Sex can be fun. Sex can be relaxing. Sex can be affirming. Any of these are fine, but when a counterfeit appears, these real desires can be counterfeited, too. We want love, but we settle for sex with a stranger instead. We want companionship, but again the sexual act is made to suffice. A good prostitute doesn't just supply pleasure; she tells the customer how desirable and important he is. She can fake an orgasm with the best of them, leaving the most ungifted of men with the feeling they're macho giants. That's what keeps a prostitute's clients coming back for more, apart from sex.

One way of attacking any addiction, including a sexual one, is to understand its roots. We're chasing something because it's a cheap substitute for other emotional longings. What we need are ways to provide real companionship and real love, not the fleeting counterfeits provided by the sex industry.

Besides the toll taken on relationships, sexual addictions often become economically devastating. Counterfeit sex can be very expensive. That's one of the things conspicuously missing in discussions among the worshippers of "smart". If people have needs, and it's legitimate to have those needs met, why do "sex helpers" always charge for their services? There are plenty of charitable organizations helping people to meet the needs of food, clothing, and shelter when those are lacking. For some reason, there are no large organizations that give away sex for free. It seems you shouldn't even need an organization. There are some who suggest this is the way society should work. Every dinner should include sex for dessert. Every party should become an orgy. Somehow, though, after years of free thinking from the sex idealists, this hasn't happened. No, sex is sold at the highest price possible to customers who can afford it.

At one point in ministerial training, I felt led to study counseling. Among my various activities over the years is one I'll never forget: I moderated a recovery group for men with sexual addictions. The stories told were sad indeed. One man lost his marriage because he "couldn't stop himself" from picking up new women everywhere he went. Another was heavily in debt to phone sex lines, which charged outrageous fees for conversations with an actress who played the role of an imaginary prostitute. Others couldn't go near a computer for fear of the uncontrollable urge to download pornographic images. The urge to do so even occurred at work where addicts could be caught and disciplined for such inappropriate use of corporate equipment on company time.

As if it's not enough to have the adult population tormented by out-of-control sex, some are trying to expand the corruption of this societal attitude to children. Some educators are attempting to introduce the idea of free sex to children in elementary school. If sex is a need, why deprive children of this wonderful experience? Educators who follow this philosophy want to hand out condoms and other birth control to children. Why make children figure out how to masturbate on their own? How can you get the supreme experience you deserve by hiding in your bedroom using trial and error? That's not very efficient. So, some educators want to include masturbation techniques in sex-education classes.

Why all this haste to move the border of sexual experience to the young? If you understand the possibility of a world in rebellion against God, the answer is clear. It's because sex makes you want more. It's addictive. As purveyors of tobacco and other drugs know, the earlier you get someone hooked, the harder it is to stop. The earlier you get people hooked on counterfeit sex, the harder it will be for them to experience sex the way God intended it. That's why it's so important for a rebellious world to advocate sex as early as possible.

Chapter 24

A Problem for Followers of the Modern "Gods": Guilt

Certain Types of Liberation Have Unexpected Costs

So, now you're liberated! You can participate in free sex whenever you want. Well, free in the moral sense, or course. Sex has a funny way of getting expensive, as we discussed. Of course, we haven't even begun to get into all the ways people seek pleasure. Drugs and alcohol always help the party, or so many think. Somehow, all the noise, all the pleasure, and all the mind-altering experiences eventually end. There in a quiet place, we're left with the gnawing feeling that something's wrong—terribly wrong.

Maybe other people just want to quietly live their life apart from God, without open rebellion or self-destructive behavior. They just want to go to work, make a living, and go home. Even here, there's something missing. There's the sense we should be pursuing something higher, something better.

This is the problem of guilt.

Guilt can be very annoying, really. It simply won't go away for most people. All people have at least one thing that makes them feel guilty if they get quiet for too long. The true God offers us a solution to guilt: confession and forgiveness. The apostle John wrote:

> If we claim to be without sin, we deceive ourselves and the truth is not in us. If we confess our sins, he is faithful and just and will forgive us our sins and purify us from all unrighteousness. If we claim we have not sinned, we make him out to be a liar and his word has no place in our lives. (I John 1:8–10)

I was careful to avoid saying God offers us an *easy* solution. Facing your sins and bringing them before God can be hard, but it's also very freeing. Confession involves looking at our actions the way God looks at them. We must agree with Him that those actions are wrong. If we're willing to ask for God's forgiveness through Jesus Christ, He happily grants it.

Counterfeit Ways of Dealing with Guilt

Sadly, there are counterfeit ways to deal with guilt, and there are lots of them. Let's look at a few.

Confess Someone Else's Sins

This one is very popular today. I've sat in on many a party where the main activity was discussing how evil *other people* are. *Other* people get involved in all kinds of bad behaviors, you know. Some of them get involved in legitimately bad things. Others get involved in new, chic sins decided upon by media personalities and the "smart" people. Oh, and don't forget those politicians. We'll get to them in more detail later, but for now they're a slippery crowd. "How did that guy get elected?" moans the partygoer as he rolls his eyes. "Why, everyone knows he's a _____ (crook, idiot, liar—fill in the blank). I've known people who must spend their entire day pressing their ear up to the television speaker, waiting in earnest for some new charge to be brought against their favorite public demon. It's as though they have a bag, and whenever something evil is announced, the statement goes into the bag. The bag grows and grows, allowing those who do this to become more and more obsessed with the sins, real or imagined, committed by the object of their hatred. Then, once every few years comes the consummation; the bag is emptied into the voting booth and the lever is pulled for the "right" candidate. On the other hand, maybe not? Voting might solve the problem. Some in this group prefer to stay home and complain rather than participate in a potential solution.

If no politicians are available, any famous person will do. Magazine racks are full of tabloids with the latest gossip on errant movie stars. Oh, and I almost forgot; the best targets are famous Christian ministers. There's something about finding dirt on a religious leader that allows those committed to a godless lifestyle to say, "See, I knew it all along—those people are *all* fakes." There are lots of sincere and dedicated people participating in ministry, but they're easy to ignore because they don't get into the newspapers. It takes only one disgrace to help the unbeliever continue his flight from God with full abandon.

Here's the problem with this approach to guilt. It doesn't count for anything. As a youngster in school, I had a friend who tried to explain a low, but passing, grade to his parents. His defense? "I know someone who failed!" He said this with great confidence, fully believing this fact made his mediocre efforts at scholarship worthwhile. Of course, his parents had to explain that finding one person who performed worse doesn't validate your bad performance. It's the same here. Obsessing about someone else's evil doesn't dismiss yours. Jesus spoke about this:

> Do not judge, or you too will be judged. For in the same way you judge others, you will be judged, and with the measure you use, it will be measured to you. Why do you look at the speck of sawdust in your brother's eye and pay no attention to the plank in your own eye? How can you say to your brother, 'Let me take the speck out of your eye,' when all the time there is a plank in your own eye? You hypocrite, first take the plank out of your own eye, and then you will see clearly to remove the speck from your brother's eye. (Matthew 7:1–5)

Jesus is clear; deal with your own heart first. After that, you can move on to others—if you still want to, and if you still have time. Those who deal with their own hearts are often less judgmental of others.

Punish People Who Practice Certain Sins

This is an extension of "confess someone else's sins". People who go this route proceed one step further than merely obsessing over the sins of others. They think if they identify a given sin as "the worst" and then go out and persecute people who practice this sin, somehow this action makes their own sins go away. Homosexuals are big victims of this practice. Punishers decide somehow that homosexuality is the worst sin—certainly worse than any sins committed by the punisher. The punisher then waits outside of bars and clubs where homosexuals are known to gather and attacks people who come out. Punishers are usually accompanied by enough friends to greatly outnumber victims. Apparently, courage is not a requirement for people with this mindset.

We are commanded to love those with whom we disagree. I mentioned earlier that the Bible clearly teaches sex is only to be enjoyed in marriage.

Biblical marriage is one-man-one-woman. However, you can read through the gospels as many times as you like, and you won't find any situations where Jesus instructs His followers to beat up gay people—or anyone else for that matter. There is no verse that states, "Jesus and his followers waited outside the gay bar and fell upon all who came out." We are to love people and seek the salvation of their souls, not the destruction of their bodies. If finding other people who are worse than you fails to take away your sins, certainly beating those people fails, too. Punishers of this sort belong in jail, not on the honor roles of the faithful.

Improve on Old Ways of Removing Guilt

Again, there is only one way of removing true guilt. You must confess your sins to God and ask Him to forgive you. For some reason, this doesn't seem good enough for many. As people throughout the years have looked for more practical ways to remove guilt, one item has popped up repeatedly: *help the underprivileged.*

Before going too far with this, I should stress that one of the signs of a spiritual rebirth is concern for those less fortunate than you. I would love to write a book about all of the wonderful acts of charity and mercy that have been shown by believers throughout the years, large and small. Hospitals were built and maintained long before there was any talk of public funding for such organizations and certainly before they became businesses. Orphanages were created when the streets of major cities were full of children whose parents were either dead or unable to raise them. Whether a handout to a needy individual or a major institution helping multitudes, history is lined with the generosity of believers who reached out to the less fortunate in God's name.

Unfortunately, this is a book about the ways that people have gone wrong over the years. One of the ways they've gone wrong is to abuse charity.

This problem is summed up in one statement by the apostle Paul: "If I give all I possess to the poor and surrender my body to the flames, but have not love, I gain nothing" (I Cor. 13:3).

When someone confesses sins to God, God renews their heart. When God regenerates a human heart, He places His love there. Driven by that love, the regenerated person gives, expecting nothing in return—least of all salvation. Salvation is first in line *before* we commit acts of charity. Salvation is not the *result* of those actions. Without the love of God in a person's heart, no act of charity matters for any eternal purpose.

People who misunderstand this go wrong in several ways. The first person believes forgiveness and salvation are purchased on a "pay as you go" plan. This person gives regularly, believing such giving is accumulating credit for heaven. This is like making regular deposits to a retirement fund to provide a safe retirement. It's a nice idea; however, scripture is clear in saying this isn't how things work.

Another person lives life any way they wish. They realize late in life that perhaps this wasn't the best way to spend their years on earth. As the entrance into eternity looms near, they decide to make a few big gifts. Some wealthier individuals even set up huge charitable institutions to give away riches after their death. Now, many people have benefitted from such giving, but sadly, the greatest of endowments doesn't provide a ticket to heaven. Even if you could purchase salvation, the idea that you can live off your wealth for most of your life and give it to the needy after you're through with it, leaves something to be desired from a spiritual perspective. It's like drinking most of the beverage from a bottle and offering God the last sip before throwing the bottle away.

The third problem is the oddest. If you get it into your head that forgiveness and salvation are commodities to be bought and sold, it makes sense that you would try to purchase those things with large sums of money. People in the third group, though, appear to be bargain hunters. In fact, they're just plain cheap. There's something about throwing pocket change into a collection plate at church or handing a can of food with a questionable expiration date to a homeless person that makes these people feel they've done plenty to get into heaven.

To each of these groups, Jesus tells a story:

> Jesus sat down opposite the place where the offerings were put and watched the crowd putting their money into the temple treasury. Many rich people threw in large amounts. But a poor widow came and put in two very small copper coins, worth only a fraction of a penny. Calling his disciples to him, Jesus said, "I tell you the truth, this poor widow has put more into the treasury than all the others. They all gave out of their wealth; but she, out of her poverty, put in every-thing—all she had to live on." (Mark 12:41–44)

If it were possible to purchase salvation, there would be only one price: everything you have. Anything short of this is a joke.

Did I say that the last group above was the strangest? I'm sorry, I'm wrong. There is one more even stranger. In order to introduce this group, let me share a story about the great Hebrew king David:

247

> On that day Gad went to David and said to him, "Go up and build an altar to the LORD on the threshing floor of Araunah the Jebusite." So David went up, as the LORD had commanded through Gad. When Araunah looked and saw the king and his men coming toward him, he went out and bowed down before the king with his face to the ground. Araunah said, "Why has my lord the king come to his servant?" "To buy your threshing floor," David answered, "so I can build an altar to the LORD, that the plague on the people may be stopped." Araunah said to David, "Let my lord the king take whatever pleases him and offer it up. Here are oxen for the burnt offering, and here are threshing sledges and ox yokes for the wood. O king, Araunah gives all this to the king." Araunah also said to him, "May the LORD your God accept you." But the king replied to Araunah, "No, I insist on paying you for it. I will not sacrifice to the LORD my God burnt offerings that cost me nothing." (II Samuel 24:18–24)

What's going on here? At one point during the rule of King David, a horrible plague broke out. Although plagues can break out randomly for reasons unknown to us, this particular plague was clearly identified as having been the result of sin. As such, David was instructed by a prophet named Gad to offer a sacrifice at a given location. The owner of the property offered to give it to David for free, but David refused. What was his reasoning? David shared a very important spiritual principle:

Spiritual sacrifices can't be made with other people's possessions.

For a sacrifice to be eternally effective, it must be made by *you*. It should involve your resources: your time, your money, and your possessions. By definition, a sacrifice should be something that's valuable to you. If it's not valuable to you, it's not a sacrifice.

Many miss this point; I call them the "Somebody-Elsers". I often hear people say something like, "I just heard about some really unfortunate people. It seems *somebody* should do something about that!" Somebody? How about you? Somehow, people in this very curious group can spend great amounts of time wringing their hands about all the "somebodies" who fail the needy of the world. The "somebodies" are usually the rich. "Those rich people just aren't doing their share to care for the poor" laments the Somebody-Elser.

The media is happy to help here. Somebody-Elsers love to watch TV and hear about desperate people at home and abroad. Pictures of starving children and victims of distant wars appear as often as the media can find them. People who watch this steady stream of victims develop a condition I call "caring constipation". They see a needy person and feel deep concern. They *care*. Unfortunately, the caring and deep concern doesn't motivate them to do anything. Who can help all the needy people who show up on TV? It seems a strange development has taken place. It's not necessary to do anything with these emotions. It's only important that you care. For people in this group, there is only one virtue: caring. If you care, you're a good person, and that's enough. Whether something actually gets done about the problem appears to be totally irrelevant.

Like many other substitutes for dealing with guilt, even the highest levels of caring leave a hole in the heart. Wait—did I say, nothing is done? How wrong of me! There's a group of people happy to see that something happens. They represent yet more gods of the modern age.

Chapter 25

Politicians and the Modern "Gods"

Politicians: we love them; we hate them. We'll discuss both in this chapter, but mostly the "hate them" part. Politicians are complex, but let's focus on one point: politicians love guilt-ridden people. Why? Because of the following principle:

Guilt-ridden people and their money are easily separated.

Imagine you're walking down the street one day and you see a needy man sitting under a tree. You feel bad for him. Maybe you feel guilty that you have money, and he doesn't. Now enters a man we'll call Pat the Politician. He sees your obvious concern and offers help. "Give me a hundred dollars, and I'll see that the needy man over there gets help." You give Pat the money. He walks away. You feel better. About a month later, you walk down the same street, and you see the same needy man. The problem is, he still looks needy. This time, you decide to talk with him personally. Let's call him Ned Needy. You walk up to Ned and say, "Hello." Ned answers back, "Have you got any spare change?" You answer, "I gave you all my spare money last month." Ned looks confused and says, "I'm sorry. The only person who gave me any money last month was Pat the Politician. I love Pat."

Now you're the one who's confused. Ned Needy has no idea you were the source of his income last month. He thinks it was Pat the Politician. You go on, "Well, I guess the hundred dollars helped?" Ned looks more confused. "No, it wasn't a hundred—it was something much less."

You gave Pat a hundred. What happened to the rest?

You decide to ask Pat about this. He's speaking at a rally downtown, so you go and take your place in the audience. You notice upon your arrival that Pat's clothing has improved a lot since you last saw him. He's obviously been employing a more expensive tailor since your first encounter. Pat walks up to the podium with a stern face and begins his speech. "There's a horrible problem in our country," he laments. "There are too many people who *don't care*. All around us are needy people." He goes on, "Elect me and I'll see that we battle this plague!" The crowd cheers. Pat continues, "Isn't it obvious my opponent doesn't *care?* He helps all of the uncaring, the greedy, and the selfish. But I know *you're* different! You *care!*"

Next to you, you see a man and women both very emotionally involved in the speech. The man wipes a tear from his eye. The woman cries out, "We love you, Pat." When finished, Pat rushes off the podium and disappears into a limousine with dark windows. He speeds away before you can ask him any questions.

Before going on, let's give the standard caveat: politicians with good hearts are helpful people. Unfortunately, lots of politicians lack good hearts. Their goals involve serving themselves rather than their fellow citizens. Sadly, I don't have to give examples. I don't need footnotes. Selfish and self-serving politicians are so common, everyone understands.

Here's how politics works: politicians take money from people and do things with it. Hopefully, they do things like fund police forces and fire companies. Hopefully, they build and maintain roads and other forms of infrastructure. On a national level, they fund a military. On all levels, politicians create laws making the lives of their constituents better—hopefully.

Somehow, though, the role of politicians has expanded. Over time, some people realized a lot of money was changing hands. Some who noticed this were dishonest, so money started getting funneled to them. Another time, someone noticed that public funds could go to things like "helping the needy". This sounds good on the surface, but the day politicians acted on this, some bad things happened.

To understand the problem, you must understand a scriptural view of charity. When people with the love of God in their hearts see a needy person, they could feel moved to offer help. As I've said, they would use their own resources. If asked by the recipient why the giver is offering help, the believer might respond, "God loves you, and He spoke to my heart." Perhaps the person receiving the help will be touched by this; perhaps they'll feel encouraged to seek God who, they're told, encouraged one of His followers to help them. In this way, people receiving help aren't just helped in this world; they're helped in the next, too. It's not just stomachs being fed; it's souls.

Or, the receiver could choose to do nothing; it's his/her choice. True charity doesn't come with coercion.

Having said this, givers sometimes notice something about "the needy". Some needy are truly needy; they lack the resources to help themselves.

Perhaps it's a health issue. Perhaps it's a mother abandoned and is left to raise children alone. The list goes on. Help is often offered no matter the response.

On the other hand, some "needy" people could help themselves if they wished to; they just don't wish to. For this group, it's easier to accept help than go out and work for a living. Or perhaps they've tried to work; they just haven't tried very hard. They don't like waking up at the same time every day and showing up to work at the agreed-upon time. They don't like to work very hard or very fast. They like to say nasty things about their employers when their employers look away. Maybe they like to drink or take drugs, despite warnings from friends that those indulgences are getting out of hand. Again, the list goes on.

For this last group, too much charity is a bad thing. When I first started reading through the Bible, I wasn't surprised to see examples of believers who felt led to help the less fortunate. I was very surprised, though, when I ran into the following:

If a man will not work, he shall not eat. (II Thessalonians 3:10)

From this we learn a simple, and to the modern ear, a stunning truth: *believers are under no obligation from God to help people who can work but who don't want to.* Some people need to run out of resources before they realize something is wrong with their lives. It's then they may appreciate help and decide to make a change. They may even choose to repent of their sin that is manifested in selfishness, laziness, and personal dissipation.

Do you want to know something even more stunning? Believers aren't under any obligation to help anyone. There's no need to feel guilty about having extra when others have less. There's no crime in that. Believers don't give out of guilt (or, at least they shouldn't). They certainly don't give expecting anything in return, either from the recipient or from God. *They give because they want to.* They give because they desire to be like God in ways God intended.

God is generous. His true followers desire to grow in qualities like this. They're motivated by the knowledge that it's pleasing to God when His followers seek to be like Him. Also, charity can be a wonderful way to grow in virtues like faith. If we give, believing God will continue to provide for us even after we've sacrificially provided for another, our faith grows.

Another important point: if we respond to the pain of others with personal action, we escape "caring constipation". Our emotions have an outlet that works the way God intended. Our compassion allows us to understand better the compassion and generosity of the Creator who placed the seeds of virtue within us. True compassion from a heart of love is very different than guilt-motivated giving.

Let's get back to our topic. As I started to say before, when the government takes over the function of charity, much goes wrong. Here's how:

1. Most modern Western governments function in a "religion neutral" mode. As such, when a government worker hands out funds, they're not allowed to say, "You're receiving this in God's name." People who receive such funds don't realize God ultimately provides.

2. This kind of giving is very inefficient. With Pat the Politician, one hundred dollars given to a politician resulted in a lesser amount received by the needy. What happened to the rest? In one word: overhead. There are armies of lawyers, social workers, accountants, and others involved in distributing funds to the poor. Many government workers are sincere but fail to understand how much their roles contribute to massive waste. Others are just crooks.

3. This kind of giving is highly ineffective on the whole. What's the result of all this spending? In the 1960s, President Lyndon Johnson declared a "War on Poverty" in the United States. Numerous programs were created to help poor people. Estimates of amounts spent since that time vary, but most place the figure in the trillions. (The War on Poverty 2014, 3) Yes, that's *trillion* with a "T." The result? We're still treated to regular images of "the needy" among us. Millions are still classed as poor. It's not that we lack an occasional success story. If you spend a trillion dollars, sooner or later you'll have a few people who feel a program helped them. Overall, though, government is very inefficient when it comes to charity.

4. Unlike God, who is infinite, governments are not. They run out of money. When this happens, they must increase taxes, or they must go into debt. When citizens protest, they're often told that they're selfish. The government, assisted by the media, creates a shame machine designed to keep the populace in a state of constant guilt. Images of children in wheelchairs abound just before elections.

5. Givers lose the benefits of giving. Money is taken in the form of taxes. Another principle of sacrifice is that sacrifices must be given willingly. No one happily pays taxes. Money taken with the threat of punishment for noncompliance doesn't count as charity. Even if it were possible to purchase God's favor, you wouldn't be able to turn around after the tax collector leaves and say to God, "That counts, right?"

6. It's not good for politicians. As I said, you don't get spiritual credit for giving away other people's money. Many politicians miss this! I can't

help but think some of them sincerely believe they're purchasing a ticket to heaven through their actions.

7. People who are previously independent become dependent. When I was young, we had a bird feeder in the backyard. It was fun to watch birds. It was also gratifying to think life was easier on the birds in wintertime when finding seeds was difficult. One day, though, I learned about the problem of bird feeders. Previously, the birds figured out ways to feed themselves in the wintertime. Then someone sets up a bird feeder. The birds start coming to the feeder *and forget the skill of foraging for food in difficult seasons.* If you forget to fill the bird feeder for a few days, the birds starve! Previously, the birds were independent; now they're dependent on you. If you fail to provide, the birds, who previously knew how to get along, are hurt. In years gone by, many people learned how to survive tough times without help. Perhaps they did with less. Perhaps they went to friends, family, and church. Once government programs replaced these resources, people stopped using the former and become addicted to the latter. Many don't even remember days when there were other ways of getting along. As such, millions of people have been turned into something like the birds in my old backyard. The lists of those receiving "entitlements" grow with each passing year. If someone in government realizes the problem and attempts to cut back, millions of people cry out, sincerely believing they have nowhere else to turn. In previous generations, they had many places to turn. Those days became forgotten with growing government handouts.

8. When the government acts as the middleman, the true source of funds is hidden. This may be the worst problem. Politicians rarely inform recipients of charitable funds that those funds are from hard-working people who pay lots of money in taxes. The recipients just assume the money comes from the government. In fact, recipients believe they're "entitled". In the Western world, we often hear the phrase "government money"; in fact, there's no such thing as "government money". If you pay taxes, it's *your* money. Lacking an individual face for this wellspring of resources, who winds up getting credit? Politicians. Yes, Pat the Politician gets full credit for "helping the needy". Pat gets his picture on magazine covers as "Man of the Year". Pat gets banquets in his honor and buildings named after him. Why is this perhaps the biggest problem? Because, ultimately, we are to go to God for provision and help in times of need. When politicians step in and provide funds taken from others, they replace God. In fact, *they become gods* in the eyes of the citizenry. Did I say politicians may think they're purchasing salvation from God? Maybe it's worse. Maybe they think *they are* God! The problem gets bigger when politics becomes a lifetime job. Playwright George Bernard Shaw once said,

"A government that robs Peter to pay Paul can always depend on the support of Paul." Helping the needy becomes a way to use money taken from people who work hard for it to purchase votes from masses of people who receive it. With handouts aplenty, the political gods never go away.

Some readers, especially those who think of themselves as believers, want to stop at this point. "But isn't it important that government is making the world a better place?" they ask. "Doesn't the fact that the poor are receiving help make government programs worthwhile in the end?" "Doesn't that mean believers should support politicians who talk about government helping the needy?" "Shouldn't believers support politicians who *care*, rather than those who don't?" "What's so wrong about *caring* anyway?"

Imagine you're on the Titanic, the great ocean liner that sank in the frigid waters of the Atlantic in 1912. On the upper levels of the ship were the wealthy and privileged. They wore fine clothes. They ate fine food. They enjoyed the best of everything. Then there were the people on the lower decks, callously referred to as "steerage" by the upper classes. They had enough food for the voyage and enough clothes to wear, but enjoyed much less luxury than those above them. Imagine we could do something to improve the social status of the steerage class? Imagine we could attack all the wealthy and redistribute their wealth to the poorer people. Now everyone would have the best! Sadly though, the ship will still hit an iceberg. It will still sink. No improvement in social status will help the people in steerage. They don't need a better cabin—they need a lifeboat.

Should we care about those less fortunate than ourselves? True believers do; and they often do what they can to help the needy. However, believers understand that feeding only the stomachs of the poor and neglecting their souls is the same as class upgrades on the Titanic. Everyone will die someday and stand before God. They will either pass the judgment because they sought him during their lives, or they'll fail the judgment and enter a horrifying eternity. It may sound idealistic, but people need salvation more than food. Forgetting this important principle hurts the recipients of charity more than any of us can imagine.

Chapter 26

The "Gods" of America, Part I

Questions about American History

When I was a youngster, I learned the following rhyme:

> In fourteen-hundred-and-ninety-two Columbus sailed the
> ocean blue.

Having been brought up in a somewhat creative environment, I then learned this additional verse:

> In fourteen-hundred-and-ninety-three his ship fell off the
> edge of the sea.

The "discovery" of the New World by Columbus marked a major pivot in world history. I say "discovery" in quotation marks because recent years have seen discussion about who really reached the New World first; Columbus, Leif Erickson, or someone else. There were lots of people already living there, and they matter, too. Having said all that, Columbus marks the point in history when large-scale travel started between Europe and the Americas.

The combatants in the battle for the hearts of mankind lost no time booking a ticket.

This was a complex period of history. With some fear of over-simplification, I'm going to divide European visitors to America into two groups. First, there were people like the Pilgrims. The Pilgrims had a deep faith in Jesus Christ. As they looked at their home, England, they saw a country that was supposedly Christian but was filled with people who acted in ways the Pilgrims considered contrary to the cause of Christ. They worked for return to a purer form of Christianity. Instead of seeing a return, they saw persecution from the establishment of their day. They came to America hoping to create a community of faith. There, they could practice Christianity as they understood it in safety.

To this group was later added the Puritans, whose name symbolizes a pure Christian faith. To the south of these groups landed William Penn, founder of Pennsylvania. Penn was a member of the Quakers whose worship became so intense participants shook during meeting times. This colony's cornerstone was Philadelphia, the "City of Brotherly Love". Penn wanted this city to be ideal in both design and philosophy, a place where people loved God and each other. All these groups longed for a world where the name of Jesus was revered and where His teachings were fervently followed. All of them wanted to introduce paradise on earth in God's name. They saw the New World as the place to do this.

The second group of visitors to the New World had different motivations. The continent they came from may have been influenced in varying degrees by Christianity, but they had no interest in following God. This group of people was interested in taking what they could in whatever manner seemed most profitable. If you asked them about their religion, they'd mention the name "Christianity", though they had no idea of its meaning.

This is confusing for anyone trying to piece together a history of the United States. Depending on your personal view of God and Christianity, you can come up with profoundly different views of this nation.

I was in college when I became a follower of Jesus Christ. At that time, I learned about people who believed the Pilgrims and Puritans had a profoundly positive effect on America. Those people felt that many problems faced in America today were caused when the culture abandoned its religious foundations. People in this group say things like, "America needs to return to her Christian roots!"

Armed with such rhetoric, I ventured into the world of the modern college campus. At one party, I remember hearing someone lament about problems facing our country. I boldly interjected, "Well, that's because we need to return to our Christian roots!" I was very proud of myself for solving that problem in such a concise way. At this point, a man of African descent felt led to interject something from his perspective. "Christian roots, huh? Are you referring to the 'Christian roots' that allowed white Europeans to kidnap people from Africa and make them slaves? Do you mean the 'Christian roots' that made slave traders pack human beings into the holds of ships like sardines, causing many of them to die in filth on the voyage, with their bodies being tossed overboard to the sharks? Or how about the 'Christian roots' that caused slave owners to whip slaves senseless and shove them into dirty shacks while their masters lived in fine homes?"

This went on for what felt like an eternity. With each new pronouncement, I wanted to say, "Well, no, I don't mean *those* Christian roots," but I knew that would have sounded ridiculous.

What happened to America? How could there have been so many people dedicated to living a godly life at the root of this nation, but with horrors like slavery appearing in the branches of the tree? It's not just slavery; I remember one historian giving a talk concerning a study of diaries written by early inhabitants of the United States. With a wry smile on her face, she said, "Christian nation? Let me tell you about this 'Christian nation'!" She went on with an almost gleeful demeanor describing women who had casual sex with men they met on the street. There were times when more couples showed up at marriage altars pregnant than otherwise.

Again, what happened? The beginning of the answer has already been stated: America has always had two kinds of people; those who wanted to follow God, and those who weren't interested in God at all. The godly built hospitals and orphanages. The ungodly built slave ships and houses of ill-repute.

How did the second group prosper so much? Why were they dominant many times in this country's history? Of particular concern to many modern believers is the question: how did all the evils wrought by this group of people get blamed on Christians?

Let me suggest an answer. It's a hard answer, but I think that it explains the situation. To understand this dilemma, we need to revisit the Pilgrims.

The Missing Part of the Pilgrims' Journey to America

As a child growing up in America in the 1960s, the following was my understanding of the Pilgrims: The Pilgrims were people who wore black all the time. The men had buckles in their hats as well as their belts. They left England because they were persecuted for their faith. They came to America so that they could have freedom of worship. They met the Indians. They all ate turkey, mashed potatoes, and popcorn. They called this meal "Thanksgiving". The end.

There are lots of children in America who don't learn much more than this, based on what I've heard. There are more than a few things wrong about this collection of observations. Some are inconsequential. For example, the Pilgrims didn't restrict their clothing to black. They often had more colorful attire. There is one piece missing from the story, though, which is significant.

Some time ago, I visited Provincetown, Massachusetts; this was the first place the Pilgrims landed when they came to America. To commemorate the landing, there's a museum that includes historical items documenting the voyage. While looking through the displays, I was surprised to learn about a section of the Pilgrim's trip I hadn't heard before. The Pilgrims, it seems, didn't leave England and travel straight to America. They traveled first to Amsterdam and stayed there for years.

What happened during this little-reported time in the journey of the Pilgrims? The Pilgrims encountered two big problems. The first, oddly, was a byproduct of their quest for freedom. They enjoyed the freedom of worship they craved, as the Dutch hosted a very open society by the standards of the day. Unfortunately, societies that allow freedom of worship often allow freedom *from* worship as well. This meant the Pilgrims, a people who loved pure living, were surrounded by many whose desire for purity was notably lacking. To our friends who've read this far but haven't bought into the ideas of this book, this phenomenon is difficult to understand. When you're a believer, it's painful to watch people live their lives in disobedience to God. It's even more painful to watch such people influence your children.

The second problem can be understood by anyone. In England, before the Pilgrims suffered persecution, they were established members of society. Some were highly educated. Others were landowners. Although you can't take away an education, property is fair game in lands where rulers dislike certain members of the population. Lands and possessions were stripped from the Pilgrims. The more fortunate were made to sell at rock-bottom prices. Others did worse. As such, the Pilgrims lived among the Dutch as an underclass. Some of the more educated could attain teaching positions and such, but others took whatever work they could find. Many lived off meager savings or proceeds of undervalued properties sold in England. After a time, the Pilgrims began running out of money. These noble people had become poor. Some gave up and moved back to England, blending back in as less-zealous practitioners of faith. Other wondered what to do.

Then, the Pilgrims learned about something unheard of by previous societies; a portion of the "New World" had been claimed by the King of England. The land of this new acquisition was full of wealth. It was waiting to be mined and farmed. The waters of its shores teamed with fish ready to jump into nets. There was only one problem: to have farms and mines and ports, the king needed residents. Apparently, it wasn't easy finding willing people to go over and colonize. So, the king made a generous offer: To those willing to sign the right contract, he would grant land. The Pilgrims had no property to give up, no farms to abandon, and no sentimental ties to the homeland. They weren't hapless, uneducated poor people. They knew how to run farms and businesses. They were ideal candidates for this venture; and the problem of an unpopular faith? Kings can be very practical at times like this. Unpopular faith several thousand miles away was much less a problem than unpopular faith closer by. This was a good deal for everyone. So, the Pilgrims found themselves on a little ship called the Mayflower sailing into the future as landowners once more.

To most people, this is the practical end of the story. The Pilgrims took their place as icons of America, with their story repeated in grossly stereotypical fashion by countless schoolchildren every year at Thanksgiving.

The Problem Facing the Pilgrims and Other People of Faith in America

For those who want to dig deeper into the causes of spiritual decay America, there's more. When the Pilgrims landed on the shores of the New World, they had two desires—two passions. The first was to build a new society based on faith and devotion to Jesus Christ. The second was to gain property and wealth. You know something? Those two goals aren't necessarily incompatible. The Scriptures say in multiple places that wealth attained by godly means is a good thing (Proverbs 8:17-18); but the Scriptures also teach that wealth and the quest for it can be deceptive. (1 Tim 6:9-10)

In the minds of the Pilgrims, they walked off the Mayflower with one God, Jesus Christ. I believe they were mistaken. There were in fact two gods who arrived on that famous ship. The second was a stowaway, a god I'll call the "*god of the Better Life*".

The "God" of the Better Life

If you grow up in America, you hear a lot about something called "the better life". I remember seeing educational films in elementary school showing images of immigrants from all over the world coming to the shores of America. Why did they come? Because America, the films said, offered "a better life". Some immigrants left their homes because of poverty, and they wanted opportunity. Others left persecution and bondage, wanting the freedom offered at that time only in this unique country. All wanted something better. This tradition was started by the Pilgrims, who left both poverty and persecution for the better life offered in this new land.

Let's present the usual caveat. Is it wrong to want a better life? If you suffer pain and persecution in your homeland because you hold unpopular beliefs, is it wrong to escape? Of course not. If you're poor, is it wrong to long for a place where you could better provide for yourself and your family? Again, no. The problem, as I've stated several times now, is this: *some desires become gods*. The problem with any god appears when we make *choices*. From the earliest settlers of America up to the modern age, the question is: *when pursuit of the better life comes in conflict with pursuit of God, who wins?*

As far as the Pilgrims were concerned, their earliest choices often demonstrated greater love for God than property. Although the Pilgrims made mistakes along the way, there's evidence God miraculously provided for them. They weren't perfect, and their story is complex. However, their success and their many sacrifices happily place them at the roots of the American story.

What kind of choices came later for other early American settlers? How did temptations from the god of the better life influence those who followed the Pilgrims?

Flags and Crosses

Before going on, let me mention that my admiration for the Pilgrims outweighs my criticisms. However, let me share a negative observation about them and the other godly people who populated America in its early days. It's not really their fault so much because it involved a common belief of the day, but it's something that caused problems for all who followed.

In those days, many people believed it was proper to fuse religion, government, and society in general. As such, early American believers proceeded to make the same mistake their forefathers in England made. They all assumed that the one major requirement for a "Christian society" was to walk onto a beach, plant a cross, and declare the new territory to be "Christian". Somehow, this was going to solve all problems and result in a Christian paradise.

The problem: This has never worked anywhere. England and the Netherlands, the countries left behind by the Pilgrims, should both have been Christian paradises. Both, at one point in their histories, had residents who declared those nations to be Christian. However, both fell into some level of spiritual decline. This pattern has been repeated throughout history. Adam and Eve saw the murder of their child Abel only one generation into the world. The godly line of Seth became corrupted by the ungodly line of Cain after some centuries, leading to the great flood. Moses led the children of Israel into the Promised Land with incredible signs of God's power, yet they fell into cycles of disbelief that eventually led to their deportation into neighboring lands.

Let me make an important statement here: *I don't believe it's the proper goal of believers to create a Christian nation.* It's the proper goal of believers to share their beliefs with all around them. It's certainly their goal to influence others in positive ways. We're reminded of Jesus' commands to His followers that they be "salt" and "light". If believers influence large groups of people, and if those groups of people come to belief, rejoicing is appropriate.

America has enjoyed the powerful influence of godly people. In fact, I would agree with those who say America is an amazing place. It's one of the best on Earth and one of the best in all human history because of this influence. However, when people walk onto a beach and declare a nation to be Christian, the results tend to be short-lived.

Many people desire something other than what their parents want. Some children choose the opposite of what their parents desire for them. When the children of believers act in unbelieving ways, it's a very sad thing. Worse though, when residents of a nation declared to be Christian act in ungodly ways, *Christians get blamed for it*. Sadly, there was a lot of blame to come for the young land of America.

Chapter 27

The "Gods" of America, Part II

Slavery

Slavery has existed for a long time. Many societies from the earliest recordings of history had slaves. In the early days of America, many participated in a technical form of slavery called indentured servitude. I say "technical" because an indentured servant agreed to enter a limited time of service for payment. After the time was over, the indentured servant was free. During the period of the contract, though, the indentured servant, for all practical purposes, belonged to the contract holder. Still, choice governed the contract. Many gladly entered this kind of service to gain needed funding for travel to the New World.

This was different than forced servitude. In ancient times, forced servitude was often the cost of losing a war. Societies in those days gave losers a choice: die or live as slaves. Many of the vanquished chose the latter. This may seem harsh to modern ears, but at the time it was a form of mercy. As such, you can sometimes see this kind of slavery tolerated in the Bible when believers interacted with surrounding societies. The apostle Paul, for example, didn't declare that all slaves should be freed, but rather encouraged believing slaves to make the best of bad situations. Doing otherwise could result in severe punishment or even execution for slaves. As outsiders and a minority in their society, early Christians had to work with a bad system. When slave owners became Christian, however, Paul encouraged change (Phil. 1:8–21).

One kind of slavery, though, was clearly forbidden in scripture: forced servitude as the result of kidnapping, sometimes called "chattel slavery". Moses was explicit: "Anyone who kidnaps another and either sells him or still has him when he is caught must be put to death" (Exod. 21:16). Kidnapping for enslavement was a death penalty offense. Later, Paul wrote to his protégé Timothy:

> We know that the law is good if one uses it properly. We also know that law is made not for the righteous but for law-breakers and rebels, the ungodly and sinful, the unholy and irreligious; for those who kill their fathers or mothers, for murderers, for adulterers and perverts, *for slave traders* and liars and perjurers—and for whatever else is contrary to the sound doctrine that conforms to the glorious gospel of the blessed God, which he entrusted to me (I Timothy 1:8–11; emphasis mine).

So, it should be clear to anyone that the Scriptures disapprove of chattel slavery. As I mentioned above though, declaring a "Christian nation" doesn't stop some people from behaving badly. From the earliest interactions between Europeans and the New World, some fell to the temptation of this practice. Some Native Americans fell victim first. Fortunately for them, enslavement was difficult. The natives didn't look much different than Europeans. Many learned English. So, if a native escaped, they were hard to find. They could blend in with the Europeans. Add to this, many natives previously lived in the territories where they were enslaved. If they escaped, they could find their way home easily.

Africans were a different story. For them, when Europeans gave into the temptation of kidnapping for slavery, it was harder to run. It was easy to pick out a dark-skinned African. Most came over knowing no English and had no way of getting home unless they went on a ship. Because of all this, it was easier for some Europeans to give in to evil.

Wait—America was a Christian nation, right? What would the residents of a Christian nation do when a ship full of slaves pulled in to the harbor?

- The slaves would be freed.
- The ships would be burned.
- The owners and operators of the ships would be arrested, and it would be they who wore chains for the rest of their lives instead of the Africans.

Why didn't this happen? Some regions leaned that way, especially those in the North heavily influenced by the Puritans, Pilgrims, and Quakers. In those regions, slavery was outlawed in the early 1800s. The Quakers were leading abolitionists. Other American Christian organizations distributed the writings of people like the English minister Charles Haddon Spurgeon, who was highly critical of slavery.

So why didn't America see the end of slavery sooner? Why was there a fight at all?

Because slaves brought the "better life".

Or, at least it was thought. For many, the two major "gods" of America hit head-on when the institution of forced slavery took hold. Many Americans made a tragic choice; they followed the god of the better life. As stated above, many didn't. Conflict ensued, culminating the American Civil War of the 1860s between the northern and southern states.

As a child, I was taught the Civil War was fought over slavery. In fact, it was fought over several things, but slavery was a major factor. Many citizens of the southern states didn't care for the constant drone of the northerners against slavery. What made the southerners hang on to slavery so tenaciously when so many voices were raised in opposition? To understand this, you must understand two things.

First, remember that God created us to be like Him. He wants us to make choices by exercising godly virtues. These virtues make us do things like value others more than ourselves. False gods move us in the opposite direction. They encourage people to act selfishly and to value self over others.

Second, the god of the better life promises three out of the five human wants, what I've called the "Five 'P's". The god of the better life was born of the desire to be prosperous. We all like to own things. We all hate living in a state of want. The New World offered an abundance of opportunities to be prosperous, but fear of want isn't the end of what possessions bring. Possessions also bring power. The more you own, or the more you control, the more powerful you feel. The more you own, the more popularity you acquire.

Power and popularity may have been more important factors than prosperity. Let me explain: when a person is kidnapped from a foreign land, beaten, imprisoned, and brought to a foreign shore, something happens. They come off the boat disoriented, weakened, and unable to communicate. This creates the illusion that *they're something less than their captors*. They appear to be less intelligent and less concerned with the higher things of life. For Africans, add to this a noticeably different skin color, and it became possible for slavers to imagine the slaves *were not human beings*. They were imagined to be a higher form of animal. This sounds ugly, but it was the reality of the day.

When people visit the zoo, it's fun to watch antics of the animals in their cages (or "habitats" for better zoos). Often though, the antics aren't merely cute. On our lesser days, we're reminded that we're *higher* than the animals.

We achieve a sense of smug superiority by watching them. If we want to insult someone, we compare their behavior to those caged creatures. "You're acting like a monkey." "He's like some kind of wild animal." "Why can't you close the door behind you; were you born in a barn?" This sense of superiority was heightened with "creatures" that looked human.

Although not cheap, slaves were affordable for many. If you weren't prosperous enough to own slaves, you could manage them. You could be the lowest of what the southerners used to call "white trash" and still be placed in charge of slaves. Many members of the corporate world fear something called a "glass ceiling", a point in the hierarchy some people can't pass. Conversely, the presence of slavery provided a "glass floor" for society. There was a point the privileged couldn't fall beneath. Individuals who'd normally be at the bottom of the societal ladder were guaranteed some level of status even if they could achieve nothing otherwise. Therefore, slavery was supported even by those who didn't directly profit from it. It was this weakness of human nature that caused problems for slaves and their descendants long after the slaves were freed. Many Caucasians clung ferociously to their desire to feel superior. They withheld education and other benefits of society from Africans, which perpetuated the belief that people with dark skin were somehow lower than they were.

The perpetration of the "lower life form" lie was central to the existence of slavery. In societies heavily influenced by scripture, people develop a sense that other people should be treated in certain ways. They should be treated with fairness and some level of respect. To circumvent this, you need to have an excuse. In the case of Africans, the belief that you weren't dealing with a human provided the cover most people needed to quell their consciences.

This tragic attitude infested two important institutions of American society. First was the legal profession. Early drafters of the American constitution wanted to outlaw slavery from the first moments of the young nation. They were forced to compromise with slave owners in the South. Lacking restrictions on slavery, some of the greatest legal minds in America rationalized the institution in the highest statements of law. One of the most tragic decisions of the American Supreme Court was *Dred Scott v. Sandford*. Dred Scott, a "man of color" and a slave, sued for his freedom. After going to the highest levels of American law, Scott lost his case. The reason? He wasn't considered a human being; he was simply property. (Dred Scott v. Sandford 1856, 60)

How could some of the most intelligent people in the United States at that time miss something that's considered a fundamental truth today? A person's skin color doesn't determine his/her humanity. How could they assign nonhuman status to a human based solely on that person's appearance? I'm afraid it's quite easy when intelligent eyes are clouded with idolatry.

The second infestation was even more tragic. The churches of the northern states correctly preached the dignity of all people based on scripture. However, the churches of the South gave in to idolatry, even reading perversions of racial prejudice into scripture. As I mentioned earlier, there are plenty of statements in scripture identifying slavery as evil. Sadly, those who worshipped the god of the better life missed those passages and misread others. Worse, much of this errant teaching continued into the 1900s, complicating the healing that might otherwise have occurred had southern white ministers been faithful in seeking scriptural truth.

To summarize this whole sad state of affairs, the god of the better life did two things related to slavery: (1) It encouraged people to value possessions and status above all things, including God; and (2) It taught people to value themselves over others, even to the point of denying the humanity of a whole race of people.

Before moving on, let me stress something very important. Like my friend in college, many African Americans today attribute slavery in America to the Christian church. There is little that breaks my heart more than hearing this falsehood repeated. I, along with many American believers, want to emphatically state that chattel slavery was not created or endorsed by Jesus Christ, and it is not endorsed in the Scriptures. It was created and maintained by the god of the better life. It was not supported by those who came to America hoping to create a world influenced by belief in God. Rather, it was created and maintained by those people in America who came wanting to take whatever they could by whatever means available. Sadly, some of those perverse people placed on their faces masks with the likeness of Jesus. In adding this perversion to their evil practices, they've put a stumbling block in front of the victims of their godless trade. One of the greatest tragedies of American history involves the fact that many African Americans, who now live free because of the work of Christian abolitionists, are taught to overlook the hard work of believers that brought freedom for their ancestors. Instead, they're taught to look to the idolaters who created slavery and to assume those monsters are one and the same with Christians.

If the horrors of slavery perpetrated by idolaters against the people of Africa weren't sufficient, the descendants of those idolaters now work overtime to prevent the descendants of slaves from discovering God. In one of the vilest of distortions, the infamous hate group, the Ku Klux Klan, adopted as their symbol a burning cross. The cross is a symbol of the act that freed all followers of Christ from the bondage of sin. These thugs have turned the cross, the symbol of ultimate love, into a symbol of oppression carried by some of the most hateful people our sinful world has ever produced.

Chapter 28

The "Gods" of America, Part III

The "God" of the Better Life in Public Education

Slavery, a creation of the god of the better life, was a dark blot on the soul of America. Even after its abolition, racial tension continues to the present day.

The work of the god of the better life wasn't finished. He's subtle and deceptive. Do we need to state it again? There is nothing wrong with hard work and enjoying the fruit of your labor. Prosperity is not bad in itself; but with each new generation of Americans, and with each new wave of immigrants from other countries, the drumbeat grew ever louder. Come to America. Why? To find faith in the one true God? No. "Come to America to find *the better life*".

At some point, a funny thing happened. Merely having a better life than you had in your home country became insufficient. We began to hear that each new generation of Americans was to have a bigger share of the better life than the one preceding it. It became the responsibility of each citizen to sacrifice for the next generation. OK, do I need to say it again? Is it wrong to sacrifice for your children? Of course not. The question is: what are you giving your children by your sacrifice? Is prosperity in ever-growing quantities the chief purpose of humanity?

During this time, it wasn't that faith disappeared. Instead, it became increasingly subordinated to the better life. Of course, it's not that the country lacked noble people and noble acts. America is a country founded by people convinced that humans have a high calling; but, more and more people bought into the notion that nobility has limits; one such limit was a sacrifice of status. One by one, every institution quietly transformed to comply with this all-consuming god.

With education holding the keys to higher levels of prosperity, the institutions of higher learning slowly became temples of secularism. In early years of elementary school, the three "Rs", "*R*eading, w*R*iting, and a*R*ithmetic", became the goal of all students. Although the Bible was encouraged among the curriculum in the early days of our nation, "religion" was not heralded as one of the "Rs" at any time I can recall.

Throughout the early history of the United States, it wasn't unusual for schoolchildren to be required to listen to Bible recitations. This practice was stopped in 1963 by the U.S. Supreme court (School Dist. of Abington Tp. v. Schempp 1963, 1). Many believers felt stinging disappointment at that moment of American history. Although I would recognize it as a sad moment, I wouldn't do so for the reasons held by many. Forcing public school children to listen to scripture when their families have no desire for it has no place in the goals of a faith that recognizes the importance of choice. It only has a place when believers fall to the mistaken notion prevalent since the time of the Pilgrims that believers only need to plant a cross and declare a given piece of real-estate as "Christian" to have completed their earthly tasks. No one can be coerced into true faith. No attempts should be made by people who call themselves believers to participate in coercion.

However, this moment does mark the moment in American history when we became honest about our beliefs. The best legal minds of the nation decided the following: The purpose of public education is: (1) the acquisition of knowledge for the sake of knowledge; and (2) training armies of young people to march in step with the ever-growing quest for prosperity. My sadness comes from the fact that the influence of scripture had already been waning for years, not in the fact that it had become apparent.

A Strategic Error

At this point, many people of faith make a strategic error. They associate the loss of prayer and Bible reading in our schools with negative things like a growing crime rate. People who follow this track often quote a survey reportedly given to educators every year. Among the questions in the survey is, "What's a teacher's biggest problem?" When the survey was given in the 1940s, before prayer was removed, teachers reported their biggest problems as gum chewing and swearing. In more recent surveys, the problems include drugs and guns in schools.

Unfortunately, the biggest problem with the "biggest problem survey" is that it's likely a fable. No one can find the actual survey. There are better sources for the discussion, such as articles from major newspapers documenting metal detectors in public schools ("New York Schools"). These detectors catch thousands of weapons every year. That's serious. The presence of such measures in modern schools clearly indicates a decline from the 1940s.

However, there are problems with believers pointing out things like this. First, people who aren't interested in spiritual solutions can find numerous ways to fix problems. Are children bringing guns to school? Put metal detectors in the doorway. Voila, problem solved. The crime rate goes down. If all you're concerned about is the crime rate, there are plenty of solutions that don't involve introducing children to God. When prosperity without God is the goal, the condition of children's hearts becomes irrelevant.

A more serious problem lies in the inappropriateness of assuming crime rates and other societal ills should be our focus. What are we talking about, really, when we introduce figures about the crime rate? We're discussing safety, and safety is related to one of the five "Ps": protection.

It's appropriate for believers to ask God for protection. However, when believers allow their thoughts and arguments to be dominated with statistics like the crime rate, safety can become an idol. It's possible we're treating God as though He's no more important than the other major god of our land. When we pray, we're saying something like, "Lord, please keep us safe—so we can spend our time pursuing the better life."

As important as it is to live in a safe world, safety is not our main goal. Our goals are to grow in our relationship with God, to enjoy the wonderful gifts He offers to us, and to share our joy with the world. When increasing numbers enjoy God's love, they treat each other better. Sadly, the god of the better life still influences American churches more than they realize. All of this had a heavy influence on societal trends of the 1970s and the 1980s.

The Sexual Revolution

In the 1960s, our society became more accepting of behavior that was, shall we say, not preferred by the Pilgrims. "Free sex" dominated the media. Concerned believers wanted to speak out, but what tone should they use? I can't examine the hearts of everyone in the faith community who addressed this issue, but I often heard the following line of thinking: "God hates sexual sin. God sent terrible judgments upon societies who endorsed this practice, like Sodom and Gomorrah. America is a great country with many blessings, but those blessings came because we honored God in the past. If we as a nation stop honoring God, He may send judgment upon us, too."

Many who said this often added the following: "Although God hates sexual immorality, He loves people no matter what activities they choose.

He's willing to forgive any sin, no matter how offensive." That was an important closing, but I'm not sure I always heard it. What I think I heard often was something like this: "There are people out there (*"those* people"). If we don't get them to stop doing what they're doing, something bad will happen. Right now, we're prosperous and free. But if God unleashes judgment, we may lose our prosperity and freedom." In other words, "We enjoy the *better life* here in America. If we don't do something, we'll lose it." So, what were many people who called themselves believers really trying to achieve? Did they pray to God because their hearts were broken with concern for friends and neighbors? Did they weep over the impending judgment against all who rebel against God and follow idols instead? Or were they, like many in America, caught up in worship of the god of the better life? Were they concerned primarily in keeping *it* strong? If people prayed this way, it's no wonder the sexual revolution kept growing. It did so because people who called themselves believers were praying to the wrong god. They were praying to the god of the better life, and as a partner to the other idols of the world, he likes free sexuality very much, thank you.

Abortion

Sex often results in pregnancy. A strange thing happened during this time. In poor societies, children are often considered valuable. If you live on a farm, every child is a potential farm hand. In civilizations that achieve only low levels of technology, unskilled labor is vitally important. You need armies of men wielding shovels and pickaxes if you're going to build roads and buildings. Today, America and other Western countries have experienced prosperity unrivaled in any other age of mankind. Technology is growing at lightning speed. With these new developments come an ironic new trend: children are not as valuable as in the past. What do you do when your society endorses free sex, and sex often results in pregnancy? Birth control is an option for the technologically advanced society, but many found birth control methods to be less dependable and convenient than they wanted.

The next step is abortion.

What happens in an abortion? By pure definition, abortion is the purposeful interruption of the gestation of a human embryo. The phrase "termination of pregnancy" is also popular. Abortion is vitally important in a society where the god of the better life is worshipped along with the god of pleasure. Most people today want to enjoy sex with little thought to the results. *Since children are no longer vitally important, unplanned pregnancies must not be allowed to develop into children unless parents feel the children will enhance their enjoyment of the better life.*

What I just stated is very dry. Words like *abortion*, *termination*, and *interruption* give any thoughtful person the notion that abortion is a simple act. We "interrupt" many things in life.

At the age of seven, I was given a packet of seeds and some dirt. The instructions on the seed packet stated I should plant seven or eight seeds in a small area. When the plants began to grow, I was to select the strongest and "thin" the rest. Maybe I was too sensitive as a child, but I found this difficult. It seemed a waste to allow something to experience life and then "interrupt" it; but these were plants, not higher life forms. Farmers, who deal with life forms higher than plants, often "cull the herd." Of course, farmers harvest all plants and animals at maturity. This all works because we're dealing with plants and animals.

What about the result of sex between humans? What is in a woman's womb when she's pregnant? We have another dry term for this: it's a *fetus*. Here's an important question: Is the fetus a plant that sometimes needs to be thinned? Is it a lower life form that can be culled at the discretion of the farmer?

The Bible says something amazing about the mysterious thing growing in the womb of a pregnant woman. King David pondered the wonder of the human body, and penned these words:

> For you created my inmost being; you knit me together in
> my mother's womb. (Psalm 139:13)

David said human life, from its formation in the womb, is a creation of God. It's never an accident or an oversight in God's mind. David wrote a few sentences later:

> Your eyes saw my unformed body. All the days ordained for
> me were written in your book before one of them came to
> be. (vs. 16)

David states even more strongly that life in the womb is created with a purpose. The purpose of each human is known by its Creator, long before procreation starts. There are more complete explanations of these principles available to any who want to research further, so I'll have to stop here. The Bible is clear: human life begins at conception. The fetus is a human being, not a plant or animal to be thrown out at the whims of parent or society.

Many argue the words *abortion* and its parallels aren't seen in the Scriptures. Why not? I suggest abortion isn't seen in the Bible for two reasons. First, medical technology wasn't very sophisticated in Bible times. There were ways to "interrupt a pregnancy", but they were dangerous. More importantly, that was a different world. Children were valuable. The idea that you would throw one out simply didn't occur to members of agrarian cultures.

There is an even more important reason why abortion didn't occur (at least not often enough to be considered) in ancient biblical society. The reason lies at the core of the revelation contained in the Scriptures: All human life is highly valuable. In fact, human life may be the reason this planet exists.

This is the problem with abortion. At its core, the acceptance or tolerance of abortion in a society means the value of human life has diminished. Let me illustrate: imagine someone you care about is involved in a car crash. A drunk driver slammed into the vehicle carrying your loved one. Once the accident is reported, two ambulances arrive. The drunk driver is alive and screams for help. Your loved one is also alive but unconscious. If they receive immediate help, they'll survive and enjoy a healthy life; but if help is delayed, they'll die. The two sets of emergency workers, upon leaving their vehicles, appraise the situation. They see one person obviously alive and calling for help. They see another person motionless. You'd hope one team would help the person calling for help, and the other help your loved one. Imagine that the latter team says, "We're not sure the person over there is alive because they're not moving. Let's go home." Because of this choice, your loved one dies.

How are you feeling right now? Most people would be enraged to hear that a loved one was ignored by medical workers simply because they lacked any easily-observable appearance of life. *Because your loved one is important to you, you'd want the emergency responders to assume the victim is alive.* You'd want them to pull out their stethoscopes and listen for a pulse. You'd want them to work on the assumption the unconscious person is worthy of help, even if onlookers aren't sure. *If an error is to be made, you'd want them to err on the side of life.*

In a society dominated by idols, human life isn't valuable. Many people, some of them the most intelligent of our modern world, look at a fetus and say, "We're not sure whether it's a human life or not." It's only considered to be a human being after it leaves the mother's body.

There is amazing evidence on the side of life. After only a few months, the fetus has a recognizable heartbeat and human features such as arms, legs, eyes, and fingers. Brainwaves are discernable well before birth. However, this evidence falls on deaf ears. If human life were valuable, people who viewed a fetus and who were still uncertain about its humanity would err on the side of life. Instead, the status of a preborn child is left to its mother. If she thinks having a child is valuable to her, the pregnancy is permitted to continue. If she (or society) feels otherwise, the fetus is labeled as nonlife and can be terminated at will. It is to be removed, like an annoying wart.

If things weren't hard enough yet, let me ask a hard question; What words do we use when one human being ends the life of another? If one human angers another, and the second gets a gun and shoots the first, we have a word for that. The word is *murder*. If you have an annoying growth, and someone removes it for you, what words do we have for that? We have words like operation, procedure, and so forth.

So, for the preborn child, the big question is *"What is it?"* If it's a lifeless piece of tissue, it can be removed at will, and words like abortion and termination are appropriate. If it's a human being, well, we have very harsh words for someone who destroys another human being based only on convenience. *The life or nonlife of the fetus is the core issue.* We can state all kinds of evidence pro and con, but then the bigger question becomes "How valuable is human life?" If human life is valuable and we are unsure, we err on the side of attributing humanity with all its privileges to the fetus. If life is not valuable, if human life is something less than divine, we allow individuals and society to attribute value to it as seems appropriate at the moment.

In the 1970s, this issue was addressed by the Supreme Court of the United States. In the landmark case *Roe v. Wade*, the highest court of the land, populated with the best minds our society could produce, made the following pronouncement: The fetus was not to receive the protections of law normally given to human life. The mother's right to control her body was more important than the life of the preborn child. (Roe v. Wade 1973) There were other associated cases, but Roe stands as the summary legal decision. Since that time, millions of abortions have been performed.

We stand at a vital juncture. If you don't understand why this issue is important to people of faith, you probably don't understand very much else of what we believe. If you still don't agree with my reasoning to this point, please humor me. You can go to the library or go to the Internet and within seconds see amazing pictures of a fetus in the womb. Some of the pictures have captured preborn children doing very human things like sucking their thumbs. If we add the knowledge that these "objects" have heartbeats and brainwaves, do you understand why some "misguided" people like myself might get it into their heads that we're dealing with human life? If you can at least acknowledge the possibility our arguments have merit, you then understand why we're horrified.

We see our friends and families, people whom we otherwise like and respect, look us straight in the face and tell us that any woman has the right to destroy the child in her womb based only on what she feels at the moment. I must put this in dire terms: if a fetus is lifeless, then we've had millions of procedures since *Roe v. Wade*. If it's a human life, then we have committed millions of murders.

The picture gets worse. In ancient societies, some of the gods demanded extreme sacrifices. One of the gods battled constantly by the ancient Hebrews was Molech, whom we learned about in Chapter 11. This god received the sacrifice of young children, who were made to "pass through the fire." (2 Kings 23:19) Why did adults agree to make their children die in such a horrifying way? You know the answer from the earlier chapters of this book: they sought prosperity and protection. Children were sacrificed for a better harvest or victory in a war. In a tragic parallel between our society and ancient societies who endorsed such barbaric practices, it could be said that followers of Molech sought a *better life* for themselves.

Here we face the issue confronting mankind from its inception. The issue is choice. Prosperity and "the better life" aren't problems by themselves, but, what do we do when we face choices between practices offensive to God but profitable for us? As individuals, most of the believers I've met have no problem. They choose to express their sexuality only in marriage. If a pregnancy results from sex, whether planned or not, parents regard life in the womb as valuable to God. As such, they do their best to welcome the resulting child into their families. If a friend or family member makes the unwise decision to have sex outside of marriage and a pregnancy results, I've seen many believing families encourage the mother to allow the child to come to term, later welcoming mother and child into their own homes.

What about society? As I've stated, I don't believe our job as believers is to take over society and force people to comply with our beliefs. However, our job is certainly to influence. We must proclaim our belief that God created all human life with a purpose, with the hope that people will choose to honor and obey Him.

On the other hand, though, all civilizations have treated some behaviors seriously. Murder is one such behavior. I believe I've demonstrated that abortion is the ending of an innocent life. Because of this, many believers participate in the *pro-life movement*. On this issue, we believe it's our responsibility to protect innocent human life. If we can, by simply raising our voices, save children's lives, it's worth our time. More, we must consider our place in a democratic society. We can choose to elect politicians who promise to uphold the value of human life through legislation.

Some ask, "What if a mother's life is in danger?" That's an important question. There are some situations where the health of the mother or infant is so dire that an attempt to bring the child to term will possibly result in the mother's death; or worse, both mother and child will die. Fortunately, advances in medicine are making such instances rare. However, if such instances occur, many in the pro-life movement would grant that intervention is an extreme but permissible action. Having said this, we must remember the fundamental question: the humanity of the fetus. If such an action is considered necessary, we're saying we must destroy one human life to save another. This is always tragic. Such decisions must be approached with the utmost gravity. I must add, I've heard numerous stories of women who carried a child to term even when warned that doing so might be dangerous. They felt the reward of a new human life was worth the risk.

Others argue, "What if physicians determine the child will experience ill health, deformity, or retardation?" I wish we had time to discuss this in more detail, but once again we must ask, "Is a sick child, a child with a handicap, or a child with retardation a human being?" Humans are always valuable even if they're sick. What this person really says is, "The goal of every reasonable human being is to have a better life. Allowing sick children to be born prevents parents and child from obtaining this." If you believe the goal of humanity is the better life, then this makes sense. If you believe humans have a higher purpose than the pursuit of riches, comfort, and pleasure, you side with every human life born on this earth.

Politics and the Issues

Having mentioned voting, we need to discuss the relationship of politics and faith. Put simply, most people in biblical times didn't vote for their leaders. The Romans had a form of democracy, but only for citizens of Rome. Israel, the home of early believers, had no such system. As such, there's no clear command to vote or abstain from voting. Believers have debated the relationship of faith and politics for a long time. We won't solve the issue in only a few paragraphs. However, I can try to quickly summarize pertinent history and principles.

Politics is a complicated subject. Politicians are a strange mix of honesty and dishonesty, passion and indifference, and noble service and self-service. Voting is a privilege unheard of in human history much before the time of Christ. It's not always allowed today. How does a believer use it? How does an idolater use it?

America Chooses

One of the pivotal battles between faith and nonfaith, and pursuit of God and pursuit of idols, occurred in America in 1992.

A number of events had taken American believers by surprise. With the belief that America was a "Christian nation", many who attended Christian churches, Protestant and Catholic, were appalled to hear the Roe decision had established a "constitutional right" to an abortion. Believers also saw troubling developments in the legal and educational systems; developments which endorsed and even encouraged movement away from faith.

With this, believers in America became politically active. With their influence in the voting booth, they started electing individuals who supported their beliefs on issues of faith. It was hoped these new politicians would do two things. First, they hoped to prevent bad legislation on faith issues. Second, believers realized the importance of the federal government's judicial branch. *Roe v. Wade* was thought by many to be the result of politically liberal justices who "discovered" rights not stated in the American Constitution and who "legislated from the bench". Many hoped better justices would be appointed to more accurately interpret law. People with these goals saw a lot of progress.

Then came the election of 1992. Two candidates, Republican George H. W. Bush and Democrat William Jefferson Clinton vied for support from the American people. Following is a summary of arguments presented by the candidates from my perspective:

President Bush, the incumbent, said he was open to the ideas of believers. He had to represent a lot of diverse people, but he appeared to listen to people of faith. He included people who were respected in the community of faith in his decisions, along with constituents from other groups. He promised to appoint justices who would interpret the law, not legislate from the bench. Finally, he said he didn't approve of abortion, and that he would work to end it.

The other candidate, then Governor Clinton, said he felt abortion should be legal. His Supreme court would contain liberal justices who would continue the tradition of *Roe v. Wade*. He didn't appear to have a lot of time for conservative expressions of religion.

Of course, both candidates had views on other things, too, but these are the items of importance for this discussion.

How would American's choose? A growing number considered the views presented by President Bush appealing. They were troubled by the moral direction the nation would take under the Democrat. President Bush displayed solid knowledge of international affairs. He successfully organized forces of the civilized world in a war against Saddam Hussein, the Iraqi despot, whose military invaded the neighboring nation of Kuwait. Mr. Bush presided to that point over an economy that provided jobs and prosperity for many. It didn't look like a hard decision, and the sitting president didn't give the appearance of being in any danger.

Then came the recession. In 1992, the United States entered what is now known to be a minor economic downturn. At the time, the media portrayed it as the end of the world. Ten years of remarkable growth ended. Jobs were lost. The stock market faltered. It was then Governor Clinton introduced two of his most famous statements. First, "I feel your pain." The governor was skilled at looking into a camera and making viewers imagine he spoke directly to them. He was able to portray the current president as unfeeling, a man who didn't care about hurting people. Next, "It's the economy, stupid!" All these moral issues like abortion didn't matter. The only question "smart" people asked of their president was, "Are you going to get me a job?" During his announcement speech, Clinton stated his public efforts were all about; "a *better life* (emphasis mine) for all who will work for it, a better future for the next generation" (Clinton 1992).

With this, Bill Clinton got what he needed. He hit the vein many Americans considered to be their lifeblood. The sitting president, George H. W. Bush, had offended the god of the better life. This trumped his qualifications, experience, and moral attitudes. He needed to go.

With this, the election went to William Jefferson Clinton. After his victory, he appointed some of the most liberal justices the courts have ever seen, and vetoed legislation created in bipartisan agreements that would have curtailed some of the worst types of abortion. This all was fine for many because the American economy boomed in the 1990s. People were back to getting the better life again.

Now, America is a diverse place. There are people who vote all kinds of ways on all kinds of issues. What concerns me deeply is people who call themselves believers. They attend churches, Catholic and Protestant. They may attend faithfully. Many would tell you they want to honor God. Many say they're troubled by practices like abortion and would never do it themselves. On the day of the national election in 1992, though, many of those people became idolaters. Their part in the better life was threatened. Because of this, they rationalized voting for someone who advocated things they knew were abhorrent to God. When given a choice between God and the better life, they chose the better life.

Was it more complex than that? In some ways yes. The issue of homelessness concerned people in 1992. Some felt a caring government should be elected; but, as I've pointed out, big government programs tend to be bad ways to help the needy. If people feel compassion for the poor, the best answer is to reach into their own pockets and help with their own funds. Delegating the responsibility of helping the poor to government resulted in people coming into power who insured that millions of abortions were performed.

This raises another question. Does the presence of homeless people promote compassion in people's hearts, or does it cause people to worry that they could be next? Perhaps concern for the poor was only a rationalization to cast off trust in God. Instead, people turned to a growing federal government that became more god-like every year.

Here's another problem: Sometimes, when you fail to pursue righteousness, pursuing it in the future becomes more complex and expensive. People who called themselves believers in 1992 could have influenced a whole nation to abandon the abhorrent practice of abortion by merely trusting that the nation would recover from a recession, just as it had numerous times in American history. There wasn't a war at the time. The environmental movements that later developed into widespread concerns for global warming were only in their infant stages. Believers in those days could have trusted God to provide for them and protect them at a time when it was relatively easy. Instead, they looked to the federal government to carry them through bad times.

Later elections brought more complex issues. With the terrorist attacks of September 11, 2001, people had to be concerned about new threats. How should the nation respond to this danger? President George W. Bush and his advisors chose harsh responses, which turned out to be controversial. Not being an expert on the military or international relations, it's not within the scope of this book to respond to the reactions of the American government when threatened by terrorist forces. It's clear, though, numerous issues arose, which sapped the energies of a nation growing uncertain about its moral center. Global-warming alarmists warned that the earth could become uninhabitable in only a few years if massive amounts of political energy weren't directed to that cause. A major economic collapse in late 2008 further undermined the energies of anyone trying to encourage the American people to follow the one true God.

And Now

With this, we arrive at the present. We've taken a whirlwind tour of American history together. We now understand how America changed over two hundred years, from a nation that enjoyed the strong influence of Christianity to a nation relegating the Pilgrims to misconceptions of school-children at Thanksgiving. A god called "the god of the better life" is winning the hearts and minds of America. The God of the Bible gets the blame for everything that ever went wrong.

What can we do?

We are ready now to turn our gaze away from the past and look forward. What choices lie before us as we face the future? We'll consider that in our closing chapter.

Chapter 29

Choices for Today

From the earliest appearance of men and women on earth, all human beings have shared a common experience: choices. From the moment we awaken until the time we sleep, we make choices. I even seem to remember making some choices while deep in sleep, dreaming.

I guess we never get a break.

Each day, we're offered opportunities—the same opportunities offered to humans for millennia. We can choose based on values pleasing to God, or we can choose based on our own values. In this last section, I'll present some essays on what I believe are the major choices standing before people of the world as we walk into the future.

To Choose, or Not to Choose?

Some Choose to Avoid Choosing

Almost two thousand years ago, the apostle John saw a vision he later recorded in the book of Revelation, the last book of the Christian New Testament. Among the things God showed him in that vision were seven churches. God said something important about the church in a city called Laodicea:

> I know your deeds, that you are neither cold nor hot. I wish you were either one or the other! So, because you are luke-warm—neither hot nor cold—I am about to spit you out of my mouth. (Revelation 3:15–16)

The people in Laodicea had a problem: they didn't want to make a choice. God compares them to a meal. Hot food is great. There's something about the sizzle of food from the grill that spurs you to dive into your meal. Chilled food can be great, too. However, there's something about food meant to be enjoyed hot or cold, but which has been sitting around at room temperature for too long, that can make you feel ill. If you can find a reasonably polite way to spit it out, great; that's what napkins are for, right? God uses this picture with people.

We have three choices concerning what God offers us. First, we can choose Him and know our choice brings pleasure to His heart. Second, we can choose to refuse. That's bad. Refusal, though, is sometimes the action of people who aren't ready at the moment. There's still hope for those who choose badly—maybe they can be reached later. Last, we can choose to avoid choosing. In this case, we make God want to vomit.

How does one "refuse to choose"? There are several ways.

Probably the best way to avoid making a choice is using phrases like "all roads lead to God". It's tempting to say that in today's world. It sounds so open-minded, benevolent, and sophisticated. *To God, it sounds nauseating.*

This gets worse. It's bad enough when a given "person on the street" says all roads lead to God, but it's worse when the statement is made in buildings once dedicated to worship. All over America and the Western world, every Sunday morning, men and women stand up in pulpits of churches and tell their followers that Jesus Christ is a fairy tale and Moses is a figment of some shepherd's imagination. Somehow, though, you can still have faith. Just keep donating money, so the minister can have a job.

Maybe it's not quite that bad; maybe Moses and Jesus aren't quite fairy tales. Many of these people would say Jesus and Moses possibly existed. It's just they existed as mere men, not as individuals who had dealings with God. They certainly weren't more significant than prophets of other religions. The more open-minded will say something like "I'm sure *something* happened that made all those people follow Jesus; we just can't know what!"

The first decision you must make is this: Decide whether to seek God, reject God, or content yourself with "playing religion". The word *Christian* literally means "little Christ". A Christian is someone who wants to be like Christ. If you don't know for sure who Christ was, how can you be like Him? If there is no authoritative history of Jesus' life, and if the Bible is a collection of distorted folktales, we have no real way of knowing who Jesus was. If you want to walk into a building, open your mind to the universe, and worship whatever feelings you have, then you must take the word Christian off the outside walls. Christianity without Christ is one of the most asinine concepts ever to cross the minds of modern people. The ministers who stand in the pulpits of such buildings, encouraging people to replace conscious brain activity with mental fluff, are at best intellectually dishonest. At their worst, they're reincarnations of the ancient pagan priests and priestesses from whom Abraham fled and with whom Moses fought. We may never fully know the damage done to the souls of people who trusted their eternal security to these false prophets.

To members of these religious organizations: start being honest with yourself. Walk out!

Choosing Only in Part

Another way to avoid choosing is to choose only in part. There are lots of people who love the idea of a loving God. They just dislike the idea He's also a God who pronounces judgment on people who disobey. Others like the idea of God judging, so long as He doesn't judge *them*. In fact, these people like judging so much, they become judges themselves. Finger-pointing at others becomes their reason for living. There are lots of people deserving punishment in the eyes of these judges. However, the idea that these judges could be among the guilty flies over their heads, like a lost balloon drifting in the summer breeze.

I can't help returning to illustrations involving cars and driving. I live under a government that requires three things (at least) from people who want to drive. First, you need to pass a driving test and obtain a license. Second, when you drive, you must obey posted speed limits. Finally, you must make annual visits to an approved inspector to ensure your vehicle is safe for transportation on public roads. You must meet all three requirements. Imagine a man happily cruising the highway at a speed significantly above the limit. He sees bright lights from a police vehicle in his rearview mirror and pulls over. When told he's about to pay a fine, he argues, "But I have a license and my car is properly inspected." Likely, he'll find the officer unresponsive to this argument. Seconds later, another officer pulls over a woman in a vehicle just ahead. The driver of the first car overhears that she was speeding, too. Add to that, the she failed to keep her vehicle properly inspected. "See," says the first driver, "I'm much better than that woman. I'm only guilty of speeding." To his dismay, he finds he still has to pay a penalty. A few seconds more, and a man in a third car is pulled over. The first two drivers take some hope when they hear this new driver was speeding, driving a vehicle that failed inspection, and driving without a valid license. "There you go," chime the first two, "We're both better than that guy!" All three drivers, though, leave the scene with penalties. Each pays a different amount based on individual levels of lawbreaking, but all are guilty. So, all pay.

Let's push the illustration further. Imagine a man quietly driving past the previous scene at the posted speed limit. He has a properly inspected vehicle and a current license. Unfortunately, he's driving to a bank with the intention of robbing it. When he gets there, he pulls out a gun and uses it against the bank security guard, killing him. The police arrive and overpower this dangerous criminal after a gunfight. What kind of a reaction would this man get if he argues, "But I drove here obeying the speed limit every inch of the way"?

You don't get to pick and choose with God. The Scriptures aren't like menu offerings in a cheap restaurant. God isn't like a trip to the amusement park, where you choose only rides that excite you while skipping others. God offers all of Himself to us; it's all or nothing.

If there are parts of Him you find difficult to comprehend, that's understandable. He's willing to give time to any sincere person who'll start down the path. He's happy to work with people willing to chew hard on the food He supplies. God said through Jeremiah the prophet, "You will seek me and find me when you seek me with all your heart" (Jer. 29:13).

You must choose. All roads don't lead to God, and once you get to God you're getting all of Him.

It's an odd thing, but many who fail to choose think of themselves as sophisticated and superior. After scolding the church of Laodicea, Jesus offers these words:

> You say, "I am rich; I have acquired wealth and do not need a thing." But you do not realize that you are wretched, pitiful, poor, blind and naked. I counsel you to buy from me gold refined in the fire, so you can become rich; and white clothes to wear, so you can cover your shameful nakedness; and salve to put on your eyes, so you can see. Those whom I love I rebuke and discipline. So be earnest, and repent. Here I am! I stand at the door and knock. If anyone hears my voice and opens the door, I will come in and eat with him, and he with me. To him who overcomes, I will give the right to sit with me on my throne, just as I overcame and sat down with my Father on his throne. He who has an ear, let him hear what the Spirit says to the churches. (Revelation 3:17–22)

God knocks on your door. You can open it and invite Him in; or, you can cover your ears. God offers Himself to us. You can take Him or leave Him. That's the choice God gives. It's one thing to ponder, study, search, and then come to a conclusion after a time. It's another to use common clichés to avoid making a choice. Someday, you'll stand before God who offers all of Himself to you. At that time, you'll have to answer the question: Why did you give Him little of yourself?

If you've read this far and still haven't accepted Jesus Christ as your Lord and Savior, what's keeping you? There's no better time than now. Turn away from the false idols of this world and turn to the one true God, your Creator. He wants to share His love and His heart with you. He wants you to walk with Him forever. Why not take Him up on it?

When You Choose, Know What You're Getting Into

What happens if you choose to accept God's offer? Two things: one is very good; the other, frankly, is often unpleasant.

The Good: You will have pleased God. Here are the things God gives to people who come to Him, asking His forgiveness for their sins and acknowledging Him as their rightful ruler. God grants anyone who does this total forgiveness. It may not always feel like it, but our feelings don't matter. "Therefore, there is now no condemnation for those who are in Christ Jesus" (Rom. 8:1). You are now free from the penalty of an entire life spent away from God. At this point, God adopts you into His royal family (Gal. 4:4-5). He guides you. You'll now be able to see the choices that lay before you as opportunities to exercise the divine nature God gave you.

The Unpleasant: You're leaving being the gods of this world. In short, they want you back. Previously, you went through life making whatever decision seemed right at the moment. You "drifted with the current". Now, you're changing course. You're moving toward God. You'll now be faced with choices you'll recognize as either trusting the other gods of this world or trusting the one true God. You'll feel something like a strong current pushing against you as you move through life.

Let's start with approval. In America and the West, your first conflict will involve the god of smart. I'm afraid I have some terrible news for you. From the time you become a believer, you're stupid. I say this not because I think so, mind you. However, based on your decision to follow Christ, the rest of the world will think you're a dummy, a waste of intellectual resources, and an embarrassment to any secular educational institution you've attended. As such, you'll be treated with something less than excitement by your contemporaries. Your popularity will fade in direct proportion to the amount of dedication you display for God.

You'll be perceived as intellectually lacking because "properly educated" people are taught certain things. They're taught God either doesn't exist or He is so mysterious no one will ever understand Him (her, it, etc.). Therefore, there's no such thing as a Creator God who actively monitors the universe. Therefore, the universe and everything in it is a product of random chance. Therefore, life simply happened at some point in some place and eventually grew complex. Therefore, smart people believe the theory of evolution as the only reasonable explanation for life. If you question this, you're just plain stupid.

"Smart" people also believe the following without question:

- We are sexual beings. Consenting adults should be able to have sex with anyone they want whenever they want. The only restrictions should be safety issues, such as the use of condoms to prevent transmission of disease. If for some reason you don't want to be sexually active, you're a little strange. As long as you don't insist on others being like you, you'll be tolerated.

- When sex results in an unwanted pregnancy, reproductive freedom demands that a woman be able to choose abortion. It is a right.
- No belief system is better than anyone else's belief system. Well, in actuality, some systems are better—the ones that encourage followers to subordinate their beliefs to all the above. If a belief system isn't willing to subordinate, it's invalid.
- People with invalid belief systems can be tolerated if they're useful to society and if they don't suggest others believe in their invalid belief system.

If you disagree with any of the above, you're stupid. You will learn about the new "Rs" of education. The old "Rs" were "Reading and wRiting, and aRithmetic." Whenever someone challenges the smart people, you will see *R*olled Eyes, *R*ocked Heads, and *R*aised Voices. The minute someone suggests evolutionary theory may not be all it's cracked up to be, you'll see the educational elite and their disciples roll their eyes. It is just a little short of what you'd see if someone were having a seizure of some kind. Next, they'll rock their heads back, notably elevating their noses. Finally, the elites will often jump past any attempts to cite the "mountains of compelling evidence" they believe exist in their favor—they'll run directly to attempts at intimidation. Hence you will hear loud voices proclaiming, "Well, we've got another one of *those religious* people here" or, "I never thought *you'd* fall for that religion nonsense."

"But wait," you say. "I'm not a dummy. I'll study and work hard and show them I'm intelligent. I'll get good grades. I'll do research—maybe I'll even make some sort of discovery that will show everyone I'm not intellectually lacking." I know this seems harsh, but please understand: This rarely works. There are a few exceptions, but in general there's no place in the unbelieving mind for an intelligent believer.

Now, some who are more open-minded among the educated elite have a mechanism permitting a small bit of latitude here. Intelligent people who have faith that makes them challenge accepted norms may be *weak*. This comes into play if you find a way to make yourself useful to the educated elite. For example, let's say you surprise them and make a useful discovery of some kind; or, perhaps you're a very competent and diligent worker. In these cases, they may forgive the fact that you go to church, pray, and disbelieve the core system of the smart ones. If you don't challenge what they believe on a regular basis, you'll merely be pitied as opposed to despised. In this case, you may encounter only mild persecution.

Sadly, there's another option. You could also be regarded as *mentally ill*. There simply must be something wrong with your head if you base your life on what the elite consider superstition. This kind of mental illness, it's believed, makes its victims mean-spirited and domineering. People with this illness inevitably become "control freaks" who use religion to intimidate others. You see this theme often in movies. Now, there are in fact people who are mentally ill and who have odd ideas about religion. On the other hand, there are also mentally ill people who are atheists and agnostics, too; and they also behave badly. You just won't hear much about this latter group from the gods of smart.

The only other exception to this rule isn't really an exception, but it's another way for the educated elite to rationalize intelligent people who choose to dwell in the realms of religion. Unbelievers hold that such people are *dishonest*. Since smart, mentally healthy people can't have faith in the Bible and its teachings, intelligent and strong people who claim to believe in religion are only doing so to perpetuate some sort of scam on the unintelligent and weak.

This is all old hat to people who've been believers for a long time, but if you're new to this, you may be surprised. If you look around, though, you'll see this kind of thinking infects most of modern Western culture.

For example, if you like watching movies you'll soon discover Hollywood has little time for balanced presentations of believers. From this point forward, count how many times you see people who believe the Bible portrayed in a positive light. Decades ago, movies were full of ministers, priests, and nuns who were viewed as gracious charity workers. They helped people in need and offered wise counsel when people had problems. Today, it's different. As long as faith is portrayed as a nebulous belief that a higher being might look down from Heaven every now and then, characters may receive some sympathy from Hollywood writers; but, most believers are portrayed as weak and/or annoying. In worst-case scenarios, they're monsters who lead the bad guys' team.

Science fiction movies are probably the most blatant. In the 2007 movie, *Sunshine*, the story starts with the statement that earth's sun is dying. (Warning: "Spoiler Alert") A spaceship is sent from earth with a massive device thought to be capable of reigniting the sun and saving the earth. Actually, this is the *second* ship; the first disappeared for some mysterious reason. The crew has trouble getting along with each other, creating all kinds of tension. Should I get sidetracked by mentioning that most astronomers place the death of our sun billions of years in the future? Should I suggest the crew of a ship meant to save the earth would likely be checked before departure to make sure all were of sound mind, as well as body, and that they would all know that getting along was paramount if the world were to be saved? Let's not get confused with mere facts. We're trying to create drama here.

Well, lo and behold, the ship finds its lost sister. Eventually we discover the first ship was sabotaged. By whom? A religious fanatic who believed God had ordained the end of humanity, and no one should be allowed to get in God's way. The saboteur was the only survivor, and he gets onto the second ship. Will this deranged individual succeed in sabotaging the second ship and preventing it from completing its mission? Fairness prevents me from giving away the whole plot, but for now you can see the template—humanity is capable of fixing any problem thrown in their path with the help of science. Only religion and the religious get in the way.

This movie is a modern parable, representing what all the "smart" people think about religion. It's not merely inconvenient. Religion is dangerous.

People who believe in the Bible are the most dangerous of all. As such, it's extremely important for members of the "smart" cult to make sure people who believe in the Bible are kept out of any positions involving power. If you feel led into politics, prepare yourself for constant hints and statements from the media that you're a total dolt. Make certain you are never, ever seen pushing on a door with a sign that says "pull" or pulling on a door that says "push". If you do, someone will catch it on video. The video will be played by comedy shows with never-ending glee.

At this point, one reader protests: "You know, you're being a bit negative, aren't you?" Sadly, negativity is sometimes called for. Furthermore, I'm not more negative than Jesus. Matthew quotes Him, "A student is not above his teacher, nor a servant above his master. It is enough for the student to be like his teacher, and the servant like his master. If the head of the house has been called Beelzebub, how much more the members of his household?" (Matt. 10:24–25)

Actually, the last few paragraphs are tame. Paul wrote of believers throughout the ages:

> Some faced jeers and flogging, while still others were chained and put in prison. They were stoned; they were sawed in two; they were put to death by the sword. They went about in sheepskins and goatskins, destitute, persecuted and mistreated—the world was not worthy of them. They wandered in deserts and mountains, and in caves and holes in the ground. (Hebrews 11:36–38)

If you're only considered stupid for your beliefs, you may be getting off easy. With all seriousness, though, you'll find times when it seems you're surrounded by the Cains of the world: people who are unhappy with God and who choose to attack Him through you. Abel saw something much more serious than attacks on his intelligence. You may, too. Fortunately, you'll also find times when you're surrounded by God's encouragement. This may come through fellow believers, or it may come from the quiet assurance God gives to His followers. You'll never be totally alone.

Before leaving this section, let me mention that I'm not suggesting you avoid study or that you should disrespect knowledge and intelligence. One of the wisest men ever to live was King Solomon of ancient Israel. As a young man, he learned he was going to be king. God appeared to him one night in a dream and encouraged the young leader to ask whatever he wanted. Solomon asked for wisdom, so he would be a good king. Because he asked for the ability to serve his people well, God rewarded him with wisdom beyond any of his day (I Kings 3).

Pray about what you think God wants you to do with your life. Then work hard to be the very best you can be. If you believe you should be a physician, scientist, teacher, engineer, or anything else involving study, then study hard: but study because you want to honor God with your life, not because you want followers of the god of smart to accept you. Along the way, you'll find a few people open to your beliefs. Share with them. Enjoy them, and let them encourage you. Do what you can for them. Once you've completed your degree, go about the business of using your God-given intelligence to serve God and others.

Priorities for Believers

O nce you choose to follow God, what are your priorities?

If you randomly select someone off the street and ask what he/she thinks "religious people" should be doing, you'll hear things like: "They should feed the poor," "They should help people," and "They should be 'nice.'" I'm not sure what "nice" is, but it supposedly describes believers.

So, what is the top priority for a believer, according to scripture? One day in the life of Jesus, someone put the question this way, "Which is the greatest commandment in the Law?"

> Jesus replied: "'Love the Lord your God with all your heart and with all your soul and with all your mind.' This is the first and greatest commandment. And the second is like it: 'Love your neighbor as yourself.' All the Law and the Prophets hang on these two commandments." (Matthew 22:36–40)

Jesus was clear and direct. Love God, and love the people He created. The application of this may vary from person to person, but can I suggest a starting place? Perhaps if Jesus was speaking today, He might have said, "*You* love the lord with all your heart" and "*You* love your neighbor as yourself." There are lots of people who think their jobs in life are to make *others* love their neighbors, but others aren't the issue. It starts with you.

Personal Tools

Individually, loving God involves what many call your "devotional life". There are many excellent books on this topic, but I can summarize in just a few paragraphs.

One of the most important things to remember as you enter the great battle is this: not all of it occurs on earth. Much of it occurs in spiritual places, places we can't see. Because of this, we need more tools and weapons than we can find in the earthly realm.

The first heavenly tool is scripture, the "Word of God"—the Bible. This is where we start to understand God and His power. Read it. Study it. Understand it. Remember it.

Second is prayer. In its simplest form, prayer is just talking to God. The apostle James tells us, "The prayer of a righteous man is powerful and effective" (James 5:16b).

When they're available, fellow believers are an indispensable help. Find a good church, one that teaches the Bible as the authoritative revelation of God. It's difficult to follow God by yourself. A good group of believers can help.

Turning to the World

Like many believers through history, sometimes when I pray, I use the famous "Lord's Prayer" (Matt. 6:9–15) as a pattern. It's certainly sufficient alone, but sometimes for my own reminder, I add the following amplifications. Let the text of the prayer be "T" and let the amplifications be "A":

T: Our Father in heaven, hallowed be your name,
A: And let your name be hallowed in some way because of me.
T: Your kingdom come,
A: And may it come because I add to the work of those who cleared the way.
T: Your will be done on earth as it is in heaven.
A: And may my hands be among those who implement it.
T: Give us this day our daily bread.
A: I acknowledge that I am totally dependent on You for my provision, and gladly so.
T: Forgive us our debts, as we also have forgiven our debtors.
A: (This is a good time to confess anything that God has pointed out in your life).
T: And lead us not into temptation, but deliver us from the evil one.
A: Because my heart is no better than anyone around me, I need Your help to turn away from Satan and idols. I will be better at helping others after I've dealt with the idols in my own life.

Once again, I would love to write books about all the people who fed the poor, built hospitals and orphanages, and fought social evils in their day. I've met many "nice" people among believers; but on a high level, I can't help but believe a major task of all believers throughout the ages has been to battle idols. Idols are the main things preventing people from loving God.

Helping the Needy, Healing Injustice

One of the challenges of modern idols is they've infected otherwise good and noble practices. Once, while having dinner with friends in a restaurant, I sat next to a college student. She ordered a vegetarian meal. She ordered loudly, making the point her meal was different than everyone else's. I asked why she chose to be a vegetarian. Was it for religious reasons or maybe health reasons? Her response: "American farmers feed grain to their cattle. Grain should be fed to hungry people. I'm protesting by avoiding meat."

There are lots of people who hold these kinds of beliefs. Maybe they don't lodge this kind of protest, but many believe poverty in Third World countries is the result of oppression by people in richer nations. Since we're supposed to care about the poor, it's the job of good people to repeat this common wisdom to any who will hear. In response, let me retell a story I once saw in a documentary.

A village in Africa was filled with poor people; there was little fresh water. Because of this, children were dying of dehydration and diseases related to bad water. Images presented in the documentary were heartbreaking.

There was a reason the cameras were there. A group of people from a Western country felt compassion for this little village, so they raised the funds needed to send a team of relief workers. Among a number of things they did for the village, they dug a well and fitted it with a modern mechanical pump. The sad pictures from the village changed overnight. The health of the children improved. The health of everyone improved. Previously, villagers spent hours walking long distances, so they could haul heavy containers of semi-potable water back to their homes. With a well nearby, everyone had more time. This meant they could spend it growing food or making things they could sell. The result? Not only was everyone healthier, everyone's standard of living improved.

Unfortunately, the story didn't end there. The people of a neighboring village became jealous of their neighbors. This, in their minds, was a highly inequitable situation, and they decided to do something about it. They drove in one day with Russian-made AK47 rifles and did a lot of shooting. During the attack, they ripped out the pump and threw it onto their truck. The pump was damaged in this process and rendered useless. Even if it hadn't been damaged, these men had no idea how to reinstall it when they arrived home. So, it sat in the neighboring village gathering dust.

The final pictures of the original village quickly reverted to their former desperate shades. Children became sick again. People went back to spending hours walking to sources of potable water, so they no longer had as much time to grow food or make things for sale. Poverty and death returned to this tragic little village.

Question: Are the children of this village dying because Western farmers feed grain to their cattle?

The answer is *no*. These people are dying because of the effects of sin, expressed through the wicked hearts of their fellow man. Now, let me declare yet one more caveat. Am I saying the desperate plight of the poor throughout the world is exclusively their own faults? Are these people all bad people who're getting what they deserve? No, of course not. What I am saying is this:

Until the day the hearts of humankind change, we'll never cure poverty.

I can't peer into everyone's heart, but I'm suspicious my young college friend's food protest was nothing more than worship of the god of smart. She believed her actions made her look intelligent and caring. Unfortunately, her actions didn't change much in the world.

What can change things? The gospels include the following story:

> While he was in Bethany, reclining at the table in the home of a man known as Simon the Leper, a woman came with an alabaster jar of very expensive perfume, made of pure nard. She broke the jar and poured the perfume on his head. Some of those present were saying indignantly to one another, "Why this waste of perfume? It could have been sold for more than a year's wages and the money given to the poor." And they rebuked her harshly. "Leave her alone," said Jesus. "Why are you bothering her? She has done a beautiful thing to me. The poor you will always have with you, and you can help them any time you want. But you will not always have me. She did what she could. She poured perfume on my body beforehand to prepare for my burial. I tell you the truth, wherever the gospel is preached throughout the world, what she has done will also be told, in memory of her." (Mark 14:3–9)

In the passage above, Jesus says something very curious. "The poor you will always have with you." Why would He say something like that? It sounds rather uncaring, doesn't it? Does He want us to give up on helping our fellow man? No. Jesus reminds His followers they can help any time they like. This woman, though, understood something vital. She understood who Jesus was. She knew that pouring out expensive perfume at His feet was an act of worship. In a moment of personal pain, she turned her heart to God and honored Him, giving Him a sacrificial gift intended to bring pleasure to His heart. In that moment, she showed what the world needs: people who seek and honor God. By accepting this gift, Jesus communicated that He was aware of the poor and their suffering. However, as horrible as poverty is, it's not the world's biggest problem. The world's biggest problem is sin and alienation from God.

Why do we have poor people in this world? Why does oppression exist? Because the world is filled with broken people. As long as there are broken people in the world, there will always be those who look with envy on their neighbor's possessions. There will always be people willing to steal and those willing to oppress. There will always be people who strike out in anger, killing those around them merely because that's how they deal with their problems. There will always be those who are simply apathetic, who turn their ears from the cries of their neighbors. Most sad, there will always be innocent victims of the groups mentioned above. If people merely behave badly, this results in pain for individuals. In the worst of days, this explodes into the wars that have plagued humanity for millennia.

So, what is our priority for the needy and the oppressed? Jesus gave it in the last words His disciples heard from Him before He ascended into Heaven:

> Then Jesus came to them and said, "All authority in heaven and on earth has been given to me. Therefore go and make disciples of all nations, baptizing them in the name of the Father and of the Son and of the Holy Spirit, and teaching them to obey everything I have commanded you. And surely I am with you always, to the very end of the age." (Matthew 28:18–20)

Christians refer to this as the Great Commission. Our priority is to encourage others to become followers of Jesus Christ. Once that happens, their hearts change. Once people's hearts change, they treat others better. So, our main job is to point people to God and to clear the idols blocking the way. After this, we can help the needy and oppressed with our voices and our resources.

The Great Theological Questions

Until our hearts change, poverty isn't the only thing humanity will be stuck with. Pollution, war, crime, and a host of other evils will remain.

Sadly, one of the symptoms of our sinfulness is a heartfelt distrust of God, and even anger toward Him. For example, the great minds of our time ask, "Why is there suffering in the world?" Another variation is, "Why do bad things happen to good people?"

These questions miss the point in their very statement. Here's the problem: The questions assume that each of us are good people. If we're good and bad things come along, whose fault is it? Someone else's, obviously.

Does the fault belong to some evil person? That's certainly the next step of reasoning; but, if so, why doesn't God do something about the evil "someone else"? If God has the power to stop evil and He doesn't, the following conclusion becomes apparent: if we're good people and evil exists in the world unstopped by God, *then evil must be God's fault*. We're victims of a supreme being who's callous, incompetent, or just plain mean. Perhaps He's even evil Himself. The polite people suppress that thought. The braver state it openly.

We aren't wonderful people. We're broken. We're sinners. This brokenness in our hearts radiates to all the creation and causes more brokenness. Imagine the worst scene you can. Imagine a starving child in a poor Third World country, emaciated and in pain. Imagine victims of a war—the injured, the crippled, and the dying. Who's at fault when people experience all this pain?

It's my fault. It's my fault, because I'm a broken sinner.

It's your fault, because you are, too.

We're products of the sin of mankind, and we're sinners ourselves. We add to the evil of the world every day; perhaps not each to the same degree, but we're all guilty. You may be an axe murderer, or, you may be a very polite person who simply acts in self-interest sometimes, rather than considering the good of others. Maybe you're even a kind and generous person, who believes your good behavior is buying something from God. The correct way to state the question of human suffering isn't "Why does God allow pain?" but rather, "Why does God allow you and me to cause pain in others?" The question isn't "Why does God watch without concern as brokenness rampages in the world?" but rather, "Why does God allow you and me to break the world more each day?" The question isn't "Why does God allow bad things to happen to good people?" but rather, "Why does God allow anything good to happen to bad people who have sinned against Him and others?"

If you're offended at this point, please remember this: I put myself first in this problem of sin. So did the apostle Paul:

> Here is a trustworthy saying that deserves full acceptance:
> Christ Jesus came into the world to save sinners—of whom
> I am the worst. But for that very reason I was shown mercy
> so that in me, the worst of sinners, Christ Jesus might display
> his unlimited patience as an example for those who would
> believe on him and receive eternal life. (I Timothy 1:15–16)

You see, God's goal isn't the creation of a sterile world. If it were, He could have cleaned up all the messes made by the human race long ago. Unfortunately, creating a completely evil-free world would require removing us all! That's why God hasn't done it. His goal is something much more important. His goal is you and me: we are the goal. God wants to offer us the gift that allows us to share in His divine nature—the gift of choice. In order to exercise this gift, we must be allowed to choose. Unless there are real choices, there is no real choice. In order to have real choices, we must be allowed to choose badly; and badly is how many of us choose most of the time. The result is a broken world where evil exists in abundance.

Many ask, "But what about the people who end up on the wrong side of choices—what about the people who are the victims of evil? Is that fair?" Here is why you must understand the visit of Jesus Christ to the earth. In the incarnation, God the Son left heaven to be born as a human being. He was born in a nation oppressed by a powerful and often cruel invader. He was born to a poor family, and He walked among the poorest of the world. Throughout His life, He felt the sting of all mankind's evil. Finally, He died a torturous death alone on a cross, accused of crimes He didn't commit.

No, God didn't clean up the evil of the world. The evil of the world is the result of the human beings who inhabit it, beings whom God dearly loves. Instead, He chose to enter into the world and walk through it with us. He chose to feel the pain we feel. He chose to feel that pain more intensely than any other human has experienced it. Because of this, He can truly understand us. Because of this, He has earned the right to put His arms around us and hold us when we suffer. Because of this, He can console us and wipe away the tears we shed when we're injured. There are even times when He heals us, but there are other times when He allows us to feel the sting of the broken world we helped create. Know that on those days, He weeps with us.

Because of this, our first priority is the Gospel of Jesus Christ. Until our evil hearts are changed, no evil in the world will ever completely go away. Further, without the revelation of Christ, we have no context for our pain and suffering. The best we can do is quote little Orphan Annie and sing, "The sun will come out tomorrow." The problem is, sometimes the sun doesn't come out. Even when it does, we still hurt. Without the work of Christ, fixing the world is temporary. It just gets broken again.

Even if we could fix things for any length of time, there is the problem of eternity. Assuming we could make the world a perfect place, we would just have to leave it one day when it's time to stand before God on the Day of Judgment. That's a frightening proposition. It's only with the work of Christ that men and women can enter eternity without fear.

As we said, it's not just poverty that will remain unchanged. It's a whole host of things we consider evil. Here's where sin has infected the otherwise good process of changing the world. As much as I would like to praise all people who get involved in attempts to make the world a better place, I'm afraid I've run into too many people who use activism to cover their sinfulness. "I may be sleeping with someone I'm not married to, and I may think myself better than everyone around me, and I may speak with utter disdain about people who want to follow God, but *I recycle!*" I've run into numerous people who believe loud protest is sufficient to change the world. They become heavily involved in activist causes, thinking they're making the world a better place. In fact, their energies have only one focus: taking their eyes off their own sin and focusing on the sins of others.

Currently, the world's biggest problems involve two people. To change the world, we must start with them. Those two people are *you* and *me*. As such, personal love and commitment to God become our priorities. We must first preach the Gospel to ourselves. We then preach it to others.

I've heard many suggest that people have a hard time listening to the words of the Gospel if they're hungry or sick. As such, it's appropriate to include relief to needy people. If someone's in pain because another dumps junk into the water upstream, it's certainly good to speak out for the victims. However, without the Gospel leading our way, feeding the poor, cleaning up the world, and all the other things done by activists become worthless.

The Role of Government

I f it's a bad idea for us as individuals to change the world without changing hearts, it's even worse when governments try to do it. We've spent time considering the problem of people who look to government as the final solution for all problems. It seems every generation has a new group of people who attempt to rebuild the Tower of Babel. Individuals who never deal with their hearts and who try to solve the problems of the world are often merely ineffective. When large numbers of people who fail to deal with their hearts join together, only danger follows.

We mentioned earlier that politicians have a bad habit of taking on god-like qualities when they handle social evils. Today in the West, however, we've reached a point where people have been looking to government to solve their problems for so long, the government itself has become a god. The government is viewed as an infinite entity capable of curing unemployment and poverty. It can provide health care for any who can't (or won't) pay for it. This is, in addition, to more traditional roles of government, like providing a military to fend off invaders, establishing police forces to fight crime, and operating a legal system.

In the United States, this burden is amplified when our neighbors and allies look to us for help when they're threatened. The United States' military forces stand at alert near the borders of numerous far-away nations, protecting them from their warlike neighbors.

Again, the caveat: Is it wrong to feel concern for the needy, or for a strong nation like the United States to help its weaker allies? Of course not. I might add I have great respect to the members of the United States military. They spend significant portions of their lives far from friends and family because they believe they're protecting freedom and justice; not just for themselves and their fellow citizens, but for people all over the world.

At some point, though, the money runs out. The government isn't infinite. Governments are only representations of their limited people. For decades now, the state and federal governments of the United States have increased services to constituents in all manner of ways. Those services continue to increase, even though the taxes gathered from constituents fail to meet the expenses involved. Because of this, politicians have borrowed to pay for them. The national debt is now incredible.

At what point do people say, "We don't have the money to do all the things we want to do"? If the government is merely an institution, fiscal constraint becomes a vital reality. If the government is a god, then requests for services go on and on and on. Because government isn't a god, debt grows and increases until it become disabling.

For this reason, I believe it's important for charitable work to move back to private organizations. I have seen organizations that will, for a relatively small donation, take in a child and make sure he/she's fed and educated. Some organizations move into poor villages like the one I mentioned earlier and build wells, so people can begin the process of caring for each other instead of hauling water jugs long distances. I've seen private organizations do all kinds of things to help the needy. In some cases, they're traditional; in others, they are very creative. A lot of them do their work without any government money.

If we want to, we can stress the dangers of delegating charitable work to the government in practical terms, like the loss of freedom that inevitably occurs when governments become too large. We can discuss financial disasters created when governments borrow too much money. This is more than practical, though. It's a heart matter. When people choose to be generous with their neighbors through charitable organizations, they build the spiritual virtues God intended for His beloved creation. Conversely, there's something about the current business of state-run services that may take care of people (at least until the money runs out), but which leaves both givers and recipients without the opportunity to grow in virtue. The tax man takes the money, the government worker doles it out, and the government grows in debt. In the meantime, citizens sit around at parties, lamenting the plight of the poor and imagining themselves to be righteous people because they voted for someone else to take care of the problem.

So, am I suggesting that you avoid caring about people less fortunate than yourself? Of course not. I'm simply suggesting poverty is complex. Government isn't the best solution for it; and there may be other important priorities for believers.

Sexuality

once watched an interview involving a man identified as an "evangelical leader". During the discussion, he said something like this: "We believe God cares more about human suffering than what people do in their bedrooms." This sounds very enlightened, but consider this story about a man called John the Baptist:

> Now Herod had arrested John and bound him and put him in prison because of Herodias, his brother Philip's wife, for John had been saying to him: "It is not lawful for you to have her." Herod wanted to kill John, but he was afraid of the people, because they considered him a prophet. On Herod's birthday the daughter of Herodias danced for them and pleased Herod so much that he promised with an oath to give her whatever she asked. Prompted by her mother, she said, "Give me here on a platter the head of John the Baptist." The king was distressed, but because of his oaths and his dinner guests, he ordered that her request be granted and had John beheaded in the prison. His head was brought in on a platter and given to the girl, who carried it to her mother. (Matthew 11:3–10)

John the Baptist was highly regarded by Jesus. When asked about him, Jesus said, "I tell you the truth: Among those born of women there has not risen anyone greater than John the Baptist" (Matt. 11:11). To Jesus, John the Baptist was right up there with Moses and Elijah. In the view of the Master, John's name belonged among the greatest of God's prophets. So, if something was important to John, it was probably important to Jesus. As such, it ought to be important to us, right?

Now look at the situation leading to John's death. He said very troubling things to Herod, the king of Israel. They were so troubling, Herod had him arrested. What was John saying? There were lots of poor people living in

Israel. Did John accuse Herod of insensitivity toward them? The Jews in that day were politically oppressed after being invaded by Imperial Rome. Did John accuse Herod of being a coward, who should have resisted the Romans? Did John accuse Herod of being an oppressor himself, collaborating with the enemies of his own people? All these charges would have merit.

No, it was none of these things. Here's what John said to get himself into so much trouble: he criticized the king's personal life. Herod was married to a woman named Herodias. Herod stole her from her previous husband. Because of the way the king's marriage happened, it was little more than whitewashed wife-swapping.

By today's standards, this is nothing. There are millions of people who don't even bother to get married, much less worry whether a divorce meets ethical standards. John took this very seriously. To him, it was worth being imprisoned—and this was no weekend incarceration. There were no international societies checking to see if prisons were clean or that prisoners were properly treated. Prisoners were chained to the walls and fed minimal fare. John knew this lock-up would eventually lead to death. At any time, he could have said, "You know, it's pretty nasty in this prison. Maybe I was wrong. King Herod, can we talk?" He didn't do that. He remained loyal to his beliefs, even to the grave.

In today's parlance, John was willing to die for something called *the sanctity of marriage*. Marriage was an institution ordained by God since the first two humans. One man marries one woman for life; it is one of God's greatest gifts. Today, there's discussion among various Christian groups as to whether divorce is ever permissible. Many view it as allowable in some circumstances; but whatever those circumstances are, Herod's didn't count as one of them. To Herod, marriage was a formality, an old-fashioned restriction to be practiced by those less powerful or less smart. The rules applying to others didn't apply to him. John called him on it. To John, marriage was to be honored, especially by one who called himself king of a nation descended from Abraham.

Because John felt so strongly about the sanctity of marriage, he was willing to die rather than see it abused by his leaders. That's why this is still an important issue for believers today. Our sexuality is to be expressed only through a one-man, one-woman, lifelong union. Sex is not to be casually experienced when convenient. When people marry, it's serious. Adultery is a matter of the utmost gravity, not a small dalliance. Attempts to change the definition of marriage are abhorrent to God.

We don't live in an age where abuse of sexuality is met with imprisonment or other punishment, and I don't believe our goal is to change that. On the other hand, the sanctity of marriage is very important to God, and *part of our job to let people know this.*

I can only imagine a day when people are standing in line for heaven, waiting their turns at the great seat of judgment. The "evangelical leader" of the previous paragraph sees John the Baptist passing by and runs over to say hello. John says, "So, you were a leader of believers." He then asks, "What kinds of things did you tell people while you were on earth?" The leader proudly answers, "I taught people the sanctity of marriage wasn't a big deal." John ponders for a moment and then quietly replies, "I died for that."

What does God care about more? Suffering or sexuality? The answer: He cares about *both.* Telling people God only cares about suffering is a good way to gain favor at a cocktail party, but it won't impress anyone desiring to walk in the footsteps of the great prophets like John the Baptist.

The Value of Human Life

I n this book, I've made some assertions that seem impossible to many
modern thinkers:

> *God made humans.*
> *They're extremely important to Him.*
> *They're so important, they may be the main reason for the*
> *existence of Earth.*

As such, the protection of innocent human life is of utmost importance
to believers. One of the most important fronts in this battle involves abortion. *Abortion* is the act of ending a human life before it can leave the womb.

There are only two questions in the abortion debate. First, *what is a fetus?*
If a fetus is a lump of nonhuman tissue that only becomes human when it
leaves the womb, removing it from the mother's body is simply a "proce
dure", on the level of removing a bad appendix or an ugly wart. If a fetus is
a human being, then ending its life is a grave matter.

The second question is *how valuable is human life*? This question is
important for any uncertain of the answer to the first question. If humans are
the product of a random universe, then to be blunt, they aren't important. The
only important thing in that case is how any individual human feels about
his/her existence. With billions of humans inhabiting the planet, what's one
more or less? If humans aren't important, why trouble people at parties with
controversial topics? Why make people think about issues like abortion when
they have other, more important concerns? If humans are important to God,
we must consider even the *possibility* that a fetus is a human being.

In scripture, human life begins at conception. For a believer, that's enough.
We don't need to get into the presence of heartbeats, brainwaves, and so on.
We don't need to argue about the time at which a fetus becomes capable of
living outside the womb; but others may need to hear positive arguments for
life from scientific evidence, so we should learn them.

People of good faith can debate whether abortion should be allowed if the mother's life is in danger. In this situation, if abortion is chosen, we must remember we're sacrificing one valuable human life for another. We aren't merely having a "procedure". For the rest of this discussion, when I speak of abortion, I'm thinking of it in those situations where it's a kind of post-conception birth control for those who simply feel they don't want to be pregnant. The life of the mother is not in question in this case.

There are many things that can be left to individual choice. As choice is important to God, you would think we'd merely encourage people to make the right choice concerning abortion and stop there. Unfortunately, the protection of life is identified in scripture as one of the core purposes of government. Noah was taught the importance of life after leaving the ark (Gen. 9:6). Moses stated in the Ten Commandments, "You shall not murder." In other words, you shall not end an innocent human life. For this reason, many believers consider the 'termination' of abortion to be an important goal for the legal system.

We may be confronted with attempts to enter other questions into the debate, such as the following:

"So, Mr./Ms. righteous, are you going to be there to help when a poor teenager is stuck with an unwanted baby?" Stated in a less critical way, a person in poverty may not have the funds to raise a child. Perhaps a woman has been abandoned by the father. Perhaps she has other children to feed, too. I'd answer with this: I've met numerous people who want to help poor women when they have children. I know people who may never have a lot of money in the bank because they insist on virtually adopting young unwed mothers and helping them through all aspects of the pregnancy. The modern stereotype of religious communities filled exclusively with uncaring people who want to throw poor women to the wolves is one of the lies of modern idolatry. Can we do more to help the poor? Sure, but telling the poor to destroy their children is a horrible way to solve the problem of poverty.

Having raised the topic of children and money, we must move on to a hard proposition. Abortion is usually performed for economic reasons. Put less compassionately, abortion is often the choice for people who want the better life but who see a child getting in the way. It's one thing to ask, "Where am I going to get help feeding my children?" It's another to say having children is inconvenient. People who ask whether you'll be there for a troubled teenager are often less concerned for the poor than for themselves. Child-rearing may prevent them from pursuing economic prosperity at some point. The better life has often been a good reason for one group of people to dehumanize another. *This is no different.*

Even more, poor children can be expensive for society. In a strange irony, it's the presence of government aid to the poor that winds up being used as a reason for the destruction of poor children. I have on more than one occasion heard intelligent people argue that the cost of an abortion is less than the cost of welfare checks.

Another question is stated this way: "So, you want women to go back to the days of rusty coat hangers and back-alley abortions, right?" This is a highly emotional way of stating that a woman with an unwanted pregnancy may get desperate. In the past, the only route for women in such emotional distress was to seek help from quack practitioners using questionable techniques. Or worse, a woman in such a distressed state may seek dangerous home remedies. The rusty coat hanger is one of the more frightening images.

The modern pro-life movement is filled with compassionate, caring people. I've met a lot of them. Their tendency is to reach out to hurting people and provide immediate relief when they see a need. The fullest answer to this kind of question lies in the spirits of each member of society. We must ask these questions: How do women get to the point where they feel so cursed by the possibility of motherhood, they consider horrific methods to escape it? How did we get to the point where there are large numbers of women who feel this way? How did we get to the point where society looks on the thought of destroying a child as not only reasonable but necessary?

There is good reason to believe a child is a human being, whether before or after birth. Obviously, a mother is also a human being. When there is a conflict involving two human beings, can't we come up with a better solution than killing one of them?

Perhaps, though, we need to revisit the idea of an "unwanted" child? If human life is important to God, then guess what? All children are wanted by God; once more, the answer lies in the values of individuals and societies. We must return to the teaching that human life is sacred. If this is so, then an important truth follows: *The ability to make life is sacred, too.*

To men: Each of you bears a sacred ability coupled with a sacred responsibility. Most of you have the ability to impregnate a woman, to cause life to begin in her womb. You simply must learn to control this. I once heard a story from a man who did a lot of work with teenagers. On one occasion, he tried to communicate the message of self-control to a youth group. One young man replied, "Hey, when I'm with a pretty girl, sometimes I just can't control myself!" The speaker asked this question: "If the girl's father walked in with a shotgun, would you be able to control yourself?" The young man laughed and replied, "Well, yeah!" It's a funny thing: *If something is important enough to you, self-control becomes attainable.*

If for some reason you get involved with a woman and find you can't control yourself, and a pregnancy results, you must take responsibility for the child. To many who think a happy, carefree life is the ultimate goal for all human beings, this seems very strict. If someone respects God and shares his value for human life, sacrificing self and taking on responsibilities is a reasonable request.

To women: You also share a sacred ability coupled with a sacred responsibility. You have within your bodies a fantastic ability: you can become the home for new human life. This ability was given to you by your Creator. You can choose to value this ability in the way God does; or, you can choose to listen to the idols of the world, who tell you the only reason for children is self-fulfillment. If you choose the first, you'll treat your relationships with men with utmost care. The only man allowed to touch you will be a man who demonstrates love for God and love for you. He'll only seek sex with you after he's walked with you to the altar. If you cannot find such a man, perhaps it's better to live your life without sex. The alternative is suffering the pain of rejection when you discover you've been abandoned.

If you have children with a good man, whether expected and planned or otherwise, trust that God will take care of you. If you make a mistake and find yourself pregnant without a committed father, know that God forgives. The life in your womb is still valuable. The path you'll follow as a single parent may be harder than if you had married. In the end, you'll have chosen a far better route than destroying your child.

Of course, there's adoption. There are multitudes of people who want to have children but can't. If you lack the assurance of a good home for your child, why not let them fulfill their dream of being parents?

To those women who've had an abortion: There have been tens of millions of abortions in the United States alone after *Roe v. Wade*. That means there are millions of women (that we know of) who've had an abortion. If you're one, you have a vitally important decision. If you're open to it, there's nothing you've done outside of God's willingness to forgive. God loves you and wants to forgive you despite your actions. To receive this forgiveness though, you must be willing to admit you've made a mistake. You sinned. Many women have reached this point. In some cases, women even use their experience to warn others against this tragic error. Sometimes, people feel so strongly about this issue, they protest in front of abortion clinics. Some women have been seen at these protests carrying signs saying, "I regret my abortion." This is very courageous. You can choose to join the ranks of those who heal through God's grace and move on to experience His love in ways you haven't imagined possible. You can choose to help others to avoid the same mistake you made.

Or, you can choose to ignore all this. You can choose to join "pro-choice" protests. You can sit around at parties lamenting all of those "superstitious religious people" who want to see abortion ended. In choosing this route, you'll live a life of increasing emptiness as you work harder and harder to suppress memories of what you've done. I hope you'll choose God and life.

To Societies of Men and Women: I'm going to paint this in a way that seems cold and harsh, but it represents a reality we must confront. Once again, it involves values. When we see a protest, and a woman carries a sign with a picture of a rusty coat hanger on it, we know it's held by a person who's very, very angry. In some cases, the signs are held by people who've been misled to believe abortion is a good alternative for women. They believe their actions make the world a better place. Sadly, they think of those who disagree as oppressors. We have to reason with these women.

Among those who carry such signs, though, there's also another type of woman. God has granted a sacred ability to her: the ability to mother a child. When offered this opportunity, she's turned to God, waived her hand with an obscene gesture, and yelled out, "I don't have time for this, Buddy! I'm surrounded by people who all have the better life. I want it, too. I don't want anything that might block it. I hate you, and I hate what you've done to me. I hate what my body can do so much, I'll stick a rusty coat-hanger into the most sensitive symbol of my womanhood to destroy the child in there. I will risk painful infection and maybe even death to avoid what you've created me to do!"

In this case, the rusty coat hanger sign essentially says, "I hate God. I hate my body. And I'm holding myself hostage until you all agree to keep abortion legal forever. If you try to make abortion illegal, I'll mutilate myself, and my injuries will be your fault!" The person who says this thinks she's making perfect sense. In reality, she has a view of life so distorted, it's incomprehensible. In a better world, this cry wouldn't be considered the result of a sane mind. It would be thought of as deranged.

What should we do with such people? Indulging them is the last thing we should do. A woman who desires to destroy her own child in pursuit of the better life has a spiritual cancer that's distorting her sense of reality. When millions of people in society think destroying children is a legitimate path to prosperity, it's a spiritual pandemic. It indicates a civilization filled with hearts desperately needing to be healed.

To believers of both genders: This is a top priority. The most powerful weapon against this evil is the Gospel. Like poverty, until hearts change, abortion will never go away; but whether it comes before or after the change of individual hearts, abortion must become illegal. Until it becomes illegal, millions of children will suffer horrible deaths in the name of the god of the better life.

Politics

What is the relationship of believers to politics? Some would say none. Many think it's possible to have government but avoid being involved in it. That was certainly the case in the Middle Ages; the average peasant had little say in what went on in the world. Sadly, it's even true in some societies calling themselves "democratic". However, in America and the West, we still have the ability to make a difference in the world through politics. We have a privilege unknown to many previous societies. We can vote. We can even run for office if we feel led.

Some feel believers should stay out of politics. This is another debate we don't have time to fully address here. Suffice it to say, I side with those who feel that involvement in politics on some level is essential for believers. Why? George Orwell was right when he said, "In our age there is no such thing as 'keeping out of politics'" (Orwell 2010, 18). Everything the government does affects everyone. The idea of believers sitting around and watching as people in power behave badly seems crazy to me. Also, believers are told to be salt and light (Matt. 5:13–16). We're to have a positive impact on the world around us. There's no restriction made on that statement. The least we can do is be aware of people who present themselves to us as candidates for office and support those willing to work with us.

Before moving on, let me set some restrictions on this. I've spent a lot of time in this book singing the praise of choice. I don't believe the goal of believers is to legislate all behavior. It's not our goal to force people who don't believe as we do to act as we think they should in all situations. For example, I have no desire to force Buddhists, Muslims, Jews, atheists, or anyone else to recite the "Lord's Prayer" daily. On the other hand, laws created by government have a purpose: the restriction or encouragement of behavior. I believe there are people in the world who don't like religion. They would gladly use the power of government to restrict believers. Why let them have full control of government when we have a choice in the matter?

Another restriction involves scope. I believe individuals should raise their voices in society. However, many feel churches as organizations should remain nonpartisan. I would agree. Churches are places of worship and training grounds for believers. As the Scriptures are studied, there's room to discuss how they relate to modern thought. Ultimately, churches shouldn't be associated with political parties or political candidates. Let me explain why: there are problems associated with getting involved in politics. The Greek writer Aesop is quoted as saying, "We hang the petty thieves and appoint the great ones to public office." Sadly, there are a lot of dishonest people involved in politics. Some politicians are experts at shaking your hand and smiling, making you think they're on your side. They have the ability to do this while, in fact, they're planning on abandoning you the next day. As individuals, being associated with a given politician who goes bad can be embarrassing; but when churches do it, an important doorway to the Gospel becomes blocked.

Back to individuals: having said that, we live in an age where politicians are often quite clear about what they intend to do with their power should they be elected. Politicians who aren't clear often have consistent voting records on major issues. Finding out how they vote isn't hard. To make things even easier, there are numerous organizations dedicated to watch for issues relevant to believers. Finding those groups isn't hard, either.

Another problem of politics is the mechanisms by which politics work. Most democracies are governed by political parties. Let me state a simple principle about them:

Political parties aren't religions.

This ought to be easy enough, but to many of my friends, political parties appear to have replaced their religions. That's a shame because parties are nothing more than collections of people with similar ideas about how to run things. In fact, in some cases, parties may be nothing more than collections of people. They may start off with similar ideas about how to run things, but it's not uncommon for a political party to find that many of its members have lost track of the party's stated goals long ago. As such, the positions of parties on important issues tend to be fluid, with life spans ranging in years, not decades. For this reason, it's unwise to associate yourself with one party for your entire life.

Those who think believers should avoid singular commitment to a political party would make another argument: No political party perfectly aligns with our belief system. This is certainly true. I would argue, however, there are times when we agree with a given party on certain important policies. We may disagree on other issues, and that's a significant concern. That's why we must *prioritize*.

The most important issues of our day involve issues of life, such as the ending of abortion, and the sanctity of marriage. Concern for the underprivileged is an important issue, but it should be handled by individuals and private charities, not an ever-growing government. As such, smaller government and lower taxes are appropriate goals for believers as they seek to affect the politics of their age.

Do you disagree with those priorities? There may be room for discussion; but here's the biggest consideration when voting. I've run into a numerous people who may or may not voice concerns for moral issues of the day. Whatever their views, whatever their faith, they don't take those into consideration when they vote. In their minds, the government has become their god. When they vote, they're voting for the high priests of this strange religion. They step into the voting booth, open their wallets, and raise them up before the names of the candidates. They inquire, "Which of you is going to put the most money in here?" "Which of you candidates is going to take better care of me?" "Which of you is going to provide for me and protect me?" They proclaim, "I'm concerned about my job and my healthcare." So, most importantly they ask, "Which of you politicians is going to give me *the better life?*" When people vote with such an attitude, it doesn't matter what their stated religion is: *When people forget the moral imperatives of the day and "vote their wallet", they demonstrate through their actions who their true god is.*

We of the United States and the Western world live in democracies. We can lift our voices and influence the laws of our lands. We can empower people who listen to the ideas of believers, or we can empower those who ignore us. In some cases, we can even empower those who hate us. We can selfishly use our power to vote for those who work for the opposite of what God desires, because those people promise to do a better job taking care of us. Once again, we must choose.

Conclusion

"Dear children, keep yourselves from idols." (I John 5:21)

A long time ago, two people stood in a distant corner of the world considering a strange plant: the Tree of the Knowledge of Good and Evil. There in the Garden of Eden, Adam and Eve were given the opportunity to receive one of the greatest gifts ever given to humans: the ability to choose. If they had chosen correctly, they would have realized their privilege as beings created in God's image. They would have awakened in their souls godly virtues, such as humility, faith, wisdom, and love.

They chose badly. They chose to listen to a voice who tempted them away from their God. The first salvo was fired in a battle that has spanned millennia: the battle for the hearts of mankind.

Because of their choice, the world was subjected to all the evils we know today, but their choice also resulted in God displaying even more of His divine nature. For since the Fall of mankind, God has reached out to His creation. He has continually offered the gifts He offered the first two humans in the Garden. With each offer comes a reminder of His love, His forgiveness, and His mercy.

Every event of history can be categorized as a part of this battle. Every age brings forth new voices, seeking to tempt humanity away from God. Every generation produces a new set of idols.

At one time in history, the idols acted like personalities and had names. We met a few of them: the gods of the ancient Middle East were Baal, Asherah, Dagon, and Molech. The gods of Egypt were Ra, Hapi, Heqet, and Anubis. The gods of Rome were called Jupiter, Venus, Mars, Neptune, and Bacchus.

We were later told by Jesus the gods would become more abstract. Money could become a god. Later, gods were born, such as the "god of smart". In the West, we have one of the most insidious of gods, the god of the better life. If humans are allowed to exist for much longer on earth before Jesus Christ returns, new idols will certainly come.

With each age comes a choice for earth's inhabitants. The choice is always the same: Choose idols, or choose the one true God. Today, we're given the same opportunity. In each life, there's one big choice. We can enjoy everything our Creator has intended for us to receive. Most of all, we can receive Him. We can participate in His divine nature—for all eternity. We can walk through each day seeing each choice as an opportunity to receive more of Him.

Or we can choose otherwise.

Now I can do nothing more than turn this over to you.

Many pages ago, I said we were beginning a journey. What a journey it was! We've traveled together across oceans and continents. We've traversed centuries and millennia.

Sometimes, when I have the time and resources for a vacation, I like to visit new places. When I go, I try to find tours conducted by experienced guides who introduce tourists to important sights. Those tours tend to go quickly. Once I've seen the memorable sights on a high level, I try to go back later for a more detailed visit.

Our journey together is like those tours; we only had time to look out the bus window and watch for a moment as we rode past the sites described in the Scriptures. Now that we're finished, I hope you'll do what I like to do after a tour: I hope you'll revisit. I hope you'll get a hold of a Bible (if you haven't already) and read for yourself. Find a good church that believes the principles of this book. There, your spiritual journey will be encouraged. Allow people with experience to teach you how to understand difficult or controversial parts of the Scriptures. Let them encourage you through the "spiritual vacuum periods" of life. Let them pray for you.

Throughout my life, I've made choices. With God's help, I believe I've made at least some well. At those times, I've learned some marvelous things. At other times, I've made bad choices. In all the times I've chosen badly, I've received forgiveness, love, and mercy from the one who enabled me to make the choice.

Because of all this, I now understand more fully the man named Joshua, who lived thousands of years ago. I now understand what he wanted for his friends, his family, his people, and the whole world. I now understand more fully those magnificent words:

Now fear the LORD and serve him with all faithfulness.
Throw away the gods your forefathers worshiped beyond the
River and in Egypt, and serve the LORD. But if serving the
LORD seems undesirable to you, then choose for yourselves

this day whom you will serve, whether the gods your forefathers served beyond the River, or the gods of the Amorites, in whose land you are living. But as for me and my household, we will serve the LORD. (Joshua 24:14–15)

Make your choice. I hope you will choose to serve the Lord.
I hope you will become a warrior in the battle for the hearts of mankind.
I hope you will find, fight against, and defeat the idols on the hills.
May God bless you.

Bibliography

Allegro, John Marco. The Sacred Mushroom and the Cross: A Study of the Nature and Origins of Christianity within the Fertility Cults of the Ancient Near East. Gnostic Media Research & Pub., 2009.

Brack, A. The Molecular Origins of Life: Assembling Pieces of the Puzzle. Cambridge: Cambridge University Press, 1998.

Clinton, Bill "Bill Clinton for President 1992 Announcement Speech." Accessed August 11, 2016. http://www.4president.org/speeches/1992/bill-clinton1992announcement.htm.

Crabb, Larry, Don Hudson, and Al Andrews. God Calls Men to Move Beyond the Silence of Adam: Becoming Men of Courage in a World of Chaos. Grand Rapids, MI: Zondervan Pub. House, 1995.

Cross, Wilbur L., and Tucker Brooke. The Yale Shakespeare: The Complete Works. New York: Barnes & Noble Books, 1993.

Däniken, Erich Von. Chariots of the gods: unsolved mysteries of the past. New York: Berkley Books, 1999.

"Dictionary.com—The World's Favorite Online Dictionary!" Dictionary.com. Accessed August 11, 2016. http://www.dictionary.com/.

Dred Scott v. Sandford, 60 U.S. 393 (1856)

Drum, Kevin. "How Many Birds?" Mother Jones. June 25, 2017. Accessed January 19, 2018. http://www.motherjones.com/kevin-drum/2011/03/how-many-birds/.

Eliot, Charles (editor). The Harvard classics: The Origin of Species, by Charles Darwin, vol. 11. New York: Collier, 1909.

Hanegraaff, H., & Maier, P. L. (2004). The Da Vinci code: Fact or fiction?: A critique of the novel by Dan Brown. Wheaton, IL: Tyndale House.

Harrison, R. K. Introduction to the Old Testament; with a Comprehensive Review of Old Testament Studies and a Special Supplement on the Apocrypha. Grand Rapids: Eerdmans, 1969.

Harvey, John F. The Truth about Homosexuality: The Cry of the Faithful. San Francisco: Ignatius Press, 1996.

Karl Marx: a reader. Cambridge: Cambridge University Press, 1988.

Levy, David H. I July 16, 2014. "Comet Shoemaker-Levy 9: 20 years later." Sky & Telescope. July 17, 2014. Accessed January 15, 2018. http://www.skyandtelescope.com/astronomy-news/comet-shoemaker-levy-9-20-years-later-07162014/.

Lewis, C. S., and Walter Hooper. Christian Reflections. Grand Rapids: W.B. Eerdmans Pub., 1967.

Lowchens "Thousands of NAMES OF GODS, GODDESSES, DEMIGODS, MONSTERS, SPIRITS, DEMONS & DEITIES for Your Dog, Horse, Cat, Pet or Child—from Chinaroad Lowchens of Australia." Accessed August 11, 2016. http://www.lowchensaustralia.com/names/gods.htm.

MacDermot, Galt, Gerome Ragni, and James Rado. Hair; the American Tribal Love-rock Musical. New York: Pocket Books, 1969.

Maslow, Abraham H. A theory of human motivation. Mansfield Center, CT: Martino Publishing, 2013.

Matthews, Alfred Warren. World religions. Australia: Cengage Learning Wadsworth, 2013.

May, Thomas "Interview with Sam Harris: The Mortal Dangers of Religious Faith" Amazon.com Message. Accessed August 11, 2016. https://www.amazon.com/gp/feature.html?docId=542154.

Murray, William J. My Life without God. Nashville: T. Nelson, 1982.

"New York City's Schools Debate Removing Metal Detectors." Los Angeles Times. Accessed August 07, 2017. http://www.latimes.com/local/education/la-na-nyc-schools-metal-detectors-20151122-story.html.

Orwell, George. Politics and the English Language and Other Essays. Benediction Classics (February 15, 2010)

Packer, J. I. Knowing God. Downers Grove, IL: InterVarsity Press, 2010.

Rahula, Walpola. What the Buddha taught. New York: Grove press, 1974.

Roe v. Wade, 410 U.S. 113 (1973)

School Dist. of Abington Tp. v. Schempp, 374 U.S. 203 (1963)

"Shorter Catechism." Orthodox Presbyterian Church. Accessed August 11, 2016. http://www.opc.org/sc.html.

The Holy Bible: New International Version. Colorado Springs, CO: Biblica, 2011.

The War on Poverty: 50 Years Later. A House Budget Committee Report. House Budget Committee Majority Staff. Report. 2014.

"USATODAY.com—Warren Buffett Signs over $30.7B to Bill and Melinda Gates Foundation." USATODAY.com—Warren Buffett Signs over $30.7B to Bill and Melinda Gates Foundation. 2006. Accessed August 20, 2016. http://usatoday30.usatoday.com/money/2006-06-25-buffett-charity_x.htm.

CPSIA information can be obtained
at www.ICGtesting.com
Printed in the USA
FFOW03n1134120518
46579724-48608FF